'Jerry Marshall takes us into a surrea endeavour entwines with business imp paced, funny and deadly accurate.'
Lord David Freud

'Jerry Marshall's witty and candid account shows how audacity, tenacity, skill, trial and error are colourful strands that weave a beautiful, unique pattern of a faithful life. His insights, hindsight and wisdom on work, family and community leave me thoroughly refreshed and challenged to lead a creative, risky and faith-filled life.'
Marijke Hoek, Coordinator of Forum for Change

'This is Jerry's story and, much like the man, it's hard to walk away from! The energy and passion Jerry has for everything he does and everyone he knows is breathtaking. A truly inspirational read.'
Rachel Gardner, Founder, Romance Academy

'Most people – and maybe you're one of them – seem to live as if their highest aspiration is to arrive safely at death! But there's so much more to life, and Jerry shows us another way in this riveting account of his quirky life – one of risk, adventure, challenge, and big hairy audacious goals.'
Simon Guillebaud, Founder of Great Lakes Outreach

Jerry Marshall has used his God-given entrepreneurial flair throughout his whole life. In this book, he chronicles it all – faith, family, friendship and fund-raising – with heart-warming highlights and occasional disappointments along the way. Laced throughout it all you can see Jerry's quick mind and deep connection with God at work. He entertains, informs, suggests, challenges – and leaves you longing not just for his insight but a measure of his boundless energy too!
Pam Rhodes, presenter of BBC Television's Songs of Praise

Peter, thank you for being part of the journey!
Jerry

Travels with an inflatable elephant

Attempts to make things happen And not happen

Jerry Marshall

instant apostle

First published in Great Britain in 2013

Instant Apostle
The Hub
3-5 Rickmansworth Road
Watford
Herts
WD18 OGX

British Library Cataloguing-in-Publication Data

A catalogue record for this book is available from the British Library

This book and all other Instant Apostle books are available from Instant Apostle:

Website: www.instantapostle.com
E-mail: info@instantapostle.com

ISBN 978-1-909728-04-2

Printed in Great Britain

Instant Apostle is a new way of getting ideas flowing, between followers of Jesus, and between those who would like to know more about His Kingdom.

It's not just about books and it's not about a one-way information flow. It's about building a community where ideas are exchanged. Ideas will be expressed at an appropriate length. Some will take the form of books. But in many cases ideas can be expressed more briefly than in a book. Short books, or pamphlets, will be an important part of what we provide. As with pamphlets of old, these are likely to be opinionated, and produced quickly so that the community can discuss them.

Well-known authors are welcome, but we also welcome new writers. We are looking for prophetic voices, authentic and original ideas, produced at any length; quick and relevant, insightful and opinionated. And as the name implies, these will be released very quickly, either as Kindle books or printed texts or both.

Join the community. Get reading, get writing and get discussing!

Dedicated to my lovely and long-suffering wife, Sue.

Contents

About the author

Jerry Marshall believes in setting at least one audacious goal every year. Recent goals include attempting to save the government £50 billion, and setting up a call centre in Bethlehem to create jobs unaffected by border closures. He's a serial entrepreneur and a sailing fanatic, has fought with Pete Waterman on breakfast TV and once won a unicycling race.

This book is about hard-won lessons in entrepreneurial leadership applied to many different spheres, including social enterprise, fighting poverty and political campaigning. It's a story of money, sex, family, faith and inflating large white elephants.

Note: To protect their distinguished careers, some names in the following account have been changed.

Introduction

> Haven't seen Jerry Marshall for nearly a week, but I know he's back in the country cos I've just seen him on BBC Breakfast having an argument with Pete Waterman.

This was my wife Sue's Facebook status on 10th January 2012.

Rather inconsiderately, the government decided to make their High Speed Rail announcement a few hours after I was to return from Palestine. I had been there to finalise setting up a call centre in Bethlehem to create jobs and develop skills.

I landed at around midnight, drove straight from Luton Airport to my sister's house in Chiswick and got a few hours' sleep before a BBC car collected me. Oliver from our PR agency met me at Television Centre and grabbed my mobile from me to field interview requests.

It wasn't the first manic media day. Two months earlier, the Transport Select Committee issued their report, which said there was a good case for High Speed Rail but was deeply critical of the specific HS2 project. The schedule was so tight I did two interviews by phone in someone's farm before jogging across to the cowshed for a Radio 4 *Today* interview. The cows mooed obediently throughout. Sue then chauffeured me to Coventry station to get to a BBC News interview at Euston, where a taxi bike was standing by to get me to ITN. I loved it.

This time, I gave a couple of interviews before being filmed live on BBC Network News as the expected announcement was made at 8am. Then on to the *BBC Breakfast* couch, with music mogul and rail enthusiast Pete Waterman. He responded to my summary of the case against HS2 by saying:

'I think they're completely bloody barmy... I've heard every one of these arguments since 1835.'

Clearly, he was older than he looked.

'We cannot look at railways financially and say it costs this because you cannot do that.'

'Of course you can,' I ventured.

'No you can't. You can never make any real case financially for a railway.'

Then he started shouting, which was perfect. I just had to keep calm and talk sense. Finally, the BBC fixed a car to take Oliver and me to BBC Millbank, where interviews had been arranged every eight minutes for two hours, as they had done before. This time, even a Chinese TV channel wanted to interview me for a business programme. I told them not to bother bidding for contracts. Whatever the government just said, HS2 was not going to happen.

Chapter 1: Goals, girls and rat food

I started life as an entrepreneur in the rat food business.

Aged 12, I acquired two rats, Edward and Fiona. 'Edward' because I felt it conferred a certain status and class to the unassuming rodent. 'Fiona', however, was after a girl I liked. I imagined she would be impressed. In my mind, I could hear the conversation:

'You know I named my favourite rat after you, Fiona?'

'Oh Jeremy, I'm so touched, what a lovely thing to do!'

'Oh, it's nothing,' I say, looking deeply into her eyes.

At this point she throws out her arms around me in undying love, etc, etc.

This conversation never happened. Sadly, the honour bestowed was never fully appreciated. Naming rats is a risky business. My eldest daughter Hannah named her rat Kevin because it seemed an amusing name for a rat. That was before she met her father-in-law, also called Kevin, a well-respected Methodist minister in Lancashire.

Fiona (the girl, not the rat) was a neighbour in Kuwait, where I was born. Israeli border control officials often ask why I was born in Kuwait. Usually I just apologise. But here's the summary.

My dad joined the army in 1940 straight out of school. He was sent to protect the Iranian oilfields with occasional breaks in Palestine before being sent off to invade Italy. This gave him a taste for the Middle East, so he joined the Anglo-Iranian Oil Company (now BP), trained as an accountant and was sent to Abadan. When Iran nationalised the company in 1951, he was seconded to Kuwait Oil Company (KOC), where oil production had started three years earlier.

My mum was torn between wealth and poverty. She started life in a large bank house with servants in Wisbech,

Cambridgeshire, where her father was a bank manager. However, when she was six, he died suddenly of a heart attack. The bank agreed to pay her fees at boarding school in Derbyshire but in the holidays she shared a room with her mother in a flat in Glasgow. She became a teenager three days after the war broke out, suffered bombing and rationing and was deeply disappointed there were no funds for her to go to university. Decades later she graduated from the Open University. She trained as a nurse, then as a secretary, and applied for a job as a medical secretary with KOC to escape post-war Glasgow.

With 600 bachelors at KOC, there was considerable competition for the small number of incoming single females. Different departments ran various scams to ensure their men got the first look-in. Dad took advantage of one of these, and the rest is history. They were married in 1952. Jill came first, then me in 1957, then Hilary, all born in Kuwait.

I have two sets of chromosomes that are at war with each other. Mum is from a family of worthy and upstanding Scots: great-grandfather was president of the Educational Institute of Scotland; great-great-grandfather was an Edinburgh city surveyor.

Dad is from a line of dodgy entrepreneurs with marriage break-ups in every generation and a colourful history of alcoholism and mental illness. Great-grandfather George was a builder and property speculator who left £300,000 (millions in today's money) to Grandfather Arthur. Arthur promptly retired, aged 32, and spent the lot. His first marriage was to Lucy Tallent, who came from a family line of fancy box manufacturers. I particularly like the story of her sister Susie who went completely off the rails. The family hired a lawyer to prevent her leaving her inheritance to a cats' home. Instead she left it all to the lawyer.

I feel torn between the desire to be a worthy and upstanding citizen and the temptations of money, sex and power. Going

15

further back, I recently discovered that I'm a direct descendant of Somerled, the twelfth-century King of the Isles and Thane of Argyll, a pivotal Norse-Gaelic figure credited with the invention of the hinged rudder. I like to think this explains my love of the sea and longing for adventure.

Kuwait was a great place to be as a kid. Until I was eight, we lived in the oil company town of Ahmadi. Home was a beige brick bungalow with a veranda, a front lawn consisting of a grass with long, wiry strands. A pale yellow plywood Wendy house with a red roof stood on one corner under a eucalyptus tree. My favourite toy was a pedal Jeep, on which I would transport a can of water along a triangular path around the lawn, pretending to be driving a water tanker. Through a trellis on the side of the house there was a bigger garden area which we called the paddock, where I drove the water and made things in mud and caught big black beetles.

When I was five, I started at the Anglo-American School, waiting at a dusty bus stop for the American-style yellow school bus. We were taught by teachers from England and played football on hard sand pitches. School outings included the Experimental Farm, where we could see real cows, though the only milk we drank was reconstituted dried milk, usually mixed with Nesquik to make it more palatable.

In the holidays and at weekends we went to the Hubara Club which had a large outdoor pool with high diving boards and grassy terraces with deck chairs. Before I was three I could swim unaided (while Mum drank coffee and chatted with friends). My largely underwater approach to swimming led to regular rescue attempts from valiant adults who dived in to save me, but they received short shrift for their trouble. In the evening, the underwater lights came on and we were left to our own devices, jumping, diving and making dens from dozens of spare deck chairs.

Ahmadi was a vibrant if rather British community of young adults and children. Mum played hockey and performed in *The Pirates of Penzance* and *The Mikado* at the Kuwait Little Theatre, a converted Nissan hut. Dad organised picnics in the desert with Fiona's family, where we lay down and rolled down Burgan Hill and tried to spot elusive flamingos around the fringes of Kuwait Bay.

We drove our Wolsey, windows wide open, down the bumpy road to Mina al Ahmadi on the coast, where we were members of the curiously named Cumberland Yacht Club (CYC). The CYC had a fleet of Fireflies, beautiful 12-foot dinghies designed in the 1940s; and an X Class fleet, classic wooden keelboats first raced in the Solent in Edwardian times. We collected the sails from a hut at the entrance to the harbour, slung them onto the bonnet, then drove further along the harbour wall. A boatman took us to the mooring, where I clambered onto the foredeck and hanked on the jib. In the heat of the summer, races were early in the morning, then we returned to the clubhouse for breakfast and to play in the sand and swim. Occasionally two or three families would borrow the company launch from the harbour and motor to Kubbar Island, a small, flat island two or three hours out, where we could swim, explore and fish.

In 1966 Dad was seconded to Kuwait Chemical Fertiliser Company, part owned by BP Chemicals. As a result we moved to a white villa in Salmiya, a suburb of Kuwait Town, which by then was called Kuwait City. This was much more multicultural and I got to know Arab children for the first time, though in the main we socialised with ex-pats, swimming in the small Embassy pool and the larger BBME (British Bank of the Middle East) pool and taking occasional Dhow trips to Failaka Island.

A rite of passage for KOC kids was being despatched to boarding school in England. I started at the age of eight. The first boarding school I attended, Branksome Hilders, was an imposing country house on a woody hill near Hindhead, but I was homesick, unhappy and didn't do well. We flew to school on BOAC VC10s, stopping at Beirut. I loved the excitement of flying, looking out the window, being with friends and feeling grown up. However, at Heathrow it all changed. I was collected by a driver and sat alone in the back seat – Mum said it was safer – while the driver tried to make cheery conversation. It always seemed to be cold and drizzling and as we turned up the long, narrow drive I was filled with a deep dread. By the time I pushed the big, wooden school door open, my dormitory would already have had lights out. There was no talking and I was sent straight to bed. I felt overwhelmingly sad and lonely.

I had friends but I felt very isolated. New boys had the choice of being thrown into the holly or the nettles. Arguments were sorted out with a fight in the gym. When there was a fight, the news spread rapidly and boys ran to the gym to watch and shout encouragement to one side or the other. In the summer, I was haunted by a fear of cold water. There was an outdoor pool and I dreaded each break time when we were expected to dive in and swim a relay. I also found it difficult to get to sleep during the long, light summer evenings and would lie awake until after midnight, becoming more and more anxious about still being awake. When I misunderstood a book club offer and started to receive letters demanding payment I did not know what to do and told no one. I had no means to pay and worried about it for months until they stopped writing. When the Six Day War broke out in June 1967, I cried. With images of World War Two in my mind, and knowing Kuwait was officially at war with Israel, I had images of Dad being called up and not seeing my parents for years.

The happiest days were the countdown to the end of term and the trip home: being collected by the driver, feeling important checking in at Terminal 3, joining a plane packed with children, some of them friends. BOAC used to put on an extra stewardess to cope with all the excited kids. We would land in Beirut in the afternoon; I would walk down the steps in the sunshine, smell the spicy Middle Eastern air in the terminal, and know I was nearly home. On the last leg it grew dark and anticipation mounted. We were given colourful tins the size of bricks, with outlines of different aircraft models on the inside lid and packed with a selection of confectionary bars. At last, we felt the plane start to descend and saw the gas flares in the Kuwait desert outside the window. Then we were climbing down the steps into the warm night, pushing through the noisy immigration hall, seeing Mum and Dad through the window and finally bursting into the arrivals area to greet them.

Waking up that first morning of the holidays, remembering I was home, and seeing bright sunshine streaming through the windows, was always a joy. Simply heading out to the shops was special: soaking up the sun and warmth, talking with Mum about nothing very much and enjoying the cocktail of Arabic and Indian sounds.

Two years after starting at Branksome Hilders, the headmaster had a nervous breakdown and the school closed. This was obviously nothing to do with me, though I have noticed a pattern of organisations I join tending to fall apart about two years later. There were only 70 pupils and it was no longer viable. So, in 1968, I was moved to Great Walstead in Sussex. This was a complete contrast and I loved it.

Great Walstead was a slightly chaotic collection of buildings: an old timber-framed building, a farm, a red-brick main school, and wooden classroom blocks gradually being replaced by smart, modern facilities. In front of the school there were lawns, with a zip wire from a platform high in a tree, a gravity railway with a small flat carriage, and a tall tree to climb with a 'Davy Descender' – a sling giving controlled descent. Behind the school there were 260 acres of woodland, fields and streams. All the staff were Christians with a living faith and a sense of fun. I remember the chemistry teacher blowing up sodium in break

19

time; and the director of music creating several small lakes by building dams with gangs of muddy boys. Throughout the year we had unsupervised raft battles on the lakes.

The rat food business started because there was a craze on pet rats at Great Walstead. The school had a 'Pets' Corner' and nobody seemed to mind if you wandered around with a couple of rats down your jumper, apart from the occasional young junior matron who screamed in such a gratifying way that it ensured further ambush attempts.

However, being a boarding school, there was no obvious rat food supply chain, and boys were largely unable to calculate their rat food requirements for the whole term. Some rats survived on the occasional boiled egg from school breakfast, and looked desperate, going completely crazy when a scrap of bacon was stuffed through the bars.

Thus, there was a market opportunity.

I exploited this by persuading a tame teacher to buy rat food in bulk, and then I 'borrowed' plastic cups from the dining hall, which I filled and sold at a shilling a cup, a 100 per cent mark-up. Business boomed and everyone was happy, especially the rats.

The lesson from this was to look for the opportunity: to start with the need, not the solution. Too often in later life I have come across engineers – both computing types and the proper metal bashing sort – who come up with technically beautiful solutions that don't actually sell. Possibly the invention gives such job satisfaction that the engineer is not motivated to develop the market and instead moves on to the next thing. Of course, there are notable exceptions. Nobody knew they wanted Facebook or a Sony Walkman until they were invented. It's almost impossible to forecast demand for a completely new concept.

School was an excellent place to run a business, but it turned out I was supposed to be there to learn stuff from teachers. That was proving problematic. Great Walstead had three streams in each year, from A to C. In the A stream were clever people like Charles Peattie, a brilliant cartoonist from an early age who went on to create the *Alex* strips. I was placed in the C stream.

However, to their credit, the school decided I was not completely stupid; the change came when I gave a class talk on Egyptology. After a short presentation I spent the rest of the lesson fielding complex questions on the genealogy of the eighteenth dynasty and whether Tutankhamen's tomb was actually cursed ('Just media hype,' I explained loftily). So they put me up to the B stream, gave me a sharp talk on my part of the bargain, and waited to see if I could extend my knowledge to anything remotely useful. It was enough to get me through Common Entrance.

I had, in fact, read some grown-up books on the subject, and, to feed this interest, my parents arranged for me to stop off in Cairo for a few days en route to Kuwait. I stayed with Egyptian friends who lived in an apartment many floors up. They had a son my age. Apart from the obvious sights – the Pyramids, Saqqara, the Egyptian Museum – the highlight was buying bombs in a local shop. These were paper packets about the size of a walnut, held together with wire. We took them back to the apartment balcony and tried to drop them on pedestrians. It was quite difficult to judge and I didn't hit anyone, but getting them to blow up on the pavement just in front of a pedestrian did cause obvious disquiet for the victim and peals of mirth from two 11-year-olds far above the street.

Attitudes to risk and safety were different in those days. It was a good time to be old enough to have some freedom and young enough to have few responsibilities. The best part of the summer term was 'Q Day'. Over this term we built camps in the woods in small teams, makeshift huts made from a wooden frame covered in leaves, branches and bracken, then waterproofed with old plastic fertiliser bags. Towards the end of term, different coloured 'Q Day' warnings were posted, building excitement to fever pitch. Then at some random point a red sign was posted and we gathered in our groups on the Tennis Court to receive food and supplies for the next 24 hours. There were lots of exercises, gathering points for each team, but by far the best was the banger exercise in the middle of the night. In this, some of the group had to prowl around the woods in the dark, creep up to other camps (difficult with cracking twigs) and chuck up to two bangers in each of the other groups' camp fires. Meanwhile others in the group attempted to defend the home camp fire. It was brilliant. In my opinion, whoever invented risk assessments should be shot.

At the next school I moved into the over-printed pens business in direct competition with the school shop. The proposition was simple: I ordered biros with the school name on them in bulk and – after adding a 100 per cent mark-up – sold them at 2.5p each. The official school biros were 3p. Distribution was genius: juniors sold them to their friends and got one free pen for every ten they sold. Utter exploitation of child labour.

Years later I was at a seminar led by Richard Dobbins, who said there are only four reasons why anyone buys your product or service: because it's better, faster, cheaper or nicer.

It's useful to know why your customers buy from you. It helps you retain them and flog more stuff to others like them. Better and cheaper are self-evident, but Dobbins said you have to be clearly better or ten per cent cheaper for anyone to switch. Faster may well be the reason you chose the supermarket you use – it's the nearest. Or maybe you buy the one that offers next-day delivery. Nicer is the most overlooked. Why do you use the plumber or the accountant you use? Because they're the best? Because they're cheapest? Probably because as well as being reasonably good and reasonably good value, you like them and trust them.

I discovered that most small business-to-business companies don't appreciate the importance of being nicer than their competitors. Over the years I've made several thousand calls to my clients' customers to find out why they buy. The clients wait with excitement to find out the reason. Is it the leading technology? The outstanding quality? The competitive price? Nope. Turns out most of my clients are pretty average, but they are nice. The company is usually quite small so you can talk to the boss if you need to. And he or she is, well, human. Not tied up with scripts and procedures designed to maximise profits. My clients simply help out if their customer is in a fix.

While establishing my business career at school I was still expected to achieve some kind of academic success. This eluded me until, at the age of around 14, I realised that exams seemed to be important in order to step onto the first rung of a decent career, and no one was going to pass exams for me.

After some consideration I decided I wanted to go to Cambridge, but I didn't tell anyone for years for fear I would be laughed at. I simply started getting up to work an hour before the getting-up bell.

Cambridge was the first of many life goals that provided a kind of trellis that my life could climb up. For every goal, however, there is a price that has to be paid in advance of receiving the benefit. Goals where we have not agreed to pay the price in advance are merely daydreams. The price for attempting to get into Cambridge was to get up early to work.

A combination of business ventures at school and a summer working as production control clerk at my uncle's carton factory in Essex convinced me that my future lay in making pots of money in business and entrepreneurship. So I decided to apply for economics, the most relevant subject on offer at Cambridge. The fallback position was business studies at Ealing Polytechnic sponsored by Metal Box Co Ltd; I knew this would be more relevant, but I sensed the Cambridge name would be a fair trade for the more theoretical nature of the course. My A level grades were just about good enough to give it a go, so I went back to school to take the Oxbridge exam in November 1975.

I travelled alone by train to the interview at Gonville and Caius (pronounced 'keys'), a college I had chosen largely with a pin. It was a beautiful sunny September day. The lawns, the flower beds, the warm stone medieval courts were stunning, a different world, full of peace and beauty. I was so awestruck I didn't stay to look around in case I fell in love with it. Telling my parents' friends that I hoped to go to Cambridge sounded good, but I didn't think I had much chance.

On 14th October 1975 an envelope arrived that changed my life. It was a standard printed letter on Caius headed paper with my name typed into the space.

> Dear Mr Marshall
> Thank you for coming to Cambridge to be interviewed.
> We have now fully considered your application for admission to Caius in 1976 to read Economics and I am happy to be able to tell you that we have decided to offer you a place.

I could barely believe that last phrase and had to read it several times to be sure I correctly understood the message and that there were no conditions. It was an utter surprise. They were offering a firm place but hoped I would still take the Oxbridge exam to be considered for an exhibition or scholarship. I only later found out that Caius had a habit of offering places on the basis of A levels and interview alone.

I phoned my mother on a reverse charge call and cut into her objections with the news. Once I had convinced her that it was an unconditional place, she was thrilled. Hearing her praise was a rare experience. Mum and Dad were from a generation that believed praise could give rise to the worst possible sin in English culture: becoming big-headed.

Reaction from the school masters was muted. I suspect it was something of an embarrassment that one of their pupils, who had never made the A stream or won a prize, had somehow been overlooked. Some of the elite pupils in my year were distinctly negative. 'If you've got a place we should all get scholarships,' grumbled one. The exception was the director of music, who announced it to all during band practice that afternoon and everyone clapped. I glowed with happiness.

There was something else I learnt in my last school term: the rewards of saying yes. I had set up a sailing club at school and was asked to find someone to fill a spare place on an Ocean Youth Club weekend. Much as I loved sailing, the idea of getting myself to Hamble, joining a crew of strangers and facing uncertain October weather while preparing for Oxbridge was unattractive. But there were no takers and I had an idea that if I went, I would look back and be glad I had made the effort.

This was absolutely the case. It was a wonderful weekend: meeting up in a pub on the Friday night, boarding late that night, heading off to Poole on a sunny Saturday morning in a force five ('perfect conditions', I wrote in my diary). I was free from the constraints of a boarding school and in my element. Many of the crew were seasick, but I and an intriguing girl called Lucy were fine and the two of us helmed much of the way. Naturally, I fell in love with her.

The lesson was: if in doubt, say yes. You don't know what you might miss.

A week after my offer of a place at Cambridge I received a letter from Lucy inviting me to her sailing club bonfire night in Emsworth. I drove down on my Puch Maxi moped and after the bonfire was lit we slipped off in the dark holding hands, wandering along the shore.

'We just stood in each other's arms in the starlight,' I wrote. 'The rest of the evening was just a dream – holding hands by the bonfire, sitting together on the sofa listening to Simon and Garfunkel.'

The following morning was a beautiful, still, clear day and we escaped her parents' observation by rowing a small dinghy into the Emsworth channel. We moored to a buoy and lay in the bottom talking, cuddling and kissing. I was overwhelmed with the sheer joy of it.

'Missed two turnings on the way back in my dreaming.'

To complete the story, Lucy was, and still is, one of a kind. She became head girl, wrote in green ink and once took a dead cormorant called Jemima to school for a biology lesson. Later she joined the Merchant Navy, sailed around the world and married the engineer on one of the ships. They settled in Nova Scotia where she runs a successful knitting business with highly original designs, and gets invited to travel the world on cruise ships holding knitting workshops. We had a family holiday with them once, exploring Nova Scotia and watching whales.

After years of not being in the bright, or popular, or sporty set, suddenly things were looking up. Other boys my age seemed far more successful than me in attracting girlfriends. I put this down to my appearance. I was medium height, with blue eyes, slim, but not very macho looking, and I thought I was let down by a mass of frizzy brown hair. I couldn't grow it fashionably long. It just grew out in all directions. I used an Afro comb and at school my nickname was 'Fungus'. Now, though, I (a) was going to Cambridge and (b) had a girlfriend. These were the top two symbols of success I could imagine, and I began to think I could achieve just about anything.

The great thing about seventh term Oxbridge is that you have to take ten months off before starting. I wanted to use some of the time to benefit my career and also to earn enough to go on an adventure. I was especially keen to work with computers; clearly they were the future. I had not seen a proper computer, but I did go to an exhibition in Kuwait in 1970 where desktop calculators could be had for not much more than £100. And in the sixth form my study mate Howard had built a kit-form four function Sinclair Cambridge for a bargain £20 (around £170 in today's money). Incidentally, I bought my first home computer in 1980, the Sinclair ZX80 with 1KB of RAM. Out of curiosity I have just created a Word document with the three letters '1KB' and the file size is 13KB. So that's progress for you.

With my hi-tech future in mind, I wrote to Fluor Nederland in Haarlem, a civil engineering company that was working closely with my father in his role as Company Secretary of Iranian Oil Services. In December the Managing Director replied, offering a six-month assignment that he thought would be interesting. I was to be a Junior Office Expediter Grade C at £55 a week, a fortune compared with my first wage picking fruit at 15p an hour and the more recent pay of £16 a week cutting and bashing metal things in a local sheet metal factory.

I also spotted an article in the Royal Yachting Association newspaper. The Sailing Club of the Chesapeake were offering Brits a chance to join them on their Bicentennial Summer Cruise as a 'no hard feelings' gesture in view of them winning the war of independence in 1776. Naturally I applied at once and was offered a place. My allocated host, Michael J Wagner, wrote to offer a berth with his family on his beautiful 1957 35ft mahogany on oak Sparkman and Stevens yacht. It was the sort of perfect vessel you see photographed on boys' birthday cards, moored on a creek at the end of their garden near Annapolis.

So I bought a Laker Airways ticket to New York and a one-month go-anywhere Greyhound Bus 'Ameripass'. After a blissful Christmas and New Year, including a trip to the London Boat Show with Lucy, I headed for Liverpool Street Station and the Harwich ferry to the Netherlands. The night before, winds gusting over 100mph had killed 24 people and caused widespread disruption, including blocking every road out of Norwich. I had a bike and a couple of cases that made progress slow and arduous as a foot passenger. The ferry eventually departed at 3am for a passage I describe in my diary as 'pleasantly rough'.

I lived for six months with a wonderful Dutch family, Jan and Marta and their young children, in the town of Heemstede, 20 minutes by bike from the Fluor office. The house had a large bay window that Marta treated as a greenhouse rather than a means to view the outside world. Apparently this is normal in Holland. When the canals froze we skated down them. When summer came we cycled to the seaside. When I had ten days of holiday, I worked as a PGL sailing instructor near St Tropez.

At Fluor, I worked in the hitherto all-female PROMPT section, part of Expediting, itself part of Procurement. PROMPT stood for 'Project Reports on Material Procurement and Transportation'. The overall aim was to buy, chase up and track all the bits needed to build very big things in faraway places and send monthly reports to the faraway manager to say how and when each bit was going to arrive. My particular thing was a $3.4 billion project in Saudi Arabia. Every day we entered information from the expediters onto worksheets which went to the punch girls who typed them into a machine that made cards with holes in them. Once a month a stack of cards was stuffed into a machine that transmitted the information to an IBM 370 mainframe in Los Angeles, which thought about it all night and spat out a tabular report we could photocopy and post to Saudi. Nowadays, I could keep an Excel file updated on Dropbox and achieve the same for a fraction of the cost. So, sadly, the relevance of the whole experience (and a later course I did at Cambridge in FORTRAN) was precisely nil.

When I left, the girls in the section typed out a greeting on four punch cards:

TO ONE OF THE GREATEST PROMPT GIRLS EVER TO INPUT CARDS
WE HOPE YOU SAIL YOUR WAY TO SUCCESS, BUT DON'T GET INTO TROUBLE WHILE
YOU'RE AT IT, DOCTORS CAN BE VERY EXPENSIVE YOU KNOW

KISSES FROM YOUR EVER LOVING PROMPT GIRLS TINA YVONNE GIL PAM AND & ANTOINET

I had a wonderful time sailing the Chesapeake from Annapolis to the Potomac, with receptions, barbecues, crab feasts, and dinghy tender races. The life experience, though, was circumnavigating North America alone on a bus pass.

Perhaps the most valuable lesson was immediately after landing at JFK before heading down to Annapolis. I was booked into a hotel for the first night and took a cab. The driver asked if this was my first trip to New York and naively I said yes. I did know how much the fare should be but when he dropped me off he demanded many times more. He was a big man; it was nearly midnight; I paid up. He even kept his hand out for a tip. Later, I thought of obvious responses: walking to reception; taking his number; even asking for a receipt, but at the time I felt completely intimidated. That night I lay awake for hours, furious with myself for being so stupid.

The experience left me with a budget of three dollars a day and a healthy dose of mistrust, though not one that stopped me taking risks. I generally boarded a bus in the late evening, blew up my inflatable pillow and tried to sleep through to the next destination in the morning. I learnt how to get two seats to myself (sit on the outside, bag on the inside, avoid looking at those getting on). For breakfast and lunch I generally bought a carton of milk, opened it up and poured in Grapenuts, the most compact and therefore most portable cereal I knew. Most evenings I splashed out on a burger.

In this way, in one month I worked my way down to Miami, round to New Orleans and El Paso (where I walked into Mexico), across to the Grand Canyon and San Diego, up to Vancouver and back east through Banff, Chicago, Montreal, Quebec and New England before returning to New York.

Not every night was on the bus. At Fort Lauderdale I slept on the beach until someone woke me at 3am. I woke up already on my feet, heart pounding, with the stranger backing off. He warned me the police were combing the beach with searchlights to remove vagrants. I spent the rest of the night on a park bench. At Banff, I arrived in the early hours and slept in the back of an unlocked car. The worst night's sleep was a $2 per night Salvation Army hostel in Calgary, where I was kept awake by the TV and snoring, coughing old men.

The lessons learnt in New York came into play in California. Perhaps it was unwise to visit the 'swimsuit optional' Black's Beach and then hitch back to San Diego. My driver claimed he had hosted the biggest nude beach party in the States and enjoyed painting men's private parts. He was keen to walk round the park with me.

'I would love to but I'm being met at the Greyhound terminal in just a few minutes time,' I lied, implying that if anything happened I would be missed immediately.

On arriving at San Francisco bus station at 11pm, a man asked if I had accommodation for the night. I had planned to stay with a weird religious group that seemed to offer free overnight stays but this guy seemed pleasant enough, and he was smaller than me, so I figured if the situation became tricky, I could run for it. As we walked to his flat he explained how, when he got home, he liked to take all his clothes off. I watched carefully as he shut the front door to make sure it wasn't locked. We smoked dope and listened to music before his intentions became clear.

'I really appreciate your hospitality,' I explained, 'but I'm just not that way inclined.'

'Okay,' he responded, 'that's cool... I just think you're missing out on a whole lot of fun'.

In the morning he gave me coffee, cereal and a map of San Francisco.

The loneliness of travelling alone pushed me into talking to strangers, and thus I experienced the rich variety of people as well as landscapes. Every day I met wonderful, hospitable people. Juan, a librarian from Eugene, gave me a fabulous breakfast in his flat, took me around the town, then to the Willamette River where we ate blackberries, apples and plums before having a meal out in an expensive hotel. Betty, a friend of a friend living on the stunning Galiano Island near Vancouver, took me in on the basis of a single phone call. We took a picnic supper across to Retreat Island and watched the salmon jumping and the sun go down. Joe, a law student, paid for a steakhouse meal in Camden, a fishing village in Maine that reminded me of Cornwall, with a beautiful harbour at the foot of low, rounded mountains. Despite the risks, saying yes to every opportunity reaped rewards.

Reflections

- Look for the opportunity: start with the need not the solution.

- Know why customers are buying your product: better, faster, cheaper or nicer?

- Set goals and decide to pay the price in advance.

- Say yes to every opportunity, unless there is a good reason to say no.

- Naming a rat after a girl you like is not recommended.

Chapter 2: Money, sex and power

Cambridge was to be the next step towards my destiny of becoming a fabulously wealthy businessman. Yet I wasn't sure I was the Cambridge type. For a start, the school careers teacher had identified my 'pragmatist learning style' and recommended I take a practical course, hence the option of a sponsored placed doing business studies at Ealing Polytechnic.

Nevertheless, I loved Cambridge. I had a room in 'O' staircase, Tree Court, which overlooks a beautiful, peaceful courtyard with a tree-lined path leading past the chapel and through an archway in a warm, stone medieval building. Yet it was next to busy Trinity Street and just yards from the marketplace. Each morning I slid down the steep bannister. In the summer I opened the sash window and lay back, wedged in the frame in the sunshine, until messengers from concerned dons told me to come in.

The staircase was famously the base for Caius engineers who, late one night in 1958, hoisted a car from Senate House Passage and swung it onto the ridge of the Senate House roof. Female students were deployed to distract passers-by, and three drunken rowers who did notice were told it was a tethered balloon. The police, fire brigade and Civil Defence Force took four days to dismantle the car and get it down. The prank was officially condemned but college Dean Revd Hugh Montefiore, later Bishop of Birmingham, left a crate of champagne at the foot of 'O' staircase, acknowledging the engineers' ingenuity. It was nearly 50 years before the details of who and how came out, by which time all the perpetrators had enjoyed distinguished careers.

To my surprise, given the goal of a business career, I was fascinated by economic history, especially the industrial revolution in Britain, and not entirely because of the wonderfully bleak Scots humour of the late great Dr Ian

McPherson who taught the course. For centuries, the UK income per head had remained more or less static. But in the second half of the eighteenth century, Britain became the first economy to move into self-sustaining economic growth. What caused this? And how had some countries – but not others – followed suit? Completely against my master plan, I went on to take every option in economic development.

My three supervision partners in economic history became close friends: fellow Caian Joe, and Newnham girls Cathy and Angela. I immediately connected with Joe, an Iranian who was as girl-obsessed as me, and apparently able to read my mind. We both fell in love with Cathy but managed to block each other's way, unfortunately allowing her to escape into the arms of someone else. Angela was a wise, lovely and caring Lancashire lass with a great sense of fun who (I say in my diary) had a life history straight from a Victorian novel. Apparently she had had to make a choice between marrying a man who lived on a scale model warship on a canal and reading economics at Cambridge.

The four of us spent Easter 1977 touring France in Joe's Ford Capri with a frame tent and a folding toilet. It was quite a squeeze to get everything in, especially the toilet, which I considered essential for emergencies. Unfortunately, Joe's rally car cornering technique of dropping a gear and speeding up was more than the Capri's gearbox could bear. It gave up near Tain Hermitage, south of Lyon, so we spent a week in a campsite on the banks of the Rhone waiting for a replacement, enduring France's coldest Easter for 50 years. It was so cold we moved into the inner tent together, enjoying the adventure and intimacy and becoming known in the village as 'Les Anglais'. Hermitage has been my favourite wine ever since. We never used the folding toilet.

Back at Cambridge, we partied and watched films, plays and debates. I joined the Union Society, tried rowing and gliding, loved punting, learnt the new sport of windsurfing, joined the college orchestra, put myself on courses in public speaking, computing and business, improved my French in the language lab and hitched around France. To gain favour with different girls, I learnt to roller skate (Alison), went to the Anthroposophy study group (Violet) and took an interest in folk music (Anne).

We ate in each other's college dining halls and explored the local restaurants. The Green Man in Grantchester, also accessible by punt. The Tickel Arms, run by an eccentric who advertised 'no queers and no long-haired lefties' and once told my two female guests off for playing with the candles, muttering 'bloody virgins'. And the Whim, which served moussaka for a bargain 63p but was later prosecuted when it was discovered that the meat used was cat food.

A high point in my first year was nominating Cathy to drive the Caius bed in the Rag Week bed race. The bed consisted of two bike front wheels linked together and welded onto a bed frame; two bigger bike wheels inserted into the back of the frame; and a mattress that rose up over the rear wheels as a back rest and doubling as a fluffy mudguard. It was difficult to steer and distinctly dangerous around corners so we gave the nervous Cathy a practice, a crash helmet and strong coffee before pushing her round to the start. A few minutes later, 22 custom-built racing beds thundered through down King's Parade at the beginning of a 12-mile race. We won and knocked ten minutes off the previous record. Cathy, Joe and I went out for a celebratory lunch with champagne and Angela joined us when she came back from pushing the Newnham bed.

My main student society focus was the Cambridge University Cruising Club (CUCrC). I joined the committee, ran the university sailing courses and organised the Caius team for the inter-college series. When it was sunny and windy I couldn't resist abandoning my books to go windsurfing. Once I sailed for the university, though this was probably because I had a car by my second year and could therefore help transport the team to the race venue. We won, mainly because as the lead boat we were in a position to slow down and cover the leading opposition boat to allow our team through to a winning combination of places. I also joined the CUCrC squash league and especially enjoyed the annual punt party to Grantchester; water pistols essential, life jackets advised.

In the holidays I went sailing: instructing at Bosham Sea School; volunteering at the Island Cruising Club (ICC) in Salcombe, a sail training charity; and taking any opportunity to go cruising.

Cruising covers a wide range of activities. At one end of the scale, I borrowed an old wooden 20-footer: four berths, a bucket for a loo and a dodgy pull-start engine. I sailed her back from Falmouth with a friend but got stuck in Salcombe after meeting a wild and wonderful red-headed Scottish girl called Kirsty at a party on Egremont, the ex-Liverpool ferry that served as a base for the ICC. Kirsty had a good heart, a laid-back approach to life and an attractively wicked streak. She was once banned from the harbour for speeding and grew cannabis in quiet spots around the estuary. The ICC, Kirsty and a growing group of friends in the area led to Salcombe becoming a second home. I loved the estuary and raw beauty of the coastline, especially out of season.

At the other end of the scale, I pushed my way into a trip from Lisbon to Cowes in a 43-footer with Charles Gardner.[1] He asked my mother if one of my sisters would be cook but I raced round and asked if the cook needed to be female. I think he was hoping for some female interest to enliven the trip but could hardly admit this. I redeemed myself by offering to take a watch, relieving him of formal watch duties.

---

[1] Charles was an aeronautical engineer who had won air races in the 1930s, competed in ocean sailing races in the 1950s and won the 1964 Cowes–Torquay powerboat race after the leading boat accidentally missed the finishing line.

We flew to Lisbon in his Cessna 340 and punched our way out into the Atlantic after three days of gales to catch the Portuguese trade wind. Scrabbling around in the bow locker to find lunch as we pitched wildly was the only time I have ever been seasick. On the trip he taught me astro navigation (no GPS then) and I learnt that a 50:50 sea water/fresh water mix is best to boil potatoes. We were in Newton Ferrers in eight days, then enjoyed a stunning 20 hours sail to Cowes, tearing round Portland Bill under spinnaker, close inshore to avoid the tidal rip, barely under control in a strong breeze, arriving around midnight at the Groves and Gutteridge marina, which he co-owned. He flew me back to his house in Sussex in his helicopter before I was dropped back home in his Porsche. I felt it was a lifestyle I could take to.

The car I acquired in the second year ensured that I had easier access to Girton College than most of my colleagues. Girton was the first women's college and therefore situated at the edge of Cambridge to keep students clear of predatory men. Through an old acquaintance from Kuwait, I came to know many of the inhabitants of her corridor and several became good friends, always ready to put a kettle on when I dropped round.

The Kirsty relationship was off and on, and what I really longed for was a regular girlfriend who didn't live 300 miles away, someone I could love and who would love me. It didn't happen, but my attempts did contribute valuable material for long, late-night discussions over a Scotch with Ralph, one of several of us who shared a second-year house in Mortimer Road. He was a man with sensitivity and a great sense of humour who liked to go punting in a traditional college blazer and straw boater. Ralph had almost identical problems of love and rejection, but with boys, an orientation that was complicated by his Christian faith. Some time before, he had taken an overdose. In sympathy, and through a sense of injustice, I briefly joined the Gay Cambridge Committee.

On the plus side for him, when he asked our battleaxe landlady Mrs T if he could have a friend to stay she asked, 'Male or female?' To the response, 'Male,' she said, 'Well, that's OK then.' The rest of us knew otherwise. When I wanted Kirsty to stay, I didn't dare ask the question and had to smuggle her in. At one point she got stuck in the bathroom for over an hour, waiting for a clear escape route.

At the end of the second year, I helped my Uncle Gerald sail his Fisher 37 motor sailing yacht from Guernsey to Malta, via Gibraltar, the Balearics, Corsica, Sardinia and Scilly. Gerald had worked for his uncle's box making company, H H Tallent, fallen out with him and set up in competition. He built it up to three factories, producing cartons for Glaxo and Boots, rigid boxes and plastic inserts for Tri-ang model railways and bubble packs for the contraceptive pill. He eventually sold the business and retired to Malta to avoid the then 98 per cent tax on income from savings. Two Girton friends joined me for the cruise, which was, unexpectedly, filled with sexual tension and discovery.

One of the girls joined the cruise in Gibraltar and, as Gerald didn't want to change the berthing arrangements, her sleeping bag was added to mine on the double berth in the saloon.

She was slim and sensual with short, brown, curly hair. Within a couple of days our goodnight kiss became more lingering. We were both embarrassed and the next day agreed that we hadn't intended on a relationship. But our friendship, intimate night-time situation and curiosity got the better of us. Sometimes we crept out in the middle of the night and swam naked. Sometimes we messed around, out of sight, on the foredeck.

It was not that we really wanted to go out with each other, but she was keen to find out what turned a guy on. She thought and acted in a very sexual way and I was thrilled to be the subject of her testing.

At the time, this sexual chemistry and the ease with which we could explore our desires was wonderful and exciting, but years later I came to regret it.

In the first few weeks of my third year, the relationship problem changed from finding someone – anyone – to unravelling a complex set of partnerships from different times and places that somehow all came together at a joint twenty-first birthday party at Girton with the girl from the Malta cruise. With a mix of horror and misplaced pride I realised I had slept with three of the guests in the previous week alone. Meanwhile, I was still in love with Cathy. Kirsty, wisely and graciously, put herself on the next train back to Totnes. It was only then that I appreciated her kind and forgiving heart, and I felt very guilty.

In that final year I had modern rooms with a wide shared balcony overlooking gardens and close to the main lecture site. The two terms were characterised by constant searching, a series of short relationships and more nightcaps with a few close friends. On at least one occasion – according to my diary – the Scotch was supplemented by both a joint and mushy peas.

The future also began to exercise my thoughts. My master plan was to learn the ropes then set up a business. My role models were Uncle Gerald and one of his friends. At the time, the only way to make serious money was by building a business. But it was not just about money, Gerald told me on the trip to Malta; it was about power. Money, he believed, could buy anything or anyone, a belief he demonstrated clearing customs in Malta.

Gerald's friend had set up Hom menswear and Loveable Bras ('It costs so little to look so loveable'). He had started in beachwear after the war but hadn't taken into account the fact that the beaches were mined so he moved into related fields. He had a sharp mind, asked lots of questions and recommended I read *Scientific American* to get business ideas. He visited me in my last term and said he and Gerald would be interested in investing in me in a few years' time.

I saw the perfect next step through the Cambridge Careers Service. A small but fast-growing precision engineering company in Coventry called Eaves and Washbourne was looking for a management trainee and offering the same salary as Mars, the highest paying 'milk-round' recruiter. They were investing heavily in computer-controlled machine tools and achieving levels of machining accuracy not then found outside Switzerland.[2]

My first interview was in a college I didn't know, and I wasn't sure which room it was in. Nervously, I tiptoed up the stairs, listened at the door and overheard MD Paul Washbourne saying, 'What we are really looking for is enthusiasm.' I crept back down and came up more noisily, knocking enthusiastically.

Four of us were selected for the next stage – two days in Coventry with a tour, a meal out and the formal interview on day two. I stayed up late preparing hard, rehearsing answers to likely questions. The first question was obvious and I prepared an answer that would appear spontaneous when in fact it was carefully crafted with lashings of enthusiasm.

'So you've had a look around. What do you think? Are you still interested?'

'Brilliant! I could watch the Sajo machines all day. And it's because I'm so enthusiastic about the possibility of working for Eaves and Washbourne that I feel I could really contribute...'

I got the job.

---

[2] The company was manufacturing Tornado aircraft lead screws with a total pitch error of five microns (0.005mm) over a metre; and three-part table sets for spark erosion machines with a total flatness tolerance of five microns. If you're not an engineer, believe me, this is accurate.

Just as the job search came to a result, the answer to my other search slipped into place. In March 1979, I met Amanda: red hair, gentle Scottish accent, pretty, a first-year lawyer. I loved the way her courage and determination covered an endearing vulnerability.

The relationship developed slowly and cautiously. We grew on each other. By the end of April I had invited her to the Caius May Ball (which naturally takes place in June). My friends thought I was nuts, as my track record suggested I would have worked through several more relationships by then. This time there was no going back, not least because she bought a £63 Laura Ashley dress for the occasion. A lot of money: the equivalent of a hundred main course moussakas at The Whim.

She wanted to separate for the duration of our exams, and when we came back together we were very much in love. Together we went round the constant series of post-exam parties in a happy and somewhat alcoholic haze: breakfast parties, garden parties, music on the backs and other evening events. On 9th June we put on fancy dress for three evening parties including Keith Vaz's 'Conspiracy Party' (the dress code was 'as Jeremy would have liked it' – a reference to Jeremy Thorpe who was on trial for conspiracy to murder). The invitation to a 'Red Adair' Party (after the oil well firefighter) to be hosted by Adair Turner, another Caian marked for success, turned out to be a hoax. The May Ball on 12th June was the highlight. 'The best evening I've ever had,' I wrote. It ended with a steel band and Auld Lang Syne at 6.30am. Amanda kept saying how happy she was.

It was sad to leave. It had been an extraordinary and wonderful last four weeks. But I was ready to move on.

I chartered a 30ft Dufour Arpège and sailed Amanda and four other friends to France and the Channel Islands. The weather was warm and sunny, and the sail from Alderney to Sark, gliding along on a beautiful, still evening at six knots under spinnaker was one of the best sails of my life. I felt a deep contentment. It was my first Channel crossing as skipper but on the way back I impressed the crew by finding Lulworth Cove, despite the early morning fog, after leaving Sark the night before. GPS is brilliant but it takes away the satisfaction of stumbling across a pinprick of a place and pretending it was down to your skill in the dark art of 'yottigation'[3].

Over the summer I went on an Ocean Youth Club week as a mate, hitched around the Loire valley and worked in a yoghurt factory. Over this time the relationship with Amanda was rather up and down. At times I felt deeply in love; at other times I had real doubts. The truth was I had no strength of will to be faithful. One night in July she asked what I was thinking, and as I had been imagining being married to her we discussed engagement and maybe getting married in a few years' time.

Just a few days later I was flirting with an old friend and kissed her a passionate goodbye. I wrote in my diary that I felt guilty and claimed that it was 'not entirely my fault', but worse was to come. In the autumn I had a one-night stand, when at the end of a night out in Nottingham, a friend of a friend fell onto my lap.

'Er, this is interesting,' I said.

'Yes, isn't it?' she said. 'We need to share the hot water bottle.'

In my diary I wrote, 'It was a horrible decision to make and I made the wrong one… we both felt very guilty ref. Amanda afterwards… I must be good from now on.'

It was hardly an accident. I knew there would be temptations and should never have gone to the event that evening. And I certainly shouldn't have spent the evening playing footsie with her under the table.

---

[3] A term coined by Bill Lucas and Andrew Spedding in their excellent book *Sod's Law of the Sea*, Stanford Maritime, 1977.

Eaves and Washbourne decided to recruit two trainees; the other was an engineer from Queens' College, called Jon. We rented the managing director's maisonette and started a three-month engineering practice course, where we had fun cutting, turning, forging and grinding metal to make useful things.

Amanda and her family were lovely. There were cards from both her and her parents waiting for me when I arrived in Coventry, and when she phoned after my first day she sounded more nervous than I was. I had a good relationship with both her parents. In retaliation for some comment I had made, her mother – aided and abetted by Amanda – put me on a mailing list for thermal underwear. I responded by writing in her name to the local naturist group to ask about membership. I assumed they would put her on a mailing list. But no. They sent a man round to visit her, clutching my letter. Amanda's mother managed to contain her laughter, claiming she couldn't think of anyone in Coventry who might have played such a trick. Apparently he was not the sort of man you would want to see naked.

I spent many weekends in Cambridge. On Friday nights I would feel very close to Amanda and in love, and the moment I left on Sunday nights I would miss her. In between, as I hung out with her and did the rounds of other friends in Cambridge, the passion faded and the relationship was often tense.

This unsatisfying situation made me want to meet people my own age in Coventry, especially girls. After all, Amanda was miles away and I'd encouraged her to enjoy Cambridge to the full, so I felt entitled to do the same.

A cunning plan soon emerged. My housemate Jon was a Christian who had been roped into a church attended by many students from nearby Warwick University. It was Church of England so I expected it to be boring, but thought it would be worthwhile going along if I could chat up a Warwick student after the service.

On 9th December 1979 I went to Westwood Church for the first time. It was friendly, full of young people and I found it curiously moving. I was stunned to discover people who actually believed that God answered prayers and seemed to be very happy. In my diary I name 13 people I met that first evening, including Geoff and Sylvia. Geoff had just been made redundant and had a family to support, and yet seemed to be at peace about it, trusting God for the future. I loved the informality of the evening service and afterwards went up to Alan, the vicar, to say I liked the 'casual' style. 'Yes,' he said in his deep voice with a smile. 'But we mustn't be casual with God, you know.'

I shrugged this off but the comment went home. Seeds of faith had already been planted in me. At Great Walstead, teachers had read to us *The Cross and the Switchblade* (a bestselling book about a minister working with gangs and drug addicts in New York), and *God's Smuggler* (a man called Brother Andrew bringing illegal Bibles into communist Eastern Europe). Both included miraculous answers to prayer that I couldn't easily explain or dismiss. In my early teens I had used daily Bible study notes and occasionally turned to prayer. The day my cousin Alastair got married, it was pouring with rain. I prayed; it cleared up, and as they left on honeymoon the rain returned. On the morning of the Cambridge bed race, it was wet; I prayed, and the sun came out. Yet this was hardly life-shattering and faith didn't make any logical sense. I'd read Lyall Watson's *Supernature*, which examines apparently supernatural phenomena in nature, and I assumed there would be a scientific explanation one day.

In the New Year, I began a tense time on 12-hour shifts operating a CNC machining centre while charged with improving productivity for the whole team. I learnt a lot about relationships. Charlie, a night-shift operator, once threatened to throw me 'into a f*****g machine'. Later I joined him on night shift and things improved. I talked with him and he seemed amazed that anyone would take any interest in him. On his stag night I saved him from being sent to Glasgow on a one-way train ticket. As I drove him home he kept turning to me to say I was his best friend. He had had a lot to drink. Chargehand Steve had directed the creation of a drink that involved a pint glass, barley wine and two of every spirit on the display.

I continued to go to Westwood Church and a student-age evening group called 'The Sunday Night Thing'. The others assumed I was a Christian, so I could listen in knowing their stories of answered prayer were not for my benefit – they were not trying to convert me. I bought a modern translation of the Bible and read John's gospel for the first time as an adult. The character of Jesus impressed me: so good, but not in a weak way. He was direct, but loving, to the Samaritan woman with a dodgy love life,[4] he challenged those about to stone a woman for adultery[5] and he was someone who stood up to polite society and said what needed to be said. 'You are like whitewashed tombs,' he said to the Pharisees, 'which look fine on the outside but are full of bones and decaying corpses on the inside.'[6] Nice.

This was the kind of man I wanted to be: loving and self-controlled with strong foundations. Someone who stood up for the oppressed, not sucking up to the rich and powerful, saying what needed to be said, even if it was unpopular. This was not who I was. I had little self-control, I yielded to the temptations of the moment; I didn't like to offend anyone and had little self-respect.

In the end, though, the question was whether the New Testament was true. If it was, it changed everything; it could not be ignored. Nothing could possibly be more important than

---

[4] John 4:1-41.
[5] John 8: 3-11.
[6] Matthew 23:27 (Good News Translation).

knowing God's guidance in this life and being certain that my long-term future, home and treasure were secure. The more I investigated, and the more I heard and read stories of God breaking into lives around me, the more sure I was that it was true.

However, there was a significant problem with becoming a Christian. I was worried I might have to give up sex. The church teaching was that sex is reserved for marriage. I went to the top for advice on this delicate matter. 'Look, God, if this is important, tell me now!' Then I allowed my Bible to open at random. This is not the recommended means of guidance, I discovered later, but God is tolerant of an earnestly seeking soul and played along. I now know there is really only one passage that could have provided an answer. And that is where my finger landed.

'Avoid immorality... the man who is guilty of sexual immorality sins against his own body. Don't you know that your body is the temple of the Holy Spirit, who lives in you and who was given to you by God? You do not belong to yourselves but to God; he bought you for a price. So use your bodies for God's glory.'[7]

The solution was, of course, to wait until I was married before I became a Christian. But something else shook me up and changed my mind.

On Monday 25th February 1980 I wrote the following in my diary:

> Mum phoned me to say that Paul Ashton had died. Paul had been one of my best friends as a kid in Kuwait and was doing well with a small company making ventilation equipment for the North Sea oil industry. Apparently he'd driven to some cliffs near Polperro in Cornwall and walked along them at about 6.30am after a party. Only a shoe and a watch were found.

---

[7] 1 Corinthians 6:18-20 (Good News Translation).

Faced with the fragility of life and death after Paul's terrible accident, I felt I couldn't wait. The diary continues:

> The second dramatic happening was that I went to visit the Westwood vicar Alan and finally decided to accept God properly – including giving up sex before marriage. That'll require a lot of willpower. I felt very spiritually uplifted and close to God, though now I'm beginning to wonder if I'll make it.

Right from the start, God had an agenda: money, sex and power. All good things but all with a dark side and, for me, all potentially damaging addictions.

The first one on the list was sex. It was a huge challenge and a significant change. However, if this God was real, wanted to be skipper of my life and would enable me to be the person He made me to be, then I couldn't be casual or half-hearted with Him. It was all or nothing, the full package and not some kind of Christianity Lite where I could opt in or out at will.

The person who got the worst deal on this was the long-suffering Amanda. I broke the news of my conversion and its implications to her that Friday. She cried. The poor girl had been involved in the Girton chapel and had taken many months to decide that it was acceptable to sleep with me in the first place.

'I think she'd rationalised it in her mind and thought it was OK, and the news that it wasn't came as a shock,' I wrote. I'd spent months convincing her of one thing and, just when that was all fine, I changed my mind.

We were both under increasing stress as 1980 progressed. I was buying a house and in charge of importing and installing a large second-hand machine from Switzerland. It was a high-profile task and at the edge of my engineering competence. Meanwhile, Amanda was working towards her finals and going for interviews. The relationship continued to be very up and down:

> Got a bit fed up with Amanda – don't really know why – except that sometimes I wish she'd stop making cutting comments and nagging, etc.

> Tried to phone Amanda because I miss her. Sometimes I get really worried about how unaffectionate I've been and I really miss her.

I went to a 'home group', a fortnightly small group where we studied the Bible and prayed for each other. They often found themselves having to pray around some complex engineering issues. When my machine finally arrived on 3rd October I wrote:

> At work at 6am, machine arrived 8.30am. I felt tremendously supported in getting the machine in and very close to God – I think I was being tested – crisis after crisis, but everything worked out in the end. It was a beautiful day, important in view of the amount of stuff we had to move outside to make room for the five-tonne Iron Fairy [mobile crane].

In November I asked the home group to pray about my relationship with Amanda. I wanted God's help to sort it out. Despite all the problems, I loved her and I was looking for a miracle. I drove to Cambridge and the first thing she said was that she thought it would be for the best if we split up. She was very upset. We went for a meal at the Three Horseshoes in Madingley, went for a walk and hugged goodbye. When I got home I was angry with God. I knelt and tearfully banged the bed with my fist. When I had asked Him to sort it out, this was not what I meant.

At the time, I thought He just hadn't heard my prayer.

I reverted to the quest to find someone to love and someone who would love me. Top of the list was Violet, a friend from South Devon who volunteered with the ICC. Violet was different from anyone else I knew: happy, loving and at one with herself and nature. In part because of her, going to Salcombe was always intoxicating. In December 1979, Violet, Kirsty, fellow ICC instructor Chuck and I walked to Gara Rock on a stormy Saturday. The sun had broken through, the waves crashed onto the shore, Violet hopped and skipped along and I felt very happy. Chuck had been offered a job as a skipper in the Caribbean at £120 a week – as much as I was earning – and I was sorely tempted to take a completely different career route.

The following November I visited Violet where she was working in a Steiner centre in Buckfastleigh for young people with learning difficulties: cheerful Suzy, who could only make whooping noises; Jean who flung her arms around everyone; Richard, who was very excitable and difficult to understand; John, friendly, quiet and helpful; Jonathan, who got violent when frustrated. We took a couple of her 'family' out and they were ridiculously and wonderfully excited. Violet earned £4 a week and I was filled with respect for her.

By the time I'd split with Amanda, Violet was going out with Peter, but I continued to visit and talk with her on the phone. I adored her but I was uneasy that she wasn't a Christian and I held back. On 26th May 1981 I was chatting with her on the phone when it went silent at the other end.

'Violet? Violet? Violet?'

An ominous voice came on.

'This is Peter, Violet's boyfriend.'

'Oh, hello… I'm looking forward to meeting you,' I lied.

'Why do you keep calling her?'

'Well, we've been good friends for years…'

He put Violet on the phone to me to say goodbye. We only had a few seconds. She sounded awkward and distressed.

A few days later I received a scribbled letter from Violet telling me to stop writing and phoning, and signed 'Yours, Violet'. It was not her letter and I was deeply fearful for her. I considered driving down and attempting a heroic rescue, but thought better of it. I never heard from her again.

I understand she married Peter and had children but then divorced. Years later, I thought I saw her on the shore as I was coming in on a ferry and she seemed to be looking at me. As soon as I disembarked I went straight to where this person had been standing but she had gone. Violet was a free spirit, a butterfly that, I fear, had been caught and pinned down.

One reason I thought better of driving to Devon to try to see Violet was that just two weeks before, I had thrown a certain Sue Ratcliffe into a ditch outside Westwood Church.

I first remember meeting Sue when I was trying to chat up her best friend, also called Sue, in her room at Warwick University. Sue R had ignored me and was oblivious to my intentions. On Sunday 10th May I'd been to a church student tea after which a group of us had gone for a walk.

'I jokingly picked Sue R up and tried to chuck her into a ditch,' I wrote in the diary. 'And it seemed to pull a heartstring.'

The next day was a make-or-break day for the church, and it was packed. The week before, Alan had said that if God was with us in a major extension project we would have raised £20,000 by the next week. That was hundreds of pounds per family. The project and his credibility were on the line. The next Sunday we had raised £20,600. It was a lesson that stuck: God honours those who take a risk, who step out in faith.

The following week I was involved in a dramatics club play. I invited Sue R to the play, and on the Saturday she cooked a meal for me and we went to the after-play party. In my diary I wrote that I was impressed with her cooking, the fact she had got a first in MORSE (Maths, Operations Research, Statistics and Economics) and that she was a committed Christian. Clearly, I was in the market for a wife.

One Saturday shortly after, I looked her up just when she was ready to be disturbed from work. We went for a walk and spent the evening together. I felt very comfortable with her.

The next day, she was looking out for me at church in the morning. We had lunch together and then went for a walk. It was a lovely hot, humid, lazy afternoon and we walked along a river near Wolston. We found a gorgeous wooden bridge going nowhere, with a handrail and a tree in flower behind. It all seemed beautifully arranged. We talked and held hands, then came back to my house for tea. One of the young girls next door asked if we were going to get married.

Sue was 'the girl next door', attractive but in a natural, ordinary sort of way. She was warm and cuddly, thoughtful with a ready laugh. She had lived her whole life in Ainsdale and those strong Lancashire roots, northern accent and clear Christian commitment suggested a stability I lacked.

My concern was she was planning to do a PGCE in Liverpool, and we'd both had enough of long-distance relationships. So I stepped out in faith and prayed that if God was in it she would stay in Coventry the following year. The next day we went to see Alan, and he suggested we go back to being good friends and wait to see what God would do.

We didn't have to wait long. The next day, Sue received a letter from Liverpool University to say they were full. A few days later, Warwick University asked her to consider doing an MA in economics. They offered her both a place and a grant. Immediately after that, a church family with a spare room asked if she knew any students looking for accommodation the following year. So suddenly she was going to stay in Coventry – a dramatic answer to prayer.

In the summer, Sue, her best friend Sue and three other friends joined me for a repeat of the 1979 Arpège cross-Channel cruise. She coped well and wasn't seasick – another key test successfully passed with flying colours. But I'm not sure whether she ever forgave me for allowing the full jar of strawberry jam to slide down the deck and into the water while breakfasting off La Coupée, Sark.

Soon I was crossing the Channel again, this time co-leading a Scripture Union youth holiday on 'Ocean Venture', a beautiful 60ft schooner with a unique and colourful sail called a Gollywobbler, set between the masts in light airs.

One evening en route to Brittany we were becalmed and took the opportunity to lead a session on the topic 'Do not worry' against a stunning backdrop of peach and hazy blue, perfectly still and peaceful. 'It's all created by chance, you know,' joked Tony, the skipper. As it got dark, there was fantastic phosphorescence, the marine equivalent of fireflies. We switched off the navigation lights and watched the fish, the bright colours bursting out in all directions like a firework display. Although Sue wasn't there she was always at the forefront of my mind, and I was very happy.

The final decision was made on the long drive back from a trade show in Hanover on 23rd September. Eaves and Washbourne had decided to save money by driving two groups out and camping in Paul Washbourne's frame tent. We emerged each day wearing our suits.

I asked Sue to marry me after a Sunday lunch together on 11th October 1981, and I shook with the enormity of it for hours afterwards We phoned our parents and Alan announced it at the evening service: everyone was so pleased. I slipped out shortly after the beginning of the service to go to the dress rehearsal of *Harvey* – I had a lead role – and saw my sister Hilary coming in. She had started a B Ed at Warwick and had become a Christian before me. I told her the news and gave her a hug and half cried. After the service, she found Sue and gave her a big hug.

We were married at Westwood on 25th September 1982, but the joy was tinged with sadness. Sue's mum was diagnosed with leukaemia just before Christmas 1981. She died in June 1982. She was warm and kind-hearted, a leading light of the Ainsdale flower show, who had told Sue she would not have a dull life with me. She had already made one layer of the wedding cake; eating it was a proud and emotional moment.

Our reception took place in the brand new church rooms, and then we headed off for a honeymoon in Tintagel, Cornwall.

My experience of God developed quickly, building my faith for what was to come. Twice I laid hands on Sue during the night because she had backache, and both times she was immediately healed. Then we bought a new mattress which seemed to be a more permanent solution!

The sex thing was never an issue during our courtship, which made my commitment about this and our relationship easier. We could be intimate without it. But within marriage, my previous experience cast a shadow. Although we never talked about it, I know that Sue worried about how she compared. And while there was no comparison, images from my earlier life came back to taunt me for many years. It would have been better without them.

At first I wasn't convinced I could remain faithful. Business people can be subject to more temptation than most, and my track record had been lousy. However, I had learnt one lesson: the decision to be unfaithful is made a long time before the opportunity to jump into bed together presents itself. The trick is to back off from that first brush of hands or touch of the feet under the table.

There were opportunities and temptations. At a two-day conference, it was flattering to be targeted for a one-night stand by an attractive divorcee. Early in the conversation – to protect myself as much as anything – I made it known that I was a Christian. She realised she'd made the wrong choice: at the earliest opportunity she went off to find someone else. I admit there was a strong sense of lost opportunity. I was alone, far from home, no one would have known. Nevertheless I absolutely knew that continuing would have been horrible, something I would regret for the rest of my life.

I'm not sensitive to the subtle communication approaches taken by women. Once a lovely Girtonian wrote to me to say that her friend was in love with someone but he wasn't aware of it, what should she do? I provided sensible advice but it was months before someone (a girl) pointed out that this was all an elaborate code to say that she was in love with me.

Despite this weakness, over the last 30 years I've been aware of three women who made it clear they were up for an affair. They all knew I liked them but I never let on that the old carnal part of me was interested. Once I got as far as picking up the phone – significantly, when Sue was out – to call someone I knew was open to an affair. I hadn't seen her in church for a while. I was just a concerned friend. Then I paused, thought about where the call might lead, and put the phone back.

Westwood Church has a policy of low control and high accountability. This is ideal for an entrepreneur. I am free to do whatever God is calling me to, so long as I have an accountability partner, someone (of the same gender) with whom I have a transparent relationship. This means that when I am away, have a drink with business contacts, come back to the hotel alone, see the advert on the TV for porn, I can text my partner and say I'm feeling vulnerable. That act in itself brings me back from the brink.

I haven't missed out. I'm glad I've made it and now I'm confident I'll remain faithful. Yet the good news for those who fail is that God always gives another chance.

The second thing on God's agenda was money. The Church worries about sex, and money gets a back seat. In contrast, Jesus talked constantly about money issues and sex barely got a look in. 'People who want to get rich fall into temptation and a trap,' wrote Paul to his trainee Timothy, 'and into many foolish and harmful desires that plunge men into ruin and destruction.'[8]

Money is a brilliant invention: it's a means of exchange and a store of value. It has great potential for good. The problem is not money, but the love of money. There is nothing wrong with possessing money: the problem is that it has the power to possess us. We can be addicted to it. With most commodities the law of diminishing marginal utility applies: the more we have of it, the less we want more. The fifth ice cream is less enticing than the first. Money can be different. For some people, the more they have, the more they want. I was in danger of being destructively addicted. I needed to learn to possess money without being possessed by it.

I needed to break the hold of money by defiling it, by giving it away. When I first became a Christian I realised I was expected to give money away, so I chose the smallest amount I thought I could get away with: £5 a month to the church. Even that was a struggle. It was as much as my sailing club subscription! However, I was also concerned about global poverty and after a while I added £5 a month to Tearfund. But money was tight. I had a £2,000 loan as well as a mortgage, and there it stuck.

Meanwhile, Eaves and Washbourne was struggling. A third £100,000 Sajo CNC machining centre was purchased because our key customer said they wanted to double production with us. A massive surface grinder was also purchased, costing £150,000 second hand. Then the recession cut in. Coventry lost two thirds of manufacturing jobs in the period 1980–82. As a result of the recession, just after the Sajo was installed, the customer halved rather than doubled production with us. In addition, the second biggest customer also cut back sharply. There were redundancies, we all took pay cuts and there was a

---

[8] 1 Timothy 6:9.

possibility we would be taken over by a partner company and become merely a machine shop.

I was sent on a sales course, and my job title changed from Project Engineer to Sales Engineer. I won some new customers but order values were low and it was a struggle to get engineering backup at times. I saw an advert for a Sales Administration Manager role at an old established firm of agricultural merchants called Lucy and Nephew. It offered a significant pay increase. I wasn't certain it was right, and I'm not sure who interviewed whom, but perhaps my caution over the role encouraged them to try to convince me and they offered me the job.

During the interview, I picked up that there was some kind of collusion going on; I had the presence of mind to say I was a Christian and would not take part in anything dodgy. This turned out to be a useful exchange: later, I reminded my employer of it.

I promised God if I got the job I'd use the extra income to make my giving up to a tithe, 10 per cent. I was appointed and a couple of months later I increased giving to £60 a month. This was a breakthrough in my attitude to money because I didn't resent it. I began to worry less about proving my success to Cambridge contemporaries. In due course, the possibility of giving more, and at times going beyond a tithe, was exciting, and I was able to increase giving to hundreds of pounds a month. The hold of money was broken, and I feel it was only then that God allowed me the opportunity to earn significant sums.

The third issue God needed to tackle was power. For me, that meant status and respect. It took an uncomfortable experience to get there.

The job at Lucy & Nephew, part of United Agricultural Merchants and ultimately Unilever, was unsuited to me but I learnt about invoicing, cash collection, computerised accounts, cut-offs, stocktakes, trading, sales and managing people, as well as about the unique aspects of the agricultural sector. I learnt you could run a profitable business on margins of under five per cent if stock turnover is high. I also learnt how not to do business plans: the regional accountant came in each year with a spreadsheet to show if we increased margins and cut costs the following year we would make more money. That was therefore the business plan for the year.

My concern about collusion with other suppliers was confirmed and I phoned the Unilever legal department anonymously to confirm my suspicions that this was illegal. It was a relief to be able to remind them of what I had said during the interview, and the Managing Director took it away from my responsibilities. I had made a stand but it seemed reasonable to limit my moral position to my particular sphere.

When I finally started to get on top of the job I grew bored. I prayed for something exciting to happen, and a few days later I was made redundant. This was not exactly what I had in mind. Having failed as an economics graduate to predict the manufacturing recession, I also failed to predict the downturn in farming in 1983–84. However, I received a generous settlement and went straight into another job.

So my first two employers went downhill within two years of joining them, but don't blame me for the third. Within a couple of days of starting work, the boss apologised and warned me that they might go bust. I was Sales Administration and Marketing Manager at Butters, a highly respected manufacturer of welding equipment. The company also installed production cells based around a Japanese robot.

There was an enthusiastic management team, the job broadened my skillset and it was only a short bike ride from home. I persuaded one of the welding experts to teach me the basics, sorted the haphazard administrative procedure and controls and started a marketing diploma. I got involved in PR, advertising, literature production, exhibiting and telesales and began to get an understanding of sales management.

Advertising and PR was a new and stimulating area for me. Like most engineering adverts, welding ads tended to focus on pictures of the product – essentially boxes. Our boxes were orange. The main competitors had red, yellow or blue boxes. We livened things up with a series of ads focussing on the much more interesting products made with Butters kit, including a TVR sports car and the Virgin Atlantic Challenger II, which beat the transatlantic record, generating editorial and making it to the front cover of *Welding Review*.

An unexpected highlight was winning the Churchill College Prize, an essay competition for graduates working in small businesses. The essay was printed in *British Engineer* and there was a double-page spread in *Management Today* with pictures that made it look like I worked in pitch darkness. The prize was £600, a dinner in Cambridge and handshake from Sir Keith Joseph (who was then the Secretary of State for Industry) at Price Waterhouse in London.

On the morning of 13th January 1986, I spent half an hour looking into the eyes of the small and beautiful child in my arms. She quietly stared back. I could barely hold back the tears. Quietly and slightly self-consciously I sang nursery rhymes and anything I could think of. The nurses, bustling around Sue, told each other I was a natural. A pink label on the cot provided identification: live child of Susan Marshall; 3.140kg; 08:59hrs.

It was moving and momentous. For us, it meant 24 hours of panic, trying to figure out how babies work, followed by a lifetime of loving and learning. For my parents, she was their first, long-awaited, grandchild. For many, this little bundle would grow up to influence, enrich or change the course of their life.

A few months later, Butters was bought by a London company that was interested in the respected brand, not the product itself. The workers, many of whom had been with Butters for decades, were made redundant, with no notice, during a holiday break. I was so angry I met with them once a month and took the new owners to court, winning a small out-of-court settlement for everybody.

This redundancy was different. The arrival of Hannah meant that Sue had given up work as a systems analyst with Warwickshire Country Council, and we had moved to a new house with a new and excitingly large mortgage. So financially it was grim.

The Bible passage on our Tearfund calendar was Jeremiah 29:11: 'For I know the plans I have for you,' declares the Lord, 'plans to prosper you and not to harm you, plans to give you hope and a future.'

Sue and I went to the Cotswolds to fast and pray for a day. We sat with our back to a tree to try to hear what God was saying and we both, independently, felt that He was telling us to wait, to do nothing.

This seemed a tall order and I thought it would be right to 'push a few doors'. I applied for several jobs and was offered the perfect role: marketing manager for a much larger company with a 40 per cent pay increase. I was given 24 hours to decide. I would have taken it on the spot but thought it would be good form to run it by Sue and have her approval.

Sue was unimpressed and cautious. I was annoyed with her. The decision was obvious and she was being both unreasonable and impractical. So I told God He would have to make it clear if this was wrong within 24 hours, which meant, in practice, by my morning Bible study time.

The passage set that morning was Matthew 16:24–26:

> Then Jesus said to his disciples: 'Whoever wants to be my disciple must deny themselves and take up their cross

and follow me. For whoever wants to save their life will lose it, but whoever loses their life for me will find it. What good will it be for someone to gain the whole world, yet forfeit their soul?'

The passage hit me hard, and I knew God was speaking to me through it. This was a job that seemed to offer the world, but the culture was to work long hours, and I sensed I would be expected to forfeit my soul for the sake of the company. I plucked up my courage and asked for more time to decide. Then I turned it down.

It was a crazy decision, especially under our financial circumstances. In particular, my career history had too many major changes and this job would have helped my CV make sense. Once again, I was angry with God. I told Him He'd messed up my CV and He had to sort it out.

Church members made all the difference. Someone put £400 in cash through the letterbox. A family decided to give us £50 a month until we were sorted. It was humbling to be on the receiving end of giving.

In these ways, God managed to break down my pride and release me from the career expectations placed on me. These first seven years after graduation were not a success. On a work level I felt there was nothing I could be proud of. My career path was broken. I was ready for it to be moulded into something new.

Was the next stage a life of fulfilment and danger, working with Tearfund in one of the poorest countries in the world? We began to explore a job in Bangladesh. Meanwhile, to stay off the dole, I considered setting up a temporary business.

What eventually emerged was completely unexpected: it was the gateway to a career that went beyond my wildest dreams.

Reflections

- Learn to treat money lightly. Possess money without being possessed by it. Defile it by giving it away.

- Find an accountability partner; have a transparent relationship with a same-sex friend you trust. Walk away from any tempting relationship right from the outset.

- Jettison pride: it will get in the way.

- God loves it and responds when we take a risk in faith.

- When four of you are touring in a sports car, don't bother with the folding toilet.

Chapter 3: The longest ever temporary business

I stood in a long queue at the benefits office. The dejection of the men around me was obvious to see. I felt that just being there labelled me a failure.

Then I found I qualified for the £40-a-week Enterprise Allowance (EA), which meant I didn't need to earn much to be better off than on benefit. Applying for EA, I was treated completely differently, and sent on a couple of days' training where the trainees were the respected clients.

Setting up a business while waiting to be recruited by Tearfund made sense. It was also an excuse to buy the Amstrad PCW, a complete word processing package with 256 KB RAM, green screen, built in floppy disk drive, word processing software and a nine-pin printer. It was selling at £399 + VAT, a quarter of the price of the cheapest PC.

In December 1986, I wrote ten letters on my new PCW, looking for freelance work.

I received one reply, from the relief agency World Vision, then based in Northampton. That year they had introduced a sponsored fast called the 24 Hour Famine and they wanted me to work with them full-time for three months to develop publicity for the second event at the end of March 1987. I said I would work four days a week, to give me time to find other clients. Not wanting to overcharge a charity, we agreed £55 a day.

My role was to maximise local press coverage. I bought the Pims Media Towns List, a directory listing press and broadcast media contacts for every town and city. Then I wrote a press release with 51 local variants, giving the number of people and youth groups signed up in each area and listing all the local schools taking part. I posted more than 400 press releases, generating more than 200 articles, as well as radio and TV coverage.

World Vision was a valuable place to develop new skills and learn about the development business. In a marketing sense, they had two main 'products': child sponsorship that appealed to older donors, reached through Sunday colour supplements; and the 24 Hour Famine, popular among teenage girls, attracted through *Just 17* and *Jackie* magazines. Each advert and promotional campaign was coded and tracked so the rate of return on every activity was known. This meant that it was easy to plan where to invest.

It was a busy, tiring, yet exhilarating time. After the World Vision contract I continued freelance PR work with an agency, so there were constant changes in gear: visiting the agency clients, writing press releases, Tearfund forms and interviews, and helping Sue look after Hannah. Money was tight but we were keeping our heads above water, and I loved being a dad.

In March, Tearfund finished their very thorough recruitment and assessment process for a post in Bangladesh to start on 1st September. In the end they had 80 A4 pages on us. They worried I might be too outspoken when faced with injustices overseas but accepted us anyway.

Then in July there was another sudden change: the Tearfund role fell through. A crisis at the project made it dangerous and the previous holder of the role returned to sort it out. The future we had mapped out vanished and we were back to uncertainty. Sue, who had taken longer to adjust to going to Bangladesh, now found it difficult to adjust to not going. Fortunately we hadn't gone too far in the preparations (except that our enthusiastic dentist had whipped out all my wisdom teeth as a precaution).

We couldn't afford a holiday but, after the hard work and emotional roller coaster of the previous year, we needed a break. I pounded the streets of Coventry visiting travel agents and was about to give up when I found incredibly cheap, last-minute flights to Malta. We stayed in my Uncle Gerald's farmhouse: the holiday felt like a special gift from God. Gerald's 'man' looked after us, Sue sat around the pool and painted, and Hannah – aged 18 months – played in a washing-up bowl by the water's edge. When we visited the local water slides, then the tallest in Europe, Hannah came down on my lap from the highest slide. After each slide, she ran from the poolside back to the steps in such a squealing whirlwind of excitement that strangers donated their unfinished books of tickets to us.

'Hi, I'm phoning to complain. There doesn't seem to be any books to help our 11- to 14-year-old church group grow in their faith.'

It was the late summer and I was on the phone to the managing editor of Scripture Union (SU). Our 'Pathfinder' members were mainly strong Christians but I couldn't find any books to help them on key issues such as prayer, reading the Bible, guidance and lifestyle.

'Well, this is a difficult age range to sell to. They're too old to be bought books but don't have enough pocket money to buy them for themselves. But why don't you write one yourself? Write me a chapter and a synopsis and I'll take a look'.

At the time I was Chairman of Coventry Youth for Christ. Our Director was a former English teacher and a skilled communicator. I tried to pass the task to him, but failed. So I had a go. It was lousy but somehow the editor saw potential and spent some time pulling it apart. My rewrite was rewarded with a contract and a £400 advance.

I enjoyed writing it, taking a fun and creative approach: stories, imaginative dialogue, a letter from God, a flow chart guide to guidance, and cartoons drawn by a friend. However, the publication process was painful. I argued with SU on which Bible study notes to recommend, how to phrase a potentially controversial section on Israel and whether or not to specify the age range for which it was written.

Get up and Grow was eventually published in June 1988 with enthusiastic comments on the back from the children's author Patricia St John and Christian leaders Clive Calver and Rob White. The biography on the back said:

> Jerry Marshall is the Chairman of Coventry Youth for Christ. He is a windsurfing instructor, is married to Sue, and hates beetroot.

A *Leadership Today* review quoted the bio, saying it hinted at the flavour of this 'imaginative and readable book' that would 'benefit new Christians of any age'.

I was excited to be a published author. I thought it was one of those things other people did but not me. If no one attempted to stop me starting a business or writing a book, was there anything I couldn't have a shot at?

Someone once said everyone should do one audacious new thing a year. This became my favourite guideline for the kind of life I wanted to live.

Writing a book meant I wasn't being paid much so we were awarded Family Income Supplement (FIS). That first year, including FIS, I earned around £12,000 to replace my previous salary. Each year after that, takings rose 20 to 30 per cent, quickly exceeding the job I had turned down. There were costs, but these were low and offset by the relatively generous tax regime for self-employment.

Talking to others who have set up consultancies, the first year is inevitably the worst, and many give up after a year or so. However, I found this to be the point when it began to get easier: repeat business and referrals started to come in so there was less unpaid time spent on sales and marketing. And, as I became busy, I could risk increasing my daily rate. Like many, I had started too low. A daily rate of £100 seemed high, but most consultants only get paid for 50 or 60 per cent of their time, with the rest lost in sales, administration and gaps between projects. Companies are also prepared to pay more to hire someone who only has to be paid when they are needed.

In 1988 I conducted a feasibility study for an inner city initiative (covered in the next chapter), worked for World Vision again, and prepared a marketing plan for a small but very impressive Christian organisation called Administry.

Administry was the brainchild of John Truscott, the most creative enthusiast for good administration I have ever met. The organisation researched and shared best practice in every area of church organisation: running effective meetings, setting up a church office, welcoming newcomers, organising pastoral care, producing newsletters. Everyone loved the witty cartoons in the resource papers while the practical and entertaining training days received rave reviews.

Administry's problem was that the numbers didn't stack up. Costs were low because the same modest salary was paid to every member of the small, hardworking team. However, only a hundred or so churches were willing to pay the £100 to £150 a year to join, churches did not expect to pay anything like commercial rates for training, and it was costly trying to promote dozens of low-price reports to every church in the country. The organisation nearly folded: if one trustee had not been held up on the M25 it probably would have been closed.

The heart of my recommendation was to introduce a new cheaper membership that was affordable for all churches, and to limit access to resources to members so there was a greater incentive to join. Existing members received a premium service at a higher rate, and I judged that most were sufficiently committed to Administry not to trade down. This meant our message to churches outside the Administry network was simplified: we only had to sell membership and a few training 'tasters'. The detailed catalogue of resources only needed to be communicated to members. The plan was adopted, membership grew to around a thousand churches, and Administry prospered.

Administry went on to hire me part time. Pay was much lower than my consultancy rate but it was fun working with John and with Lance Pearson, a creative trainer, performer and writer. It also led to a number of referrals, including a conference centre in Devon, Burstone Manor, which became a regular client and venue for occasional family visits. I took a photo of Burstone and turned it into a postcard: not rocket science but it's not usually possible to have sales material that customers pay for and send to their friends – potential customers – at their own expense.

The big breakthrough came in 1990 when I was accepted as a consultant for the Marketing Initiative, a scheme through which the government paid 60 per cent of the consultancy fees for projects of up to 15 days. The West Midlands region was administered by the University of Warwick. I was guided through what they saw as the best way to develop a marketing strategy, an effective methodology that I made my own. In time I achieved one of the highest assessments out of several hundred consultancies listed on the scheme and, therefore, received regular referrals.

The experience I had in agriculture helped me win my first Marketing Initiative client, Spalton Nutrition, a small, old-established business in Derby, run by Edward Spalton. The company produced a range of animal feed flavours and sold them to animal feed compounders and pet food manufacturers to improve palatability. In other words, their products encouraged animals to eat food processing by-products which they would not otherwise have touched with the bovine equivalent of a barge pole.

At Warwick University Library, I was able to access Key Notes reports to obtain an accurate overview of the feed compounding and pet food industries together with details of the main players. Figures from Spalton enabled me to prepare a product analysis, calculating a three-month moving average of gross profit per product.

However, the real key to this and all the other marketing strategies I produced lay in the telephone research of customers, lost customers, prospects and trade experts. On later projects I added competitors. And in general, trying to initiate anything, I found that picking up the phone and asking open questions to relevant people helped shape the project and ultimately saved time and wasted effort.

Me: My name is Jerry Marshall and I'm an independent consultant working with X from Y Ltd on a project to improve our service to customers. I'm just trying to find out what you like – and don't like – about dealing with Y Ltd?

Contact: Oh, I don't really have much to say… but I like the way that…

Twenty minutes later they were often still talking.

Unlike a rigid questionnaire, they could say what was important to them while I prodded intelligently to draw out and understand the points they were making: 'When you say there are delivery problems, what exactly do you mean?'

I scribbled down almost a full transcript and then brought together key points for each call, which appeared in the report appendix. After a while I bought a dictating machine and hired a part-time secretary to type everything up.

It didn't take many calls (just 20 or so) to get a good feel for the situation. Almost all trusted my explanation for the call. Very few wanted anonymity, though talking with a third party made it easier when it came to criticism. If anything really colourful was said, I kept it in my write-up in quotation marks rather than watering it down.

Three valuable things emerged from customer surveys.

1. The reason they used this company, which enabled me to segment the market where appropriate, develop key sales messages and prepare the sales literature.

2. Usually, some positive comments, which I wrote down exactly and used as testimonials in sales literature.

3. Details of any recurring problems, which could then be worked on and solved.

When calling lost customers and lost prospects, I explained that it would be helpful to understand why they had decided to go elsewhere. Sometimes I found that they were not actually lost customers and the call re-established contact.

The key to a prospect survey was to show that it was not a sales call, typically by saying, 'I'm trying to understand whether companies like yours buy this kind of product?' If the answer was yes, I asked where they looked for suppliers, who was involved in the decision and which supplier they used. Where they were interested, it turned into a sales call, and I immediately passed on the lead. Sometimes I would do prospect calls in several industry sectors to see where the best response rates were.

Competitors were trickier. I didn't lie but I also didn't tell the whole truth. Typically, I would phone and ask for literature. If necessary, I'd say I was a consultant and my client was interested. Once I'd given them my address, I'd ask how business was going and get into a conversation. The key was to avoid open questions (such as, 'Where do you get your business from?') as these aroused suspicion; instead, I made guesses to provoke them to contradict me if I was wrong.

'I guess most of your clients are from the automotive sector?'

'Well, no, actually our main sector is…'

'I presume you mainly find clients from trade press ads?'

'So most of your exports go to Europe?'

Sometimes I asked for a quotation, and pushed them on price as if I was buying.

In the case of Spalton Nutrition, there was an intriguing and challenging extra area to investigate. The company was supplying bio-active material which improved weight gain, food conversion and breeding performance. However, this was the middle of the BSE crisis and the bio-active supplements included meat and bone products banned in cattle feed. I carefully investigated theories for the spread of the disease, especially the spread from Scrapie in sheep, and empirical evidence on the spread of the human form, CJD. It seemed to me that the controversial theory that the disease spread and crossed species through eating infected offal was likely to prevail, and I recommended Spalton cease promoting the bio-active. It turned out to be the right call.

Edward Spalton was enthusiastic with the results and hired me for some of the implementation. In particular, we replaced the scrappy product flyers with a full colour folder and matching soft scan colour sheets that could be over-printed with the product details when required. Success also led to a stream of other Marketing Initiative projects.

Increasingly, my focus was 'developing research-based marketing strategies and practical action plans for small and medium enterprises (SMEs) selling business-to-business'. I also spent around a third of my time working with charities and Christian organisations. For these I worked at a reduced rate, but not for free: I found that when I did, my time was not well used.

I loved the variety. Most clients were engineering, IT or business service companies. They included computer room monitoring equipment, Balti cookware, confectionery, third-party debt collection, a leisure centre operator and an advertising agency. As well as Marketing Initiative projects, I worked for organisations that did not qualify for grant support: the Institute of Engineering Designers, a magazine in Hong Kong wanting to sell into the UK and Warwickshire County Council.

There were some real characters behind the businesses. There was the vicar running a print business, a feisty Irish woman running a machine tool company, and two beautiful young ladies running a successful door fittings business. There was a scrap metal wheeler dealer who had extended into dental supplies and machining precious metals; I mistook him for the forklift driver when I first visited the yard. And there was the maverick ex-DJ who built up a bouncy castle hire business before moving into corporate events. He eventually bought a farm and built a beach complete with lighthouse, getting into trouble with the local authority because the planning application just said 'lake'.

Takings steadily increased to around £50,000 in the mid-1990s while costs remained very low. I was fully booked, sometimes six months in advance. I worried that the long lead time would put prospects off, but instead it seemed to encourage them to get on the waiting list.

The most interesting projects were those looking at overall strategy. Most marketing theory is of little practical value for SMEs, but there was one piece of theory I often used to help think through business development strategy. In summary, the 'Boston Matrix' divides growth options into four possibilities:

1. Selling more of the existing products to existing customers, ie developing the core business through improved sales and promotion.

2. Selling new products to new markets, normally best avoided. (I once had a sheet metal client keen to sell teddy bears to tourist shops because margins looked much higher than sheet metal; but they had no experience of the market and were completely ill-equipped to branch out so radically.)

3. Selling new things to your satisfied clients.

4. Finding new customer groups for your proven products.

It is the last two that are the most promising. A memorable example was a pet food manufacturer that sold mostly to breeders, and was close to bankruptcy. Things were so bad I worried I would not be paid. The company needed to increase volume fast, to cover high fixed costs. We decided, first, to supply lower-margin but high-volume own brand products for pet retail chains (new customers for existing products); and second, to partner with a company selling complementary products, enabling each to introduce the other's products to their own customers (new products to existing customers). A third recommendation was to lose the aging and under-performing sales manager. I felt bad about this, but there were other jobs at stake, and my recommendation made it easier for the CEO to do the deed. All the recommendations were carried out and the company survived.

A fruitful area of strategy is to explore the profitability of different market segments. J Barnsley Crane manufactures overhead cranes, cranes that trundle on beams under the factory roof, with a chain and hook to pick things up and move them around. However, they faced strong price competition from Asia on smaller standard cranes. Their most profitable line was explosion-proof cranes for the oil and gas sector, so we focused and developed this sector. They also needed to keep their name in front of customers and prospects as purchases were infrequent, so we started a regular newsletter. As they were founded in 1809, they had a fascinating range of photos to attract attention, from pulley blocks bigger than a man to a 35-metre-long beam being gingerly manoeuvred in narrow streets.

Another take on segmentation is to produce 'market-based' rather than 'product-based' sales literature. One client had product flyers for their various offerings including PVC strip curtains. These are used by factories (to keep heat in during winter) and refrigerated food storage areas (to keep the cold in) while allowing forklift trucks to come and go. The new improved sales literature took a customer-oriented approach by focusing on markets not products: one leaflet for all the food industry products, and another leaflet for the industrial sector.

Getting the price right could be an easy win. A manufacturer of cable holders was sure that their quality metal product was the most expensive on the market. The list price for a single unit seemed to confirm this. But when I contacted competitors for a quote for 50 off, a more usual volume, their product was the cheapest, cheaper even than an inferior plastic product. So they could raise prices for bigger quantities with confidence.

Once the strategy was clear, including segmentation, messages and pricing policy, there were several fun areas of practical marketing action I could work on.

I especially enjoyed developing printed sales literature because existing literature was often poor. One client was in the cryogenic deflashing business. No, I didn't know either. This is where you freeze rubber things in something that looks like a giant washing machine and spin them round to knock off the rough edges. The company's all-purpose, one-page sales leaflet had such pithy lines as:

> We are the largest single-site user of liquid nitrogen for cryogenic finishing in Europe and the consequent purchase economics combined with high levels of plant

utilisation enable us to provide a competitive alternative even to moulders who have hitherto traditionally freeze trimmed in-house.

The starting point for marketing literature was to understand what it needed to achieve, how it was going to be used, who was going to see it and what the key messages were. Often it was about giving the average metal-bashing shop credibility and professionalism. At Willenhall Tube, the new brochure cover had a dramatic picture of a welding robot with sparks flying against a dark background. For Haden Bros, we made the otherwise dull factory and offices look good by taking the photo at night with the windows and the van headlights lit up. The text gave key benefits backed up by evidence, including glowing testimonials from the customer survey. Especially important was keeping technical information to the back page, as buyers are often general managers rather than engineers.

On promotion, beyond the obvious networking and asking for referrals from satisfied customers, the most cost-effective approach for many companies selling business-to-business was direct marketing, ie mail shots and phone calls. The golden rule was to set up a regular monthly cycle of contacts, starting with easy-to-reach targets. Several had tried a big hit then didn't have time for the follow-up. One client, exhibition stand builder Interlink Design and Display, had a feast-and-famine sales cycle because as soon as they were busy, prospecting was abandoned. As there was an average six-month lead time, sales dried up a few months later, leading to a frenzied effort to bring in sales, and eventually another busy period.

One area Interlink wanted to develop was work through marketing agencies. Getting through to 20-something creative types presented a challenge. At the time most business-to-business sales letters were incredibly boring, starting, 'May I take this opportunity to introduce ourselves… we are a leading provider of… etc.'

So I took a different approach. Later I used it as an example with a large group of 60-year-old male business advisors and received a grumpy response. 'It wouldn't work on me,' one delegate concluded. No, of course not. It wasn't written for him, it was written for young creative types.

Here's the letter.

HOW TO GUARANTEE AN ADRENALINE-PACKED EVENT

Let's face it, people who organise exhibitions, conferences, etc live on caffeine and adrenaline.

So here are five easy rules to follow for those who want the full gung-ho, seat-of-the-pants, they-want-it-yesterday experience. You could pay highly for advice like this.

1. Choose a one-man stand designer/builder, the sort that is impossible to get hold of during office hours. The fun starts six hours before the exhibition when you find (a) he's at Whoknowswotex in Beijing and (b) your 'nearly finished' stand is in his garage in Nether Wallop.

2. Or try being a small fish for a large company. Listen to the Junior Assistant Account Manager telling you how to fit in to their way of doing things.

3. Check your stand contractor avoids working weekends, so you get a chance to fill in.

4. Ensure that managers are not around during stand build, so problems are passed to you on the back of a fag packet just as the exhibition opens.

5. Do not hire Interlink Design and Display. Shocking customer comments include, 'They take an awful lot off my back... basically I just have to walk on', and

'Extremely satisfied', 'More than helpful,' etc. This company could be a disaster for your boundless nervous energy and knife-edge lifestyle.

On the other hand, if you have more than enough adrenaline to keep you going, or fancy a relaxing weekend (with Interlink making sure it all happens), then call me.

Yours...

The first time Interlink used it, a prospect phoned to say it was the best sales letter he had ever seen. And placed a £50,000 order.

Mostly, my copywriting was more conventional, following the 'AIDA' sequence (Attention, Interest, Desire, Action), focussing on 'what's in it for them?' and giving a compelling reason to act now. Favourite words were increase, improve, reduce, save, gain.

Improving presentation of price was an easy win for some. The standard quotation from a foundry equipment supplier was typical of many: a list of components that was incomprehensible to most, lots of legal terms and conditions, and at the bottom, a five-figure cost that was easy to dismiss. As part of the marketing project we designed a new 'proposal' approach, which outlined the client's situation, gave a recommendation with reasons and benefits and included an analysis of the annual savings expected to result from the proposed equipment. The quote became a sales document rather than a barrier.

Obtaining media coverage could also be a fun area. Opportunities are often missed. My favourite was the glass fibre fabricator I once visited just before Christmas. They had recently helped the local Round Table by repairing the broken ear of a GRP reindeer used on their Christmas float. There and then I called the local newspaper and told them the company had helped Santa by operating on Rudolf's poorly ear: a fun seasonal story.

Most potential projects required a sales visit. Selling, I discovered, mirrored what I had learnt about attempting to win a girl's heart. When I was 14 or 15, I thought the best way to attract a girl was, in essence, to tell them what a terrific guy I was. This approach failed completely. It was only at university that I learnt a much more effective approach: to ask the target female questions, discover her interests, then make the link with my experiences and gently test out a next step.

Consultancy selling is similar. When I first started, I gave a brief presentation to prospects on my credentials. Then I realised it was unnecessary and possibly counter-productive. Instead, I asked them questions to understand their needs, and in the discussions I couldn't help giving suggestions and quoting relevant examples from previous work. Towards the end of the meeting I would move things forward by outlining a programme of work with an estimated number of days and cost. I could then gauge reaction and adjust the programme somewhat if necessary. I won the great majority of pitches, though later I heard that the profit-maximising conversion rate was to win about one in three pitches; any more than that and it pays to increase the price.

After the first year I did very little marketing. I got involved with the local branch of the Chartered Institute of Marketing and was chairman for a year: a useful networking opportunity. I enjoyed going up to strangers, saying, 'Hello, I don't think I know you. What's your connection with this event?' The wide variety of my clients meant there was always some sort of connection.

PR can be effective and inexpensive. I wrote a series of light-hearted articles in a local business magazine, complete with cartoons. I wasn't paid but they agreed to include a box about me and my company. The first was a spoof piece on how to avoid publicity and keep a low profile, listing common PR mistakes. Another took the style of a pet care book: 'All you need to know about choosing, feeding and breeding top class customers for pleasure and profit.'

I also produced a simple newsletter with advice and information. Sales involves not just selling the product or service but also selling the person and the company. Buyers need to be happy about all three, and a newsletter is one way to spread a broader message. For good measure, I usually included jokes about marketing consultants.

'How much do you charge for market research?'

'£10,000 for three questions.'

'Wow, that's a bit steep isn't it?'

'Yes. What's your third question?'

Some projects stand out in my memory.

Hannah was excited when I came back from a meeting at Cadbury International with a big bag of chocolates. She asked if I was going to be paid in chocolate and was disappointed to learn it would be in boring old money.

The Music and Worship Foundation asked me to conduct a feasibility study to establish a national college of music and worship. The idea was to provide a blend of Bible study and music training in the wide variety of styles being used across the Church: traditional, Celtic, modern bands, etc. I concluded that it would be possible to raise the capital costs but not cover ongoing running costs and recommended that the college was set up in partnership with an existing music or Bible college. This was accepted, and I was thrilled when I heard the college had been established as a department of London Bible College (now London School of Theology).

I was cautious about working with the Israeli Government Tourist Office in London, but Amnon Lipson reassured me Palestine would benefit. Once through security – an austere hall with a guard behind a small window in the wall – meetings took place in a room with easy chairs, enhanced by Israeli fruit and good-natured banter. I researched the pilgrimage market and organised a 'Bible Discovery' tour around the country for church leaders, with talks on biblical history and a presentation from Rabbi David Rosen, a former Chief Rabbi of Ireland. He was an incisive thinker heavily involved in interfaith relations, as well as issues of peace and justice.

Warwickshire College became a regular client as they adjusted to a government initiative, Local Management of Colleges. From a marketing point of view, colleges of further education are fascinating because they face multiple target markets: 16-year-olds, their parents, adult professional, vocational and leisure students, employers who need a skilled workforce and funding authorities. The first challenge was to try to get all the directorates – which were running as separate fiefdoms with their own marketing and branding – to work together through a joint marketing committee. Research into the decision to choose the college – when the decision was made and the involvement of parents and teachers – was interesting. A key finding was that the prospectus was not a sales document; by the time potential pupils received it, the decision had been made and the prospectus was simply a reference tool. This had a direct effect on its design and on how the college promoted itself through schools to students at an earlier stage.

A sideline at Warwickshire College was a workshop I ran on advertising. Course adverts were 'product' based: the headline was the name of the course. I had faced the same problem with engineering where an advert was typically 'Air Compressors' followed by a picture of a box. Hardly attention-grabbing. The workshop tried to identify the benefit of the course and turn it into a headline:

How to earn more than £40,000 pa
(Professional qualification)

Force 10 in the Channel. Would you know what to do?
(Yachtmaster course)

Two kids and a mortgage. Now what?
(Course for 'women returners')

How much does your lack of marketing expertise cost your company?
(Marketing course)

The most significant developments – inner-city work, launching a technology company and working in Palestine – are covered in other chapters. However, there was one more modest success and one failure that stood out.

The success was the audacious idea that I could sell something to John Fenton. His position as a high-profile 'UK sales guru' had made him a millionaire and he had been described as the 'Billy Graham of salesmanship'. He advertised his 'Sell Sell Sell' Masterclass in the Sunday colour supplements with a photo of himself in a trademark white suit, passionately imploring his admiring followers. Sales, he said, was 'the most fun you can have with your clothes on'. He lived in a grand house near Stratford-upon-Avon and drove a Bentley.

The idea of selling to a leading sales guru was just a joke to amuse me one morning. I called him out of the blue, rather tongue in cheek. To my surprise, he invited me to 'fish and chips' to discuss my proposition for a marketing masterclass. This turned out to be posh fish and sautéed potatoes served with fine wine by his butler. Despite the brash image, I warmed to his openness and hospitality.

He had sold his original sales training business and had set up a franchise operation offering a range of sales masterclasses. I convinced him that marketing was the missing course in his portfolio and he paid me to spend ten days writing it, allowing me joint copyright so I could deliver it myself. I trained the franchisees but often had the well-paid opportunity to deliver it myself, which in turn provided new customers for my consultancy, including a lead that became my largest client, the International Bottle Company (IBC).

I loved delivering the course. There were anecdotes and amusing examples of both good and bad marketing. The section that gained most interest was the internet, which in the mid-1990s was a brave new world.

At about that time, I had received a simple email from a Mary Tempesta, inviting me to visit her website. Now it would be considered spam. It seems she ran a gift shop in L'Aquila, Italy, selling figures made from the modelling material Fimo. There were pictures, prices, a method of response and a button that switched the text between English and Italian. A logo advertised a small business award she had won. At the time, this was new. It blew my mind. Presumably for years she had sold to local people and the passing tourist trade. Then suddenly she discovered she could set up on the internet, write to millions of potential buyers for less than a penny per person, accept credit card payments and send the models out through the post. That was when I realised the potential of the internet for small businesses. I wrote in my course notes, 'There has been a lot of hype about the internet… but we cannot afford to ignore it.' Now, in the age of eBay, Amazon, Paypal, spam filters, social media and search engine optimisation, those early days seem a very long time ago.

The failure, at least financially, was Kuwait. My native land was invaded on 2nd August 1990. The country had been threatened before. As a small child I remember a soldier was billeted in our house. In June 1961, the Iraqi Prime Minister Qasim, who had seized power in 1958, announced that the newly independent Kuwait would be incorporated into Iraq. Britain responded to a call for protection from the Emir of Kuwait and air, sea and land forces were in place within days. The naval task force included two aircraft carriers, four destroyers and six frigates. Iraq did not attack and all the British children were ferried across to HMS Bulwark on a landing craft for a party.

Although my family had left Kuwait nearly 20 years before, we still knew several Kuwaitis, and I followed the occupation and liberation very closely. I was tearful when I heard that Failaka Island, a favourite day-trip destination, was surrounded by oil and the beaches had been mined.

Saddam Hussein's scorched earth retreat at the end of February 1991 was devastating. More than 500 oil wells were set alight. When the wind blew over Kuwait City, day turned to night and breathing filters were essential. Three out of the four main power stations were trashed, one beyond repair. The city was looted, shops were empty, public buildings needed refurbishment.

In the spring, there was a feeding frenzy around the opportunities for reconstruction with the strong view that the UK, as a main contributor to liberation, should be a major beneficiary. 'What do we need?' said the Kuwaiti Ambassador in London. 'To be precise, we need everything.'

The Department for Trade & Industry worked hard on the opportunity and set up BRIT, the British Reconstruction and Implementation Team. I attended an expensive day on the opportunities, did some desk and telephone research, and produced a report explaining where and exactly how SMEs could play a part in reconstruction. It was early days, and oil fires were still raging. The report was a labour of love. I received some very positive comments and reviews but I didn't sell enough reports to cover the time and costs.

On Remembrance Sunday in November 1991 I preached a sermon that some still recalled years later, perhaps because it was especially from the heart. It reflected on war and on the devastation in Kuwait. I said that I was proud of my dad for his role in the Second World War, and that although I realised war was always evil, I believed it was sometimes the lesser of two evils.

In the mid- to late 1990s, many of the government SME support schemes were cut back and I did fewer projects. Instead, there was a major project in Palestine (which I will cover later), and work of a more ongoing nature. I came across a fun, youthful and profitable data warehousing specialist, AKMA. On my first day doing high-level telesales, I stumbled across a massive sales lead and as a result they became a regular customer.

Another regular client was aircraft maintenance software specialist Russell Adams (RAL). Through them I learnt the value of a technology company model where a high proportion of income came through recurring licence fees. I also learnt how to use Goldmine customer relationship manager (CRM) software, which made personalised customer contact to different market segments easy and quick. Later I used it both for the technology company I established and for contacting different flavours of MPs in the High Speed Rail 2 campaign I became involved in.

While working at RAL I was involved in setting up and running stands at the Farnborough International Airshow. The key to an effective exhibition is:

1. to be at the right event, not just a trade show with all your competitors

2. to have a good location, not hidden away out of the main flow

3. to talk to everyone within collaring range.

My technique is to wave a flyer in the path of everyone attempting to walk past and ask a question that qualified leads, such as 'Are you involved in aircraft maintenance?' It's hardly rocket science but it is highly effective. Few other exhibitors seem to bother and presumed, wrongly, that prospects would spot their display and rush over to see what they were offering. Of course, some ignored me, or just took the flyer, but many paused, enabling me to read their badge and identify opportunities. At Farnborough, we had a three-stage cunning plan. I tackled passers-by, struck up a conversation and checked that they were a potential customer. Interested contacts were then passed to a more knowledgeable RAL staff member and given a brief demo. And hot leads were invited into a semi-private office to meet the boss.

Much as I enjoyed the work, it was becoming repetitive. I was bored. Furthermore, there was nothing in what I was doing that I could sell on, that could contribute to my meagre pension fund. However, in 1998, I started to work with the University of Warwick Science Park on something that transformed my career. I was asked to help with the marketing for a programme called TeamStart.

TeamStart is based on research indicating that the fastest growing companies tend to be technology based (using existing technology creatively rather than cutting-edge developments), and they tend to be formed by teams of experienced business managers rather than by individuals.

The programme helps aspiring entrepreneurs come together to form high-growth technology-based businesses. It consists of selective recruitment: ten Saturdays developing practical entrepreneurial skills and bringing teams together, and ongoing mentoring. The real value is in training by practitioners, not academics; the climate of risk-taking; and constant pushing by mentors. I was so impressed that in summer 1999 I paid the £800 fee to join the programme.

Another development that year also changed the landscape. I was contacted by Richard Gamble. He was keen to move to the Coventry area and was looking for a job. He was a complete contrast to me; a man's man and a keen follower of sport. He was someone with a touch of 'prosperity theology', happy to enjoy God's material blessings while the gap between my wealth and extreme poverty gave me some disquiet. But I warmed to him and his enthusiasm, strength of character and Christian commitment. I could see that his strengths would complement mine. I offered him six months' employment, and said that if he were successful I would incorporate Jerry Marshall Associates and give him a share of the company.

Just as Richard joined, work seemed to dry up. And Richard would be the first to admit he was lousy at the first few projects. He was disorganised, short of money and didn't seem comfortable with being trained by me. Nevertheless, he had many strengths and I was keen to push the business forward. I planned to give him five per cent a year, but he persuaded me that if he had 25 per cent, he would be totally committed to it regardless of my earnings.

So the consultancy became a private limited company on this basis, using the former strapline 'Marketing Strategy & Action' as the company name. We agreed a project fee split that gave 60 per cent to the person doing the work, 15 per cent for selling (five per cent each for the lead, sales meeting and proposal), and the rest to the company to cover overheads and pay dividends if there was anything left.

It was the biggest step forward since setting up the company, with the immediate effect of cutting my own pay. But I was excited. It felt like we now had a proper company, with unlimited potential.

Reflections

- Sales is about asking questions to see how you can best add value. Keep thinking, 'What's in it for them?'
- Talk to competitors, prospects, lost prospects, customers and lost customers.

- Don't undercharge but be generous with your time: most people return a favour.

- Grow by finding new things to sell to your adoring customers, and by finding new customers for your proven products.

- Seek fun projects with interesting people.

- Do one audacious new thing each year.

Chapter 4: Inner-city initiative

A miracle took place on Christmas Day 1972 on a rubbish dump in Mexico. In response to a prophecy, a Catholic church in El Paso, Texas, prepared a dinner for the people who lived by scavenging on the dump just across the border. At the dump, there was no water, no sanitation, no education, and no hope. Everyone had TB and the stench was unbearable. Some who worked there didn't even know it was Christmas Day. That day, however, everything changed. The church catered for 125 people but 250 turned up and were served full portions. The food extended to give everyone all they wanted and the church went on to serve many needs in the area.

In 1986, the Bishop of Coventry preached at Westwood Church to mark the arrival of a new vicar. He challenged the church to watch a documentary film on this church that reached out to those in desperate poverty across the Rio Grande.

Westwood Heath in south-west Coventry was becoming an increasingly wealthy area with a Science Park, a new business park and executive housing. Head offices, including Barclays and the National Grid, moved to the area from the South East. But although few in Coventry might be reduced to scavenging through rubbish, many areas suffer from urban poverty and high unemployment. 'Urban Priority Areas' included Canley, just across the railway line from Westwood, and much of the north and east of the city, including Hillfields, Foleshill, Wood End and Henley Green. It felt like the UK's north–south divide went through the middle of Coventry.

We were challenged to use our relative wealth to meet the needs of others in the city. Paul wrote to the Corinthians:

Our desire is not that others might be relieved while you are hard pressed, but that there might be equality. At the present time your plenty will supply what they need.[9]

I was reminded of the Marxist slogan, 'From each according to his ability, to each according to his need', and it struck me that biblical ideals of justice, compassion and individual responsibility do not fit neatly into a one-dimensional, left–right political framework.

In response to urban unrest in the 1980s, the Church of England produced a report, *Faith in the City*, which led to the launch of the Church Urban Fund in 1987. I became involved in the initial local fundraising. In time, this produced an invitation to St James' Palace, where the Queen was carefully steered between worthy contributors previously selected to exchange a few words with her. I remember thinking how small she was.

The Church had become especially involved in creating employment, taking part in government schemes. In Fife, Buckhaven Church had become the town's largest employer, employing 870 people in a trading company and rebuilding the harbour and a theatre, generating a £3 million annual turnover. In Wales, St John's Church, Penydarren, employed 1,300 people.

Following the bishop's challenge, several things came together to create an opportunity. First, the government set up an Inner City Task Force in 16 cities including the Foleshill/Hillfields Task Force in Coventry. Second, the Evangelical Alliance established Evangelical Enterprise and employed Michael Hastings (now Lord Hastings) to support church developments in this field. Third, the Director of Coventry Youth for Christ (CYFC), Steve Tash, was exploring

---

[9] 2 Corinthians 8:13–14.

ways to meet the physical as well as the spiritual needs of young people.

At the time, I was Chairman of CYFC. Steve Tash, David Depledge (Chair of the CYFC Advisory Group) and I brought people together to explore the need and opportunity to address the issue of high unemployment, and we invited Michael Hastings to share his expertise. As a result, I wrote a proposal to extract funding from the Foleshill/Hillfields Task Force, to pay me to prepare a feasibility study on how we could 'release the skills, facilities and strengths of the network of Coventry churches to provide appropriate training and employment for the neediest groups in Coventry'. I was thrilled when a letter arrived accepting the proposal.

I had no idea of what a feasibility study was supposed to be and loved inventing one from scratch for our purposes. Conducted in 1988, there were four main research elements:

1. Talking to the large number of groups involved in this space. We were keen not to duplicate existing services. What was surprising was how many groups were unaware of the others. It seemed that in their busyness and commitment to their particular task, they were failing to look up and take a more strategic view, seeing who was out there and who they might partner with to bring their broader vision to reality.

2. As well as organisations in Coventry, contacting groups elsewhere with similarities to what we wanted to do, including potential models, funders and trainers. I was especially struck by Daily Bread, in Northampton, a cooperative where a third of the staff were sufferers of mental illness.

3. Researching skills shortages and target groups and investigating recruitment and referrers.

4. Through church leaders, conducting a skills survey of church members who might be able to contribute to training, and compiling a list of church facilities and resources.

The conclusion was that the gap in existing provision was in helping those at the 'bottom of the heap' – long-term demotivated unemployed people who were simply not capable of joining a regular Employment Training Scheme and sticking with it. These were people struggling with very low self-esteem and, in many cases, recovering from alcohol, drug and solvent abuse. The study included a business plan around two main recommendations: life-skills training to build confidence and self-esteem, and a package of benefits to encourage entrepreneurs to run businesses where a third of their employees were from the training course.

All of this was developed with a project overseeing a group that comprised 25 churches, and we received support from key people in further education, industry, Coventry City Council, the NHS and from the bishop.

Not everyone, however, was happy. A minister from one of the churches in the target area was strongly against it. I have no clear idea why. One person even wondered if he was a double agent for the 'dark side'. I remember a meeting where he had taken the floor to express his anger and I could see others mouthing silent prayers. I was distressed by the conflict between the majority's wish and this one vociferous person, and the difficulty in finding a means of reconciliation. It was only later I learnt that opposition is normal, even when you are trying to do the right thing.

The Foleshill/Hillfields Task Force were enthusiastic about our plans and wanted to help us become established. However, they suggested we start with the training element before moving on to the more ambitious employment and enterprise element. So we registered CITEE (Churches Initiative in

Training, Employment and Enterprise) as a company limited by guarantee, also obtaining charitable status in due course. We extracted £64,000 from the Task Force, found premises and employed a general manager, a trainer (who developed a ten-week curriculum) and a part-time development officer to find ongoing funding.

The company was run by staff and overseen by a management committee, who were directors of the company. The committee reported to an advisory group, made up of staff and church representatives, who were 'members' of the company, meaning their role was similar to that of shareholders in a company limited by shares.

Thanks to the skill and commitment of the staff, a superb and highly innovative ten-week course called 'A foot in the door' was developed, more trainers joined the team and over time other offerings were added, including 'A toe in the water' and a programme called STEPS. CITEE gained a good reputation and a steady flow of appropriate trainees came from referrers, including Murray Lodge (a drug rehabilitation centre), Coventry Cyrenians (homeless project), Probation Services, Coventry social services and from mental health teams. Somehow, funding was always found, from various public sector and European sources, from the National Lottery and from individuals and churches.

David Depledge chaired the management committee for the first few years, which was good practice as I had been the paid consultant conducting the feasibility study. Later, I became Chair.

There was a good relationship between the staff and the committee, but one area of disappointment. Having got the training side working well, Robert, the General Manager, was not interested in developing the enterprise and employment recommendation. He felt that training was their expertise and he was not keen to have others set up a separate division under a CITEE umbrella. So while organisations such as PECAN in south London, which I had contacted as part of the feasibility study, grew in leaps and bounds in a range of new areas, CITEE stayed mainly in the training field and did not grow much beyond an annual turnover of £100,000. There was another issue that deserved greater attention: Robert separated from his wife. It seemed to me that part of the problem was that he was too close to his key assistant, Anna. It was a concern Robert dismissed.

The CITEE feasibility study opened up other doors, paid and voluntary. One was almost identical to CITEE. The Nottingham Churches Enterprise Network (NCEN) was a group of 52 churches from seven denominations in the Nottingham conurbation concerned about the most disadvantaged groups, especially long-term demotivated, unemployed people.

Thirteen of the churches were in the Nottingham inner-city task force area, Forest, Radford and Lenton, where unemployment stood at 35 per cent in November 1988. The area also suffered from low incomes, poor housing, dereliction and a shortage of open space and leisure facilities.

Working with Jane Gibbs, a former administrator of a Nottingham inner-city church, I followed a similar methodology to the CITEE project. The project had very broad support, including the active involvement of the City Council and Church Action with the Unemployed. The conclusion was to start by funding a full-time project manager, a part-time development manager and a part-time project administrator. This team would support and motivate unemployed people using the information collected in the feasibility study, especially the skills register. They would also encourage churches to provide crèche facilities for unemployed single parents and use church contacts with employers to try to change attitudes and persuade them to employ and train inner-city residents.

Once my work was done, I heard very little until I discovered the project had come unstuck over anti-discrimination rules. CITEE had specified that employees should be in full agreement with the aims and objectives of the company, aims which included 'advancing the Kingdom of God'. Fortunately we did not have any conflicts, and when CITEE's character and culture were more developed, trainers included those without church connections. At NCEN, however, the team comprised a Christian, a Muslim and an atheist. Somehow, this team fell out with the committee of church representatives to whom they reported and the whole thing came to a sticky end. I was frustrated and saw no great reason why the team could not work with the churches.

Back in Coventry, I was also hired by the council-run Wood End and Henley Green Employment Development Project. The initial project was to prepare mini business plans for an enterprise centre. It was a fascinating opportunity to look at a wide range of proven small business models: a community newspaper; hairdresser; laundrette; second-hand clothes and furniture shops; DIY tool hire; dry goods (repackaging dry foods bought in bulk); childminding; and cheap, nutritious takeaway meals. For all of these, I estimated the capital requirement, how many would be employed, space required and profitability.

The business opportunity that caught most attention, and led to a second piece of work, was babysitting and childminding. There was a shortage of day-care provision, a need for employment and a number of residents interested in training and employment in childcare. My report looked at alternatives and recommended setting up a childminding system with a resource centre and voucher scheme to subsidise some of the places. The resource centre, which was successfully established, was a place where childminders could bring their children, with space, toys and equipment where children could play. This dealt with a number of issues: the low perception of childminding; the reluctance to register as a childminder; the feeling of isolation and loneliness of childminders; and the lack of space, toys and equipment.

The 1988 Education Reform Act introduced Local Management of Schools, which gave rise to a need for school governors with financial knowledge to manage devolved budgets. I was challenged to volunteer. I felt I would be more useful in an inner-city school, away from middle-class suburbs where there were plenty of keen candidates. My link with CITEE meant I qualified to be a co-opted local industry rep and I was appointed to Stanton Bridge, a large primary school on Red Lane, just north-east of the city centre. I chaired the finance committee.

The school was around two-fifths Hindu, two-fifths Muslim and one-fifth white. Many of the governors said nothing at meetings and some struggled with English. Initially the teacher governors were concerned they were not meeting the requirement for 'broadly Christian' acts of worship and thought I would take a strong line on this. A member of staff explained they covered themes like, 'Do to others as you would have them do to you'. I pointed out that this was from the Bible and was, therefore, definitely 'broadly Christian'.[10]

The school was housed in a crumbling Victorian building but was scheduled to be completely rebuilt on a new site a few streets further north. The staff had pointed out to the local authority that Red Lane was a boundary between a Muslim and a Hindu area and that this might be a problem. It was. When the beautiful new school opened, a very significant proportion of one group left. Fortunately, there was a transition arrangement in place so the school did not have to bear the cost. Meanwhile, a new estate was being built very close to the school, just across a canal. So we campaigned for a canal

---

[10] Luke 6:31.

footbridge as a cheap way to refill the school and meet the education needs of the new community. The capital cost would be quickly met by savings on educational costs and it would save expanding another school. I was told that if it was ever built it would be called Jerry's Bridge. Sadly, it never happened, despite my befriending the City Treasurer. It seems that capital budgets are an entirely separate matter from revenue budgets; any logic around possible connections between them was met with bemused indifference.

Meanwhile, CITEE continued to flourish. In December 1999, a party was arranged to celebrate CITEE's tenth anniversary. More than 500 of the most entrenched long-term unemployed people had been helped and the success rate was high. Staff, management committee members, referring agencies and past course members joined the celebrations. It took place in Drapers Hall, Coventry, a magnificent though run-down Victorian venue with Greek style pillars and a high, ornate ceiling.

It was suggested we did some kind of performance to suit the solemnity of the occasion. As we seemed to have given birth to many long sets of initials, I penned a song based on, 'Here's a first-rate opportunity' from Gilbert and Sullivan's *Pirates of Penzance*. The staff and committee performed it at the party among the balloons.

> *We're the Churches Initiative in Training*
> *In Employment and in Enterprise*
> *But we shorten it to keep it short!*
> *So we're known as C.I.T.E.E.*
> *It's a heck of a lot of initials*
> *But we like them so you're stuck with them*
> *And it's not the only lot we've got*
> *We've got more*
> *And we'll bore you lot with them all.*

The song then worked through the various sets of initials ending with a slow, sad verse on how the National Lottery Charities Board had cut our grant.

The party was a high point: I felt I had finally helped set up something of value.

The low point came early in 2001. I came back late one Sunday from a family weekend visiting my parents to find urgent messages from Robert and Anna. They had been trying to get hold of me and wanted to see me immediately.

I really liked Anna. She was married to a Church of England minister and was bubbly, funny and always helpful. That evening, though, she was tearful as she explained she felt her marriage had failed and she had found support and comfort with Robert.

A public statement issued by the Diocesan Communications Officer explained the situation as sensitively and succinctly as possible:

> After serious thought and a great deal of anguish [Anna and her husband] have separated. Anna has decided that she wants to continue a relationship with a work colleague and has therefore moved out of the vicarage.

I found I faced what seemed like an impossible decision, and no one was willing to tell me what to do. Marriages fail – but they were living together. As Robert had stayed at the vicarage during his difficulties, Anna's husband must have felt a great sense of betrayal. I saw CITEE as part of the Church and therefore believed the company should uphold Christian values on marital faithfulness. Legally, I could not dismiss them, and if I did, CITEE would fall apart because it was too small to lose the two key people. Furthermore, however bad it looked, there was a great deal of anguish and Anna felt she could not cope alone. I didn't feel I should judge: but by the grace of God, I might have found myself in a similar position.

The following day I made immediate changes to cheque signatories as it is normal practice not to have partners as joint signatories. I listened to views ranging from doing nothing to closing CITEE, and arranged a management committee meeting where we decided to pass the buck to the advisory group. I wrote them a letter and called a meeting for 1st March. The management committee listened to the advisory group views and met immediately afterwards. We agreed CITEE should continue, that David Depledge (a trained counsellor) should meet with Robert and Anna, and that we should allow more time to take the emotional heat out of the situation and seek guidance. The Archdeacon of Coventry kindly sent me a letter of support for this position.

However, time and tide made no difference to the situation. I was clear in my mind that the situation was ultimately untenable for an organisation that was an arm of the Church. A management committee meeting immediately followed by an advisory group meeting was scheduled for 12th July. After forewarning those concerned, the committee authorised me, by a majority of three to two, to meet with Robert and Anna to reach a 'compromise agreement' to terminate their employment – in other words, to offer a package equal to the best they could get if they took us to court for unfair dismissal. My idea was then to take a hands-on role to restructure and restabilise the company. However, the advisory group did not back this approach, and the staff, who didn't want to lose Robert and Anna, then proposed a motion of no confidence in the Chairman. The whole thing felt horrible and I struggled, and failed, to hold back tears.

Under the circumstances, I felt I could not restructure the company, and that it would be wrong to start an argument with company members at an Extraordinary General Meeting. The management committee therefore reconvened, and I and two colleagues (who also felt the situation was untenable) resigned. One of the remaining two committee members agreed to be the new Chair, and Robert and Anna continued to work at CITEE. In my final mailing the next day, I wished my replacement well, and said I hoped CITEE would continue to be successful.

I was very sad and felt a sense of bereavement, though also relieved that for me the issue was closed. I went straight from these meetings to my church cell group where someone said they had a picture of me as an arrow being released from a bow with careful aim.

Under the circumstances, it was probably the best solution. CITEE continues, I have met Robert a few times since, and the relationship is cordial. I was true to what I felt was right and was released to move to other things.

Reflections

- People don't love you just because you're trying to do good.

- Talk to other people involved in your space; find out what they're doing.

- Bad relationships between staff and the management committee can destroy a project.

- Good relationships between staff can also be a problem.

Chapter 5: Sinking in the Channel and other family activities

Pan Pan, Pan Pan, Pan Pan, All stations, All stations, All stations. This is Brixham Coastguard...

The notice blared out from our VHF radio. My heart sunk: I knew it was about us. A Pan Pan message is one less than a Mayday, an emergency but where life is not in imminent danger.

It was 2am. We were halfway across the Channel, on passage between Guernsey and Brixham, with two daughters and friends from church. We were on a broad reach in a near-gale force seven, surfing down the waves, sea spray lit by the navigation light, working the wheel hard to correct anticipated boat movements as each wave hurled us forward. It was a brilliant, exhilarating sail.

But, unfortunately, we were sinking.

Years later, Hannah posted a Father's Day message on her blog giving six reasons why I was her favourite Dad. Reason number four was:

> Your ideas of fun holidays are sailing in a force seven across the Channel, staying opposite a refugee camp in Palestine and camping in Uganda – definitely more fun than the package holiday stuff.

Other reasons included:

> You have the ability to peel an apple in one go.

> You encourage my rebellious side.

> I haven't got any other dads.

Hannah is daughter number one. When she was little, whenever she wanted an apple, I was pressed into service for the one-piece-peeling challenge. Tension mounted as I got close to the end, with the peel close to breaking. Then she ate the naked apple. Then she ate the peel.

Hannah thought deeply about issues of theology. Aged five, on hearing that nothing is impossible for God, she asked, 'Dad, can God count from nought to infinity in less than one second?'

She also reflected on heaven, which she said was 'like Christmas every day but without the turkey'. Conventional Christmas dinners were not her thing. Our best family Christmas was when we had three breakfasts: a continental breakfast before church; a full English as the main meal; and American pancakes to round off the day.

Aged eight, she discovered my sister's vast store of premium ice cream. 'I'm going to live with Auntie Jill,' she said. 'Have you _seen_ how much ice cream she has?' Jill's enthusiasm for ice cream was legendary. She had once beaten Oliver Reed in an ice cream eating contest. She was a student at the time and had accepted a job on a film set in Hungary from a complete stranger who offered her a lift.

Aged nine, Hannah discovered the truth about snogging.

'Do you know how French people kiss?' she asked. 'They lick their tongues together… urghh!'

Her views on boys were so strong I recorded her on video.

'Tell me about boys?'

'Eurgh, gross! I'm going to puke up!' (Goes to waste paper bin and pretends to be sick.)

'One day you're going to marry a boy and you'll kiss them. What do you think of that?'

'No I won't! I would never kiss a boy for a million billion pounds.'

Fifteen years later I played it back at her wedding.

She was so sure of herself that we took a £100 bet (I suggested reducing it from a million billion pounds). She wrote out a contract on a piece of scrap card.

> Dad bets me £100 that I will have snoged a boy befoure I am 17 (sic).

We both initialled it and she dated it 19.5.95.

On the back, she drew a smiley face, and wrote: 'HA HA HA I get £100 off Dad'.

By the time she was 17 she had in fact snogged two boys, but I never got the £100. The vicar, Peter, an ex-barrister, told me contracts with a minor are not valid.

Hannah is unconventional and has a rebellious side that needed no encouragement. Aged ten, when classmates had pictures of pop stars on the inside lid of their desks, she had a picture of a chicken. On a church camp, she took a picture of a dead, rotting sheep and put it on her bedroom door with the warning, 'Please knock – this is what happened to a girl who forgot.' As a teenager, she experienced her first ride in an ambulance after dislocating her elbow as a result of a spectacular unicycle crash en route to Tesco. As a sixth former, she livened up a presentation on inflation by involving a sock puppet called Cedric. As a married 26 year old, she painted sunflowers on the front of her house and organised a new (tax) year party with games including Net Prophets (catching model prophets in a net) and Pea 45 (grabbing a handful of peas, and trying to make sure they numbered as close to 45 as possible).

Daughter number two joined us in December 1988. Three-year-old Hannah summed up her arrival by saying, 'I don't need an alarm clock now we've got Joanne!' As a toddler, Jo was tough and determined, with a wide-eyed curiosity, a sense of humour and an impish grin.

From an early age she developed some cunning strategies. Aged 18 months, she refused her mini milk ice lolly and reached out for my chocolate Feast. I offered her a bite but she insisted on taking possession of the whole lolly and ate the lot. Then she handed the stick back to me, said, 'Dada', pointed to the mini milk and said, 'Mine!' Somehow, she got two ice lollies that day.

She appeared to be mainly sensible. She liked school, played shops, arranged tea parties for her fluffy animals and worked through vast quantities of sticky tape. One night we decided to camp out in the lounge. We laid out sleeping bags and camping mattresses, hired a video, made popcorn and had a fun evening together. However, Jo couldn't quite bring herself to sleep in the lounge. She had a perfectly good bed and after lights out she made her way back to it.

Nevertheless, there was more to Jo than met the eye, including hard work, courage, compassion, and an offbeat sense of humour. She became an expert juggler, progressing in time to fire juggling, using small spherical cages containing an oil burner. Other skills included tightrope walking and unicycling. Her career choice was between medicine and running away to the circus. She chose the former but took classes in tumbling, leaving all options open. As a medical student she joined the City Pastors team, patrolling Birmingham's notorious Broad Street area on Saturday nights until 2am. And she apparently enjoys organised 'mud runs' and runs carrying logs or doing strange things for no logical reason.

We lived in Cannon Park, an estate built around 1970, on the edge of Coventry. On our road, houses were arranged around a green, so it was quiet, with no traffic, and there was a safe space to play in front of the house. It was a three-bed semi and the other half of the building was owned by good friends, Mike and Dorinda Holt. We removed the barrier between our front lawns, shared a lawn mower and took turns to cut the joint lawn. We led the baby alarm wires between the windows so we could go into each other's houses while the children were asleep. Their daughter Becky felt completely at home in either house. She was a big fan of playing in the bath and once wandered in, found Sue in the bath and immediately stripped off and joined her.

However, in 1991, the Holts moved to Burton Green, a village three miles up the road. With the business now occupying one bedroom, we wanted more space and we were beginning to think about being near a good school. We found a buyer for our house, the Holts told us of a house for sale on their road, and we moved to a pretty Edwardian semi next to a disused railway line in a deep cutting. Since the Beeching cuts, the line had become a popular path, lined with trees and acting as a conduit for wildlife, bringing foxes and Muntjac deer onto our lawn. Standing at the end of the garden a small Ugandan child once asked, 'Is this where your forest starts?' And peering down into the cutting, another African visitor once asked me, 'Why did your river dry up?'

Also living on this road were John and Barbara Gardner. Several years earlier, I had written a paper with Barbara, for the church PCC. Westwood Church was running out of space, and we recommended 'planting' new congregations, first in Cannon Park and later Burton Green. I was part of the leadership team establishing Park Fellowship, which met in the local primary school. Now, in Burton Green, there was an opportunity to work with the Holts and the Gardners to set up a congregation in the village hall.

The first service was a disaster. It was harvest, we asked the school to take part, and leafleted the whole village. We misjudged demand and there wasn't even standing room for late arrivals. However, a regular congregation developed, made up of both local people and those who preferred our more traditional style of worship, compared with the youthful student-focussed main church. The carol service was especially well supported by the village: its popularity may have been due to the candles and sense of community; or the mulled wine and mince pies; or our attempts to communicate the Christmas message, which ranged from puppets to a sketch with live sheep (who were not as well behaved as they should have been), to Hannah, Jo and I wearing roller skates and large cardboard boxes round our waists, pretending to be shopping trolleys.

When Joanne started school, Sue found she was lonely. And Hannah kept asking for another baby sister. We decided that with a house extension we had room for another.

Sarah's arrival in November 1994 was dramatic. It reminded me of those films where air traffic control talks down the novice pilot. It started just after midnight.

00:30   Woken by Sue. She has been checking the undercarriage. Something is up. This could be it.
00:32   Contact our destination, Solihull Labour Ward. Sister Green is controller for the night. We are cleared for approach. Neighbour Dorinda Holt is summoned to look after the crew.
00:33   Flight bag packed: check. Car out of garage: check. Cereal bar in pocket: check.
00:38   Return to ops room. Dorinda has arrived. Contractions started at 00:35 at 30-second intervals. This spells trouble. Realise we're going to have to land this crate ourselves.
00:39   *Mayday Mayday Mayday!* Controller Green remains calm. She alerts emergency services and raises duty midwife.
00:44   DH positions Sue for the final approach. I take position at the action end.
00:45   Head in sight. The tension mounts.
00:48   Cleared for landing. Controller Green talks us down.

00:51 Head is out! Anxious moment as cord is checked.

00:52 A perfect touchdown. Sarah Joy Marshall has landed, just 17 minutes after the first contraction.

00:53 The crew arrive.

'I heard Mummy say 'Ow Ow!' Then I heard 'Waa waa!'' explained Joanne later.

'I didn't know it was so messy,' said Hannah. 'I thought they just sort of popped out.'

00:54 Midwife radios for cross bearing. She's still on the M42.

00:55 Emergency services arrive and take control. We made it!

In my next business newsletter, I added 'Express Deliveries' to the range of services offered.

Sarah's arrival nearly turned to disaster two years later. We heard her cries from the garden but the back door was locked. Even in the panic of the moment logic dictated that she must have fallen out of a window, and we raced out with a cold dread, terrified she might be damaged for life, or worse. We found her lying on the concrete patio, ornamented with twists of creeper, under Jo's open bedroom window. We took her to A & E for a full head X-ray. Doctors were amazed she had got away with a couple of lumps on her head and a friction burn under her arm, probably caused by the creeper which helped break the fall. After getting over the shock, Sarah seemed to enjoy the attention. She winked repeatedly at the male nurse, said 'Don't patronise me' to the Consultant (a phrase we later found Hannah had taught her) and she went away very proud of her neck collar, sweetie and certificate of bravery.

Like the others, Sarah had a good turn of phrase. Before the age of two, she told the supermarket checkout lady that the lager in the shopping trolley was 'Daddy Juice'. When angry she had a wide and colourful range of threats including, 'If you don't help me I'll shout so loud your ears will drop off your head!'

She was a true child of the modern age. When Sue suggested that she do some painting, Sarah went to the computer. When, on a weekend away, I warmed her milk on an Aga, she didn't believe we had done it right. She shook her head and tried to explain she wanted it warm by saying 'round and round' like our microwave at home. She also challenged us with many questions. 'When does my hair grow?', 'Can I see electricity?' and 'Where do the diggers go when they're not here?'

She was an assertive child. 'Don't cut my toast into triangles; I can eat rectangles, you know,' she said when she was three or four. She often 'corrected' my southern accent ('Not 'Barth', it's 'Bath'!'). In fact, she corrected anyone she considered to be sloppy in their use of English. When I told her I'd put toast in for her, she said, 'It's not toast, you put *bread* in.' When Sue explained that a helter-skelter was a big slide except it went round and round, Sarah responded as though she was addressing an especially dim-witted pupil. 'Mummy, it's not the helter-skelter that goes round and round, it's the people!'

For a while we experimented with family democracy, to introduce the girls to discussion, reason and the joys of meetings. They all took turns to chair the meetings. We discussed fun things like where to go on holidays and more everyday issues that came up. One of the first things we did was to create 'Rules of this family' which remained pinned on the noticeboard for many years.

Rules of this family
1. All members of the family are equal but some are more equal than others (Mum's rule).

2. Everyone must be loveable (Sarah's rule).

3. Everyone must treat each other with respect even when we think their taste (etc) is sad.

4. Take care of your possessions, including clothes.

5. If you mess it up, clear it up.

6. Plan time so that all jobs are done before bedtime and so that there is time for fun things as well.

7. No loud singing before 7.20am.

It was because Sue stayed behind to look after Sarah that Hannah and Jo joined me in assorted sailing escapades. A regular crew member wrote accounts of these. 'Maritime Meanderings: An Adventure' he entitled the first, 'Starring five grown-ups who should know better and two girls who probably do but aren't telling.' This trip was between Poole and Alderney, Sark and Herm, in an old Moody 33. Hannah 'More Decibels Than the Loudest Foghorn' Marshall was given strict instructions to make sure the men didn't get drunk, a mission she carried out with enthusiasm. She also managed 1,000 cartwheels in a single day, mainly on Herm. I never asked why. But then, if you can, why not?

The memorable moment was approaching Alderney, rounding a rocky headland with notoriously strong tides. We were within sight of the breakwater and sandy bay of Braye harbour and had just taken the sails down when smoke and the smell of burning plastic began to assault our senses. Unfazed, I shut down the engine, hoisted the sails and sailed up to a visitors' mooring. Actually, I quite like picking up moorings under sail, good old-fashioned seamanship and all part of my dinghy instructor training. The crew were impressed.

The man from Mainbrace Marine shook his head and said it was the thermostat. One of the plastic pipes had melted and he was unable to replace it so we crossed back to Poole without an engine. I called the boat owner who notified the harbour authority so we had clearance to sail right up to Poole Quay. The rules say you must be under power but this was the fourth time I had sailed in without an engine. I say 'sailed' in the broadest sense: the first time was as a teenager, rowing the dinghy tender, and towing behind it a becalmed 20ft cabin cruiser.

The sinking experience was in 2003, with Hannah, Jo and a dozen others in two yachts. We were on the way home in a First 405, the sailing equivalent of a hot hatch. The day before, we had picked up some Coventry friends who had moved to Guernsey, taken them to Herm and then dropped them back en route home. So we were some distance away from the other yacht.

I was woken up in the early hours to be told the boat was flooding. I looked down groggily and sure enough there was already about a foot of water sloshing around the floor. There was a suspicious gurgling noise from the heads (toilet) area and I spent a while feeling around under the surface, looking for an open valve. But in the dark, in an unfamiliar boat, working under the water, I couldn't find anything to shut off.

There was an electric bilge pump, but it was about as effective as draining the boat with a nasal dropper. So instead we formed a line of buckets that kept the flooding under control. I called the skipper of the other boat on the VHF to give him the news, intending to keep in touch as a precaution. He suggested I inform the coastguard.

Generally this would have been fine, but unfortunately we were 35 miles off Brixham and only using a hand-held radio. The main ship radio – with an aerial on the mast – wasn't working. So while I could hear them, they struggled to hear me. Twice I emphasised that we did not need assistance, this was a precaution and I would report in at regular intervals, but they could not hear. After a few minutes I heard the Pan Pan broadcast. I felt very embarrassed.

A Royal Fleet Auxiliary ship, the Argus, was in the vicinity and heard the message. She diverted and stood by. I found out later she was a floating hospital with two full wards and mortuary. So all bases were covered whatever happened to us.

Relaying messages through her more powerful radio, it became apparent that the Brixham lifeboat had been called. All the while we were tearing along on a reach towards Blighty and bailing out furiously. When the lifeboat arrived, RFA Argus moved on. The lifeboat called us on the VHF and offered a large diesel pump, but it was clear that this was so big it would take up most of the cockpit and would nearly sink us, if we didn't drop it in on the transfer. They also offered to tow us. Suspicious about possible salvage claims, I pointed out that we were already making maximum hull speed. As you may know, displacement vessels have a terminal velocity in knots of 1.3 times the square root of their waterline length, and we were making around eight knots. They admitted we would not go any faster under tow but we might steer a straighter course. We were spinning around all over the place as we surfed down the waves. I took the hint and took the helm.

Throughout the experience Hannah and Jo seemed completely relaxed, enjoying the adventure. Either this was becoming worryingly normal to them, or they had a misplaced trust in their father. Mind you, Hannah had been sailing with us ever since she was a baby. Once as a two-year-old, halfway across the Channel and beating into a force six, she woke up in a wildly pitching bow cabin and observed, 'It's a bit wobbly.' It was just another fairground ride.

When we docked in Brixham, the charter company ('Plain Sailing') was ready with a pump. The problem was a broken inlet in the heads. They were apologetic and let us sleep off the disturbed night in a new Dufour 55, a boat with beautiful polished woodwork in all the cabins and a huge plasma TV screen. I couldn't imagine anyone risking taking her across the Channel.

Not all holidays were quite as active as the cross-Channel sailing trips. Nonetheless, they built up a bank of memories that fed our shared family history and will perhaps be our most valuable legacy.

One of the best was when Jo was a baby and we were still hard up. We paid £60 for a week in a cottage in the Cotswolds and had Mediterranean weather. Hannah delighted in walking up the river and under the bridges in Bourton-on-the-Water. In the farm park, a goat ate the food and the paper bag out of Hannah's hand, and we even found a sandy beach at Cotswolds Water Park.

Camping in France with Haven was a popular and reasonably affordable option with children. It was hardly camping: a tent with electric lighting, a fridge for cold beer, water slides and French food are surely all the essentials for a decent family holiday. And although we had to walk to the shower block, the walk was a good way to meet the neighbours. The children still remember the Tiger Club song with nostalgia.

On the way back from the ferry after one trip, we stopped for ice cream in a park in Newbury. We were minding our own business, admittedly on some suspiciously grouped deck chairs, when a couple of Portaloos started wandering across the park towards us. They plonked themselves down in front of the deck chairs and from them emerged a Mr Armitage and a Mr Shanks, who proceeded to give the growing audience a series of 'toilet safety demonstrations'. Sue was then selected for the grand finale, a wet and wild dance with mop and bucket to the tune of Abba's *Waterloo*. She was brilliant. Thankfully, we didn't know anyone in Newbury.

When we could afford it, we were well up for adventure. The summer Sue was expecting Sarah my parents did a house swap in Maine and invited the rest of the family. It was an excuse to visit Lucy in Nova Scotia as well. The cheapest route was Aer Lingus to Boston, and the leg from Birmingham to Dublin in a small turboprop was a memorable start. It was a cloudless morning with north Wales spread out beautifully below us. Hannah and Jo were in the two seats on the other side of the aisle, looking excitedly out the window. They were the only children on the mainly business flight and were spoilt rotten by the air hostesses. They were given a couple of packets of K'Nex and were so thrilled by this unexpected freebie, and had such fun making things together, that they were given all the remaining packets of K'Nex on the plane.

From Boston we got the coach to Portland and then an overnight ferry to Yarmouth, Nova Scotia. In the morning we picked up a hire car and drove up to Halifax on empty roads, with woods and forest on one side and coast on the other. Drivers were so courteous. When we stopped at a tourist office we were welcomed with free coffee and greeted so warmly we wondered if we were the only tourists they had seen all year. We spent a few days with Lucy and her family, barbecuing fresh corncobs, having a huge water fight in the garden and towing a hand truck with our things to swim in their lakes.

We continued across to the Bay of Fundy where Hannah and I had a magical evening whale watching. Jo, who was more cautious about being at sea in a small boat surrounded by whales, had a special meal out with Sue. It was the first time we discovered the benefit of one-to-one time. In the following years I booked Care for the Family's one parent/one child activity weekends with Jo, and then Sarah. These included raft-building, high ropes and orienteering. Definitely a good move.

The second half of the holiday was in a beautiful house on the shore of Woods Pond in Maine. Don't be fooled by the word 'pond'. This is a two-mile-long lake, with mountains on the far side and a sand beach at the southern end. A jetty enabled Hannah to run down the garden and jump straight off the end in a rubber ring. It also gave us access to several boats, including a flat raft-like picnic boat with an outboard, a speedboat, two canoes, a pedalo and various inflatables. We used them all, making family expeditions to the beach by canoe and letting the children steer the speedboat. We found ourselves a part of all kinds of water games. And when no one was looking, Sue and I went skinny dipping in the warm, fresh water.

There were other family adventures. After a few sails to the Isles of Scilly we decided the best way to see these beautiful islands was by staying on St Mary's and hiring a small boat. We took the helicopter to Hugh Town, and as we approached, the archipelago took our breath away: lush vegetation, sandy shores and shimmering blue sea. We stayed in a slightly run-down guest house in a fabulous position by the beach, the sand giving way to rock pools that sparkled in the light of the setting sun. At low water, Hannah 'rescued' all the stranded jellyfish and put them in a rock pool until it was one big splodge of jellyfish. We had a Skipper 14, which has a picnic table and an area in the bow where small children can sit. The islands are close together and we explored most of them: the abandoned cottages on uninhabited Samson, the beautiful beaches of Tresco, the remains of the Pest House on the quarantine island of St Helens where sick sailors were dumped, the rugged Hell Bay on Bryher, and the beach between St Agnes and Gugh, washed clean each day at high water.

A family trip to Israel was also special. Sue and I had toured Israel with backpacks, travelling on public buses before the children arrived on the scene. Since then I had made regular business trips. We took the British Airways overnight flight one February half-term and picked up a hire car from an east Jerusalem company so we could travel to the West Bank. We stayed at Bethlehem Bible College, opposite a small refugee camp. We saw the sights, swum in the Dead Sea, experienced checkpoints and ate fresh Arab bread with olive oil and za'atar. We stayed by the Sea of Galilee, explored the Golan, felt moved by the sight of rusting tanks and were awed by poppies on the lower slopes of the snowed-capped Mount Hermon.

When cheap flights came in we took advantage of them, most memorably when I spotted 'free flights' – just tax and charges – from Birmingham to Amsterdam on Sue's birthday. So we booked a day trip, first flight out and last flight back. We were in central Amsterdam by 9am and had a brilliant family day: double-decker train, the canals, a park, a market and a thoughtful tour of Anne Frank's house. Passport control at Schiphol wished Sue a happy birthday.

The backbone of Marshall family holidays continued to be sailing, and we started to venture further afield. We chartered a Feeling 29 from La Trinité-sur-Mer in southern Brittany and sailed to the beautiful islands of Houat, Hoëdic and Belle Île. In Locmariaquer we picked up good friends from Coventry (who had children the same age as Hannah and Jo) who were on holiday in the area. We had a brilliant day sailing round the Gulf of Morbihan, a kind of giant Poole harbour with several islands. At the Île d'Arz, where we thought we would stop for a cold beer, I decided to drop the crew off on a slipway before anchoring and rowing in. A bunch of boy scouts watched us as I nudged the boat into the slipway. As we drew alongside, Sue stepped over onto the slipway with the bow line. She missed. For perhaps the only time on a boat, I did feel a note of panic as she disappeared completely from sight, sliding into the water between the slipway and the boat. However, only her pride was seriously injured. It amused the boy scouts.

Flotillas were Sue's preferred engagement with sailing. She was reassured by the presence of a fleet skipper who knew where to sail, an engineer who could sort broken engines and a social host who booked restaurants and organised fun things with the kids. We went with Sailing Holidays round the southern Ionian islands then tried different bits of Croatia with my sister Jill's family. We enjoyed the freedom to do what we wanted during the day, the sheer joy of diving off the back of the boat and the sociability of being with others in the evening. We explored caves, jumped off cliffs and swum in the stunning

Krka falls. We sailed to the Kornati islands, eating at a café on an island without power, where the menu was 'meat' or 'fish', cooked by a man in a vest over an open fire as the sun set. The girls delighted in using the radio to contact their cousins and in catching giant jellyfish in the colander. ('Now what can I use for the salad?' complained Sue.)

At the end of each cruise, 'awards' were presented to each boat. On the first trip we were astonished to find we had won a wooden fig leaf award for skinny dipping. The team had been happy for us to go off on our own and so one evening we found a quiet anchorage and Sue and I took advantage of a bit of privacy when the children had gone to bed. Somehow, Hannah found out about our late-night swim, and as we came in the next day she was at the bow with the lines. Even before we tied up she shouted across, 'Guess what my Mum and Dad did!' We were at the engine end and hadn't heard. On later trips we simply sent the children to join their cousins for the day.

Nudity was also part of a shared family memory from another quiet evening. We anchored off Port Leone, a village abandoned after the 1953 earthquake. A neighbouring German boat with an elderly, naked crew caught our attention when a man operated the windless to raise the anchor, standing astride the chain. The consequence of any misjudgement was a distinctly uncomfortable thought.

The best family holiday was the last with the five of us, just months before Hannah got engaged. In December 2009, I made a speech in Kampala to an audience of bishops, businessmen and the Prime Minister, where I pointed out Uganda was potentially a world-class tourist destination and I promised to bring my family. 'You have a beautiful country,' I told them, 'Very friendly people... and amazing roads!' This brought laughter and whooping. Even major routes require travelling on cratered 'red' (ie mud) roads. A few days earlier, we had had to turn back after a main route was blocked when the track over a river had crumbled and a lorry had fallen over into the water. Just behind, another lorry driver thought he could make it, but tumbled over on top of the first lorry. Right next to this there was a new concrete bridge built a couple of years before, but due to an engineering miscalculation, there was a two-foot step from the old track to the new bridge so, for want of a ramp, it was impassable.

On the trip I had met an orphan from a care home with a remarkable story. Amos Wekes saved $50 and started a tour company, Great Lakes Safaris. Eventually, he managed to buy a 4 x 4 van, but he lent it to a friend who wrote it off. The business nearly closed but he felt God tell him to wait one more month. In that month a happy client wrote an article in the *Washington Post* and business has boomed ever since.

So, to celebrate selling CRT (see chapter six) we booked a flight to Entebbe and a Great Lakes Safaris van and driver. Han, Jo and Sarah, who love travelling and adventure, were ridiculously excited. We kept a shared diary, which gradually became filled with stories, photos and drawings. On the flight out, Jo joked that the bag of freebies with earplugs and socks on the flight made it feel like Christmas. And Sarah wrote, 'The most exciting part for me and Hannah was being allowed to watch films and eat dinner in "bed".'

My friend Livingstone gave us a lift from the airport to Kampala. Hannah wrote in the diary,

> My first impression of Uganda was that it was very colourful, eg red dirt, a lot of green plants, blue sky and crazy coloured shops. I was surprised by the number of things it is possible to take on a bicycle. When I'm on my bike I never think to transport a load of watermelons or sugarcanes although I did once cycle eight miles with an inflatable Christmas tree.

That evening, we hosted dinner for all our friends in Uganda: Livingstone, who came from extreme poverty and had lived in a slum, with his wife and children; Hamlet, another entrepreneurial friend who was chaplain to the Ugandan Parliament; Samson, who had come to Westwood Church when he was studying for a PhD and was now in a very senior position; and Anna, a friend on a gap year. Next morning, our driver Robert arrived in a Great Lakes Safaris van and we set off on our travels.

We were awed by the drama, scale and magnificence of Murchison Falls. The girls were also awed by what appeared to be a bull elephant's fifth leg and the bright blue and red colours of the Vervet monkey's bits. Hannah made friends with a warthog, Sue was scared by a chimp brushing past at speed, and we were all impressed that a three-piece suite could be fitted on a pushbike. We discovered that the Impenetrable Forest was in fact penetrable and hiked with a small group and an armed guard. We stayed in a tent with an en suite on a platform in the forest, in luxury lodges and more basic accommodation. We visited an orphanage where cannabis grew wild (so they said) in the garden. Hannah picked some and pressed it in our diary. We visited Livingstone's former house in a Kampala slum, a sticks and mud hut down a narrow corridor where the rent costs £12 per month and the charcoal for cooking, paraffin for light, use of a toilet and water from a standpipe cost another £22 a month. We swam and went white water rafting in Jinga, and discovered you could surf on a standing wave on a body board before being sucked in to the rapids. The girls had their hair braided and bought more accessories than they or their friends could possibly need. We saw hippos, crocodiles, lions, giraffes and many other creatures. Every day was a new high, a new adventure.

Later, Sue and Sarah produced a photo book with commentary as a souvenir for each of us. It was the best investment in the family we had made.

In his book, *The Power of a Whisper*, church leader Bill Hybels said he was struck by how deeply one family in the church loved each other. One day the father challenged him to

'Consider using vacations as investments in your family ... to infuse your family with adventure and joy.'

Bill was gripped by this:

> I asked a few questions for clarification and learnt that the man and his wife made it a priority to take two family vacations each year. Well in advance of the trips, they would involve their kids in the planning process and build a strong sense of anticipation for what would soon unfold. While they were gone they would squeeze every ounce of family time out of the experience, and once they returned, they'd tell stories, share memories and look at photo album snapshots as they relived the great time they'd had.

Bill went on the say that, 'For the past 25 years, that single prompting from God through that dad has had more of an effect on the Hybels family than any other counsel we've received.'[11]

Small animals were another regular theme of family life; especially rats and gerbils. One gerbil came to an unfortunate end, welded to a mains cable under the floor boards. We scraped her off with a fishing net. Her fellow inmate had also escaped under the floorboards but wisely avoided gnawing any cables. Instead, she fell into a deep crevice. In a rare moment of inspiration, I added lines of string to the top end of a Pringles tube, placed food at the bottom, and lowered it into the depths until it lay at the bottom on its side. Eventually, the forlorn creature entered the tube, which was whisked upwards and the contents duly poured back into the cage.

The marketing instinct must have rubbed off on Hannah at some point. She was the prime mover behind probably the most targeted poster campaigns ever instigated. The three children

---

[11] Bill Hybels, *The Power of a Whisper*, Zondervan, 2010, p197.

had been pushing for a trampoline for some time: one day we came back from the shops to find a series of A4 posters sticky tacked around the house, each with a picture and strapline extolling the virtues of trampolining. We conceded defeat. It was a fun investment though: three could bounce on it at any one time and, inevitably, Hannah invented silly games to play on it.

From the trampoline, we progressed to juggling, plate-spinning, clubs and unicycling. I never really managed to juggle, but I was told it took ten hours to learn to unicycle, and I took this at face value. For about seven hours I launched myself from the sitting room window ledge and managed up to one wheel revolution. Despite this, I was determined not to be beaten and, by the time ten hours were up, I was distracting drivers by unicycling down the street.

Model hot air balloons were another entertaining distraction. My brother-in-law once bought me a kit. We took it into the garden, attached cotton wool into a loop of wire under the balloon, and soaked it thoroughly in methylated spirits. Once lit, the balloon shot up over the house. We jumped in the car and followed it for a few miles. After it disappeared, we returned to read the instructions: one teaspoonful of methylated spirits. Later, I found a design using 32 sheets of tissue paper and no burner: the balloon was launched over a barbecue. I arranged a parent and child workshop in the village hall and often had groups of children chasing balloons through the village. Recovering balloons was a novel way to meet neighbours.

I love being a father. I had thought a father's love for children would be similar to my love for my parents but it is different: protective, intense, forgiving, more akin to romantic love. Now I understand why this is the analogy presented in the Bible for the Father's love for us.

Sue is a natural and excellent mother and we make a good (if rather traditional) parental team. I was the one encouraging risk and adventure; Sue was the sensible one who kept track of their schooling and schedules, did the washing and ironing and taught them to cook, bake and use the sewing machine. It was Sue who kept the family on track, on time and on budget.

Sue was the one who insisted we ate together as a family every evening at 6pm, and this was a vital foundation to family life. I know many struggle to be back from work at that time but working from home helped, and it became a priority. Sometimes I turned down work or gave long lead times to avoid being too busy, though I didn't always succeed. Despite our wealth as a country, professionals are increasingly expected to be available at all hours, cutting into family time and rest. Sue worked part-time for me doing the accounts, but otherwise gave up paid work when the children were young. It was a worthwhile investment. When I made the shortlist for a job in south-west London, I pulled out when I realised we could only afford to live there if Sue worked full-time. Now she works as an administrator for a wedding band, and contributes a great deal as a school governor and children's leader at church.

Parenting did not come without heartache and challenges. We were devastated to discover one child was the victim of bullying but hadn't told us. All three attended the local, generally excellent, comprehensive school. A youth leader knew of the problem but I missed the hints she dropped, and rules on confidentiality prevented her telling me directly. Eventually the vicar Peter was told and decided it needed to be tackled. He came round early one morning. By 9am we were in the school talking with the head of year. Other challenges included dealing with eating issues, depression and self-harm. It was uncomfortable, but we worked through it.

Marriage also had its heartaches. Sue and I are at opposite ends of any psychometric test, which meant arguments and differences of opinion. Being very different people from contrasting backgrounds gave us complementary strengths and made us a strong team, but it also meant our marriage had its ups and downs.

There were two things that significantly helped. One was our commitment to the full Christian understanding and sacrament of marriage, the 'till death us do part' bit. This meant an underlying level of trust, faithfulness and security. It also meant we were forced to sort out differences and work through the hard process of apology and forgiveness. The second related point was the need to invest in our marriage, to take time out, meals and short breaks together. Often, this was overlooked and had to be relearnt. We did a couple of marriage courses too, a sort of marriage MOT. Gradually things have got better. I joke with those getting married that the first year is the worst.

A vital component of marriage and family life is our church, which is our extended family. It's the kind of place where church members gave money when we were short, helped when we moved house, and give prayer and cake when we need it. The culture is always positive and encouraging. The youth work was especially good and the girls benefited from slightly off-the-wall leaders just a few years older than them. Beyond that, church weekends, children's camps organised by CPAS, New Wine and the youth conference Soul Survivor, which now attracts 30,000 young people, have helped them develop confidence and faith. Even better, Rachel Gardner from the Romance Academy has led brilliant Soul Sister events, which communicate a young, vibrant and positive view of Christian attitudes to relationships and sex. It would not have been the same coming from us, especially with my track record.

Reflections

- Plan family adventures together and create memories.

- Invest in your marriage: carve out and diarise time.

- Spend time with and enjoy your children, one to one and as a family. They are your most important investment, and in no time at all (it seems) they have grown up and left home.

- As a car sticker given to us by the children said, 'Be nice to your children. They choose your nursing home.'

Chapter 6: Setting up a Proper Company

On Millennium Eve we partied the night away in our church, which had been transformed for the occasion. Beautifully decorated tables were laid out in the church itself, with silver and gold balloons reflecting candles along the walls. The church rooms included a bouncy castle and a crash-out area full of mattresses for the children. After the dinner, we celebrated with an exuberant ceilidh. The world did not implode as a result of the 'Millennium bug' and aircraft did not fall out of the sky as some had feared.

In January 2000 the world seemed full of promise. The Iron Curtain had been pulled down, the internet and cheap computing were promising a step change in wealth, peaceful transition had taken place in South Africa and even peace in the Middle East looked possible. Sadly, the technology crash, Palestinian intifada and 9/11 soon poured a dose of dark reality onto the brightest hopes.

I had taken on Richard, completed the TeamStart programme and incorporated the consultancy as Marketing Strategy and Action Ltd (MSA) in February 2000. I was looking for something new, something in the marketing field but a product-based company I could build and sell. One of my life goals was to have a pension fund of at least £500,000 by the time I retired, but in 2000 I was barely a tenth of the way there.[12]

After the TeamStart programme, another TeamStart member, also called Richard, phoned me. He had been put in contact with a company in California that sold customer feedback products called 'Opinionmeters'. He wanted to use my consultancy company as a vehicle to negotiate to be the exclusive UK licensee. This was exactly the opportunity I was looking for.

---

[12] My ten life goals are listed in chapter 10.

TeamStart Richard was another economics graduate, but from the London School of Economics. For years I'd had a cartoon on my noticeboard saying that if you lined up all the LSE graduates end to end they would never reach a conclusion. From economics he had turned to computer systems, then to law, then back to computers. Meanwhile, he had flown a light aircraft across the Atlantic. I warmed to him and offered to go 50/50.

The plan was to set up Opinionmeter as a project within MSA, at least initially, to prove the model. This of course brought in Partner Richard, who owned 25 per cent of MSA and therefore would own 12.5 per cent of the new venture. However, Partner Richard was excited by the opportunity and wanted more. We agreed when we set up a separate company to give him 25 per cent and TeamStart Richard and I would share the rest.

The first stage was to check it out and sell ourselves to the Americans. Opinionmeter Inc was essentially a father and son team. Father had invented the device, was convinced it was the best thing ever and now son Morgan was improving the design further. They had had a Scottish agent who had unfortunately and inconsiderately died, so there was an opening.

In truth, the Opinionmeter was a bit clunky to look at. It consisted of a Perspex holder into which slid a paper questionnaire with multiple choice answers. Below this, a small screen and a simple keypad enabled a user to enter their responses. The screen was in fact part of a Hewlett Packard programmable calculator. The responses could then be read on the screen, or downloaded, by cable or via a modem, to a PC programme that generated the graphs and cross tabulations. The simple display meant it could be left *in situ* without a power socket. As well as the standard floor-standing unit, there was hand-held version.

To understand and evaluate the opportunity, TeamStart Richard and I agreed with Morgan that we would visit the most successful Licensee, Opinionmeter Nordic, in Oslo. The trip got off to an inauspicious start. Richard, who was to pick me up on the way to Birmingham Airport, misjudged the time by an hour. Once this fact had been established, Sue rushed me to the airport in the car, where I checked in and called him. He had made it to the car park so I waited for him instead of going through. It was only when they named me on the PA ('Will the last remaining passenger...') that I ran to departures, apologising incoherently as I jumped the queue, and sprinted straight to the gate and into the plane as the door closed behind me.

Following the trip, the two Richards and I took the plunge, signed the contract, bought ten Opinionmeter sets and began to contact potential customers. We met every week over breakfast to coordinate our efforts. I drew on my engineering experience to arrange the fabrication of the plastic questionnaire holder (we wanted an A4 version) and the steel base (too heavy to import from the States).

We had some interest from the NHS and on the strength of that decided to set up a new company, Customer Research Technology Ltd (CRT). We deliberately decided not to call ourselves Opinionmeter UK because, in due course, we wanted to supply a range of technology in the field of customer research and feedback.

We also decided that MSA and CRT would hire a secretary and rent an office at the Business Innovation Centre, a University of Warwick Science Park business incubation base. This was a smart, modern building on a new business park. Inside the glass entrance was a wide and bustling reception area, with a broad open staircase sweeping round to the first floor, where meeting rooms enabled us to look the part when inviting prospects to visit us. The centre team were exceptionally supportive and we were able to grow from a 300 square feet office, eventually to 1,600 square feet, without changing our address and contact details.

The Opinionmeter sales model was based on rental, because they were worried that second-hand units could find their way on to the market and undercut their operations. But soon we had requests to purchase. This was better for the public sector, as they were more able to find funds for one-off capital investments than extra operational budget. We decided we should serve market needs and sell as well as rent, but at a serious mark-up. The customer could then choose. Eventually, this became the business model elsewhere.

Our first big opportunity was with Burger King at Compass Group. We discussed where we should pitch the price in our proposal. TeamStart Richard's line was that Compass Group were a rich company so they could afford to pay a good rate. I was more cautious. The proposal was duly dispatched and I went down to London to meet the prospect. Later I learnt that proposals should always be presented in person. It was an uncomfortable meeting: the prospect said he nearly fell off his chair when he saw the price.

At the next breakfast meeting, TeamStart Richard kept repeating, 'You've lost that contract haven't you, Jerry?' A couple of days later he emailed to say he wanted out and wanted his investment back. It was a shock, but I also felt it was better to lose him then (at low cost) rather than later.

Partner Richard immediately phoned to ask about the situation and how I was going to reallocate the shares. I was driving at the time. He called again about the shares not long after I got home. I felt pressurised but on reflection decided it was right to be generous; it would be good to harness his enthusiasm. I said we should take 45 per cent each and allow ten per cent for key employees, starting with five per cent for Sue. We were just in the process of forming the company and he persuaded me that initially it would be easier to split the shares 50/50 and sort employees later; but later he did not recall the original offer. Lesson: make sure key decisions are in writing and filed away.

Richard asked for the role of marketing director, though I set up Goldmine, the Customer Relationship Management (CRM) system, and sent out tailored mailings. We also worked together – uneasily – on press releases and leaflets. I took on product development, Richard did a superb job on the website development and we both handled sales. I was left with a few tasks that were not my area of interest, such as company secretary, while Sue handled the bookkeeping. I was also chief technical fault-fixer and customer helpline, until we employed Dermot, who had the considerable advantage of knowing what he was doing.

The new office came into its own with our first prospect visit: a large UK car manufacturer. They could hardly have come to the former office in my house. We did various pieces of work for them – an employee survey and some events. They were terrible payers at the time. Eventually I applied our legal right and raised an invoice for interest. A lady with a condescending voice in purchasing responded, calling to say they didn't accept interest invoices. I said it was a legal right. She said they normally found suppliers wrote them off. I was shocked that such a successful and prestigious company could take advantage of small suppliers to benefit their own cash flow and flout the law on the basis that suppliers needed the work.

Richard threw himself into developing sales. A key early contract was with Welcome Break, the motorway services people. This was a complicated contract from our point of view. It involved a special walk-in unit, a scrolling display and weekly trips to Oxford Services to reset everything and take readings. Richard handled most of this. When I tried it on the way back from holiday with the family late at night, it took me forever. However, income from this kept us going in a lean time.

Another of Richard's complicated contracts was London Underground. It took literally years to get in there. After the King's Cross fire, Transport for London would not take anything that might burn and give off fumes. We had to have the units encased in steel, and we used existing approved noticeboards for the questions. A company was employed to move the units around. Richard and I attended safety training so we could don yellow jackets and work underground. We learnt that there were coded messages that could be put out on the PA, to alert staff of, say, a bomb threat, without panicking customers.

I stuck with simpler prospects and found a rich seam in the NHS, especially in Scotland, where there was a different organisational structure. I found I could get a flight to Glasgow or Edinburgh for less than the rail fare to London. Furthermore, the fact that I was flying meant that NHS trusts were accommodating in meeting with me. Typically, I would present at a meeting of senior nurses. They seemed to warm to my low-key approach and half-joking comments that patient feedback could be used for doctors' appraisals, and sales started to come in.

A GP neighbour went out of his way to help me, and through him I discovered that there was a simple but carefully developed 20-question primary care patient survey, called the Europep Instrument, which had been tested across Europe. The survey was available without charge and it was ideally suited to the Opinionmeter. Unfortunately, the NHS decided to go a different route.

The first year, Richard and I worked half time in the business unpaid, and half time as consultants with MSA. Sales were £30,000 and the balance sheet at the end of the year showed I had, in effect, lost the life savings I'd invested in the business. The second year, sales rose to £60,000 and we still didn't pay ourselves, but my life savings showed up again (on the balance sheet, not in repayment). Richard said to an advisor he didn't think CRT sales would ever exceed more than £100,000.

Nevertheless, CRT continued to double turnover every year and we started to pay ourselves. By 2004 we had 11 staff and sales of £280,000, twice the size of MSA, and we won a Deloitte 'Fast Fifty' award after four years of 100 per cent growth. Mind you, the secret to winning this is simply to have a terrible first year as a base point.

We became the most successful Opinionmeter Licensee and organised a European Licensee forum in Coventry. My main role in this was to take everyone out punting in Stratford, with a classy picnic in a wicker basket. Richard was not keen to join us, and persuaded the Irish Licensee to say he suffered from aquaphobia; the two of them went to the pub instead. There was something not right in my relationship with Richard, but I couldn't put my finger on the problem.

Fundamental changes took place over the next couple of years. The first significant threat was that the Hewlett Packard programmable calculator at the heart of the Opinionmeter went out of production, with no direct replacement. As a result, a new Opinionmeter came out, with some improvements, but less reliable and it needed to be permanently plugged in, thereby losing one of the key benefits. Software was improved but this was now supplied over the internet by licence. The benefit was that it created a small income stream from licence payments, but the disadvantage was that Morgan had the power to cut us off if he didn't think we were playing by the rules.

Meanwhile, touchscreens were improving all the time. Opinionmeter Inc were reluctant to take this route, which gave us an opening to develop our own range of complementary products. For this, I made a fortuitous discovery. We had moved to a larger unit in the Innovation Centre and on a whim I dropped in on our old office to say hello to the new tenants, a company called Initium. They turned out to be a software development company who had contributed to the lightning conductor inspection industry. I didn't know there was a lightning conductor inspection industry. Apparently, lightning conductor inspectors spent Monday to Thursday inspecting, and Friday writing up their reports. However, Initium had developed software for handheld computers that enabled inspectors to work through a series of questions which enabled them to complete their report on the spot, and then they simply had to press 'send'. Suddenly inspectors were 25 per cent more productive. More importantly for us, I could see that this software was exactly what was needed at CRT and, in due course, we bought the rights to it for the market research space. They became our IT partners.

This Intellectual Property Rights negotiation was done by Simon Rowland, a friend of Richard and a member of his church. He had been increasingly involved as a consultant with CRT and MSA, initially filming some presentations to improve our sales technique and also leading some MSA work. Simon had been highly successful as a sales director in a technology business and was then involved in taking the business to trade sale before leaving to set up his own consultancy.

We had been open to the possibility of a third partner and Simon was the perfect match. I liked and trusted him. He was a cool operator who didn't allow emotions to affect his judgement, and a strong negotiator who held out for longer than I ever dared. He also had the experience we needed: professional sales management and taking a company to trade sale.

We couldn't pay anything close to the salary he was used to, so we gave him a third of the company over a couple of years. He joined CRT as a Director in December 2005 and we appointed him CEO in 2006. It was the right thing to do. I had learnt that in Belbin team type terms I was a Shaper – good at turning vision to reality. Give me a vision I can buy into and a blank sheet of paper and I can make it happen. Once it gets to processes and procedures my brain freezes over and I want to move on to the next thing.

On the hardware side, IBM introduced a slim, robust, relatively inexpensive unit which was ideal for us. Both IBM and their European distributor Scansource were enormously supportive. Although at first we were a very small client, they could see the potential, and they provided cheap demo machines and free marketing for us.

We needed money to develop and increase the functionality of our own software and link it to the touchscreen and other input devices. We managed to win several grants, including one of £10,000 on the basis that we were a manufacturer. We were indeed assembling units but it was stretching the definition. We also applied for a small (£50,000) 'soft' venture capital investment from part of the government-funded Regional Development Agency. So for the first time we actually wrote a business plan. I was very proud of it: writing it all down made me realise we had a good business and were getting somewhere. In 2005 we won the VC deal, receiving £50,000 for 7.5 per cent, valuing the company at £667,000. In 2006 our sales rose to over £500,000, but more importantly, we had built the technical and product foundations for a strong company.

The core strength was the web-based software. Richard worked tirelessly with Simon and Initium to develop improved versions to our requirements. It was simple to use, and users could create their own survey on the touchscreen with a wide range of features, question types and design styles. The analysis end could generate automatic reports or individual graphs, provide cross tabulations (to view, for example, satisfaction by age or gender), and included a traffic light visualisation so customers with multiple sites could spot a problem outlet or a problem area across all outlets. The best feature was the quarantine system, which identified and excluded multiple entries by angry customers or suspiciously positive reports from staff trying to up their satisfaction score. One of the first customers was the Cardiff Millennium Stadium, who had to have everything bilingual (English and Welsh); this was the catalyst for a multilingual feature enabling feedback to be given in many European and Asian languages.

Alongside this, we paid a professional branding company to redo our brand and Richard worked with consultancies to develop the website and search engine optimisation. Our tag line was 'beyond question' and our in-house system was named Viewpoint.

Our big problem was Morgan, who was increasingly concerned that we were going further than introducing our own complementary range of technology. He was right to be concerned: our system was much better than his and the touchscreen began to replace Opinionmeters. He started to cut off our access to the Opinionmeter software when he was angry about something. We were concerned he might find grounds to sue us, and kept referring to the contract – which was still in the MSA name – to check we were doing things correctly. We considered buying them but there was not much worth to be had. Richard completely fell out with Morgan. Eventually, Morgan brought out an Opinionmeter touchscreen but it was too late, and we found a formula to part company.

Amid all this, MSA continued to function, with significant work from the International Bottle Company, originally won from the marketing masterclass. Richard and Simon handled and developed the contract; unfortunately, the work was too late to save them and they went into administration. At that point I was too involved in CRT, and increasingly in Palestine, to invest in maintaining and developing MSA, which rapidly fell into decline and disrepair. In due course Richard handed back his share and MSA became a personal vehicle for launching new projects.

Although there were challenges and difficulties, we also had a lot of fun. It was a nice little business to work on and we were following the original strategy while adjusting tactics along the way. IBM invited me on a trip to Future Shop in Germany to see the latest developments in retailing, and on a jolly to Portugal, with a poolside barbecue and mountain-biking in the hills. Around Christmas we had annual company parties, which steadily became more ambitious as the company grew. And daughter Jo joined me for a week of work experience, which included one of my day trips to Scotland. She helped me with some training for the Scottish Forestry Commission in Ardgarten, then we drove to the 'Rest and Be Thankful' car park to climb a mountain before a sales visit in Glasgow.

In the office, we tried to keep a light atmosphere. When Richard texted me to say that the office staff sounded fed up, I went in and taught them plate-spinning. Richard was a practical joker. Once he told a cold caller the person they needed to talk with was Mrs King – Jo King – and put them on hold. I couldn't bear to leave them in hope, so picked up the call and broke the news that it was a joke. And Richard and Simon challenged each other to get odd words – like 'Rumpelstiltskin' – into an important meeting.

Richard and I sparred in a light-hearted way on expenses and on sport. On expenses, my experience was influenced by staying in a tent on my first overseas business trip with Eaves and Washbourne. And at CRT, I once found a hotel close to the station where I was arriving in advance of a meeting early the following day. It was only £10 per night. At that price I should have realised it would be a hostel for homeless people. When we were exhibiting in Bournemouth, Richard called the PA and asked that she book the hotel before I did, but it was too late. I had already found a very convenient place a short walk away. It was full of old people on coach tours. Richard asked earnestly at reception, 'Is there a minimum age to be here?'

On sport, Richard thought I knew nothing. Certainly, I took no interest in watching sport. As a student I had a sign that said there were three types of people, 'Those who watch things happen; those who make things happen; and those who wondered what happened.' I always wanted to be the 'make it happen' type. The only football match I ever saw all the way through was Coventry winning the FA Cup in 1987. In the run-up to that, Sue and I only switched the TV on when we heard shouts from the Holts next door, a cue to look at the action replay. When the 2006 Football World Cup was on, Richard organised an office sweepstake, where we all predicted the scores for each match. I gather he spent hours on his entry. I whizzed through mine but it wasn't random. The sport round-up on Radio 4, which for years I had listened to while waiting for the 7.30am news, had sunk into my subconscious. I had a good idea of the best teams and most probable scores. Richard was deeply shocked when I won, though sadly no money was collected or passed on.

I came across the term 'kingdom entrepreneur', and in my more pretentious moments I thought it was quite a good summary of all my entrepreneurial activities, from church-planting to social enterprises to commercial business like CRT. They were all, in their own ways, part of advancing the 'King's Domain'. I thought CRT should be ultimately part of the Church in its broadest sense and therefore suggested to my partners that we place ourselves under the authority of an accountability group made up of our three church leaders. They would be a sounding board on moral issues and would also help us sort out any disagreements. The fact that one was an ex-barrister, one an accountant and one an entrepreneur certainly helped. We met with them every few months, usually over a meal.

The group was especially valuable when things started to fall apart between Richard and me.

Increasingly, I felt as though we were playing a game of Twister and I was being pushed off the mat. Richard and Simon led on the rebranding, software development and major sales.

Richard took over the IBM liaison. After providing the fruitful end-of-financial-year Goldmine mailing to NHS Trusts from the beginning, suddenly I was quizzed on why I was doing this as it was part of the marketing director's area. As a result, it stopped happening. I found myself doing exactly what I least enjoyed: policies, proposals and company secretary requirements.

In the autumn of 2006 I was involved in writing a business plan for a major call centre in Palestine. It would be finished by early January but I could see I might be involved well beyond that. I had never been paid more than half-time on CRT but I warned the board early on that I might have to pull back somewhat from the company.

The Palestine commitment and an increasingly uncomfortable atmosphere led to a meeting called by Simon in which it was proposed I drop down to two and a half days a month. I felt uncomfortable about this but I was not enjoying going in to the office, and other things had grabbed my attention. We talked it through and I accepted. Then Richard dropped the bombshell: I should give a proportion of the company back, reducing my holding to ten per cent.

I was shocked. I saw myself as the primary founder, and original risk-taker and investor. I thought I had been generous to Richard and felt I was being pushed out of my own company. I had no intention of handing my shareholding back. Richard reminded me that I had once said I would be happy just to get my money back. This, however, was simply an indication of the risk I had taken in the early days, when we were not sure whether the business would survive. I had not risked my life savings just to get them back again.

What followed was a long and painful couple of years, with much soul-searching and thoughtful support from the advisory group. The underlying problem was that neither the company nor the other shareholders could afford to buy my shares off me, but Richard and Simon wanted any increase in value from

133

the point at which I stepped back. Potentially a solution was to convert some of the equity (ie shares) into a loan. However, I would then be taking an equity risk and therefore needed an equity level of return, the kind of return I would expect from an investment in a small unquoted company. That meant a high interest rate which, of course, defeated the whole point of the exercise.

A key lesson is to have a shareholders' agreement (SHA) in place before it is needed, when things are going well, not when problems arise. In fact, we did have an agreement that had been put in place as part of the venture capital (VC) deal. This protected their investment by giving them a veto on actions such as issuing more shares to dilute minority shareholders or paying over-generous salaries to the directors. So long as this was in place, I was ultimately protected should there be a complete breakdown in relationships. However, the board wanted to buy back the VC shares prior to selling the company, and the VC administrators were open to doing a deal on reasonable terms.

So we set to work on a new SHA. The first version was a long and complicated complex standard document. We decided to abandon this and put something together in plain English. This can be a risky approach: ambiguous wording or failing to cover every possible situation can lead to massive legal wrangles and bills. However, I trusted Simon, the accountability group and ultimately God, if my conscience was clear.

At the heart of this was a 'call option' which gave my erstwhile colleagues the opportunity to buy just under half my shares at an agreed price based on what we estimated the value of the company to be at the point I ceased contributing.

The stumbling block was a veto on salary. I did not want company value to be squandered on above-market executive salaries or for the business to be lumbered with high costs. I also thought they were nuts to want to pay very high salaries, or dividends, given that we all qualified for Entrepreneurs' Relief, so we would only pay ten per cent tax on capital gains when we sold. We reached an uneasy compromise.

Our overall aim was to sell the company and we worked with ICON Corporate Finance to make sure everything was tied up and ticked off, especially IPR, well-documented contracts and good second-tier management. The aim was to be on the market when three things were experiencing healthy growth: company sales and profits, the overall business sector and the stock market. We hoped to be ready in early 2008.

As part of this, Simon and I began to look at export development. If we could show there was potential to go beyond the UK, the company would be more valuable. Richard had received enquiries from far-flung markets, but it seemed to me that the starting point should be nearby countries where English was widely spoken. I thought a franchise model would work best, given our lack of management resources, so I put together a paper. Export was also an opportunity for me to spend my small amount of time for CRT working on something reasonably independently. I worked closely with an excellent UK Trade and Investment Export Advisor, commissioned a subsidised study of potential leads in Belgium and fixed a trade visit to Brussels in June 2007. On the visit, I packed in up to five sales meetings a day with potential end customers and distributors, including the customer care director of food retailer Delhaize, who have 843 outlets in Belgium. I produced a report with recommendations for the board, which now included a non-executive chairman, a former colleague of Simon's.

It was an uncomfortable meeting. They didn't want to discuss it. It didn't fit the agenda. Despite full awareness of what was happening, Richard seemed irritated that I had found some leads, and the company didn't have the management capacity to deal with it. The leads were allowed to wither and die.

My relationship with Richard continued to deteriorate. I found another job, and in early 2008 I was asked to resign from the board. I was saddened and frustrated but there seemed little point in prolonging the agony by remaining. Furthermore, it was part of a deal to clear the decks before selling the company, including buying back the VC shareholding. With various safeguards in place, such as access to financial records, I formally stepped down at a meeting on 22nd April. Simon was disappointed with the whole issue. He had tried to bring reconciliation, but in the end he told me at that point he needed Richard more than he needed me.

The company was well prepared for trade sale. The new product range was working well, and changing the focus from hardware to software with recurring fees enhanced our value. Sales continued to grow. All the documentation was in place. Then the stock market collapsed as the credit crunch took its toll. We had been looking for £2 million to £3 million, but sales discussions were around the £1 million mark and the board pulled out.

Nevertheless, CRT continued to grow, achieving healthy profits on sales of over £2 million in 2009, with 20 staff. An investor started to take an interest, and Simon asked me what figure I was looking for to sell my share. In early summer 2009, after reflecting on this, he came to visit me with a 'non-negotiable' take-it-or-leave-it offer. The offer involved buying the call option shares straight away, then buying the rest at a somewhat higher valuation and leaving me with one 'golden share', worth about 30 per cent of the total deal, payable if and when the company was sold. The total for all these elements was around the amount I was seeking. Given that I was concerned with the way the economy was going I thought it was a reasonable offer, and I surprised him by accepting there and then. He had me down as someone that liked to sleep on things.

My parents picnicking in Kuwait 1953

Me, my friend Fiona and family and my mother and Hilary 1962

With Jill, on my way to Kuwait airport and school 1969

Chesapeake 1976

Cambridge 1979

Wedding to Sue 1982

Our girls

After delivering Sarah 1994

All of us at my parents' golden wedding 2003

The family on our boat 2005

Sarah's baptism at Westwood Church 2009

Two gingers and a ginger cake 2009

On holiday in Uganda 2010

The Opinionmeter: we then developed our own touch-screen range

TBN 'expo' trip to Bethlehem 2004

Transcend staff at launch 2012

Transcend staff

Sue and Jo at the Wall in
Bethlehem

Kibera 2008

With Jo in Mozambique

With Iris Ministries in Maputo
2008

The first HS2 interview, with Jeremy Wright 2010

HS2 march outside our house 2010 (note Jo juggling clubs)

Preparing Ele for the next outing

Ele at the Lib Dem Conference 2011

Euston poster at entrance 2011

On BBC Breakfast 2012

With Sue in Northern
Ireland 2012

In fact, the investor pulled out, but Simon still wanted to do the deal, and thought the company could afford it if payments were spread out over two years. I accepted and by 2010 was able to tick off the last of my ten life goals: to have a pension fund of at least £500,000. Suddenly we felt quite wealthy, although the pension capital was somewhat illusory: my fund would only produce a pension income equivalent to that of a middle management civil servant. However, it was there and it was flexible, split between SIPPs and ISAs,[13] and, if I invested it well, I felt it should more than keep pace with inflation.

The epilogue is that CRT did well for a time, the directors paid themselves a good dividend, and they moved out of the Innovation Centre to their own two-storey building. Richard got another job and also decided to leave, on a similar deal to mine. However, the company struggled with cutbacks in the NHS. After considering a number of possibilities, Simon decided to stick with and develop CRT. It has now turned the corner, and Simon deserves a healthy return on his efforts.

I learnt the importance of forgiving, of deliberately deciding to forgive and move on. In practice this means not dwelling on hurtful conversations, not waking up at 4am and replaying them, deciding instead to stop that train of thought. We are all sinners, or abusers, to use a more modern term. We abuse ourselves, each other and the environment. So friends inevitably let us down just as we let others down. There's no point spending our lives screwed up by whatever injustice we feel we have suffered. Richard and I are completely reconciled and he's doing well.

---

[13] A SIPP (Self Invested Personal Pension) gives tax benefits when you put money in, but it's locked in and the pension is taxable. An ISA (Individual Savings Account) can be drawn on at any time and there is no tax to pay as you take the money out. It seems to me best to have both: a small pension and a tax-free source of income and capital.

Overall, CRT was fun. I learnt a great deal. And by building something of value and generating a fund for our old age, it achieved my original purpose.

Reflections

- Whatever you do, it will take longer and cost more than you expect.

- Have a clear long-term strategy but experiment with the tactics and sales model.

- Know your strengths and bring in others with complementary skills.

- Sign a shareholders' agreement as soon as the company is getting somewhere and before it's worth anything.

- Friends will let you down: forgive and don't dwell on it.

Chapter 7: Partners in Palestine

We sped off on the Valley of Fire route, the long and winding road that meanders round the back of Jerusalem to avoid crossing in and out of Israel. The 'Service' minibus rattled through Bethlehem suburbs and villages, past square white buildings, out to hills bare but for a few green trees growing improbably out of the rock.

Round a hairpin bend, a broken down car is in the middle of the road, bonnet up, a man staring into the engine. A couple of lads in jeans and bright t-shirts sit on a rock above a flock of sheep and goats. Modern street lights line the route, each with their own solar panel, paid for by USAID. It took years to get permission from the Israelis. A massive coil of barbed wire extends a couple of hundred metres then comes to an abrupt end. On the hill there's a wall and, above this, a line of smart red-roofed villas, an Israeli settlement strategically situated here between Jerusalem and the Palestinian town of Jericho.

We slow for a checkpoint, a border between a Palestinian-controlled area of the West Bank and an Israeli-controlled area. There's the remains of a house that was demolished because it encroached a few yards into the Israeli-controlled area. We pass through the E1 corridor, a narrow strip connecting the northern West Bank with the southern. The Israelis plan to block it with settlements.

Eventually, we're in Ramallah. Advertising slips past the window: National Paint, Arab Net, Super Chicken, Galaxy Smooth Milk, a lady's leg with a snake curled round it, a sign 'Smokers' Centre' on a half-built multi-storey building with no front wall. I imagine it's a giant smokers' shelter.

I get out and switch to a taxi. There's Arabic music in the background. I ask for 'Al Hollandia', where the Dutch government has an office.

'Welcome! Where you from? Ahlan wa Salan' [hello, nice to meet you].

'Ahlan Biik,' I reply.

It's been an easy journey and I'm half an hour early. You never know how long to allow. At the gate, a security guard with a machine gun and friendly smile greets me. He pulls out a chair and beckons me to sit while I wait in the early morning sunshine.

It is October 2012 and my fourth visit of the year.

It was a church lunch with Salim Munayer in 1994 that changed my life.

Salim is a Palestinian Israeli whose father Jacob was evicted – 'ethnically cleansed' – from Lod in 1948, along with the rest of a thousand-year-old Christian community. Salim was the dean of Bethlehem Bible College and had set up an organisation called Musalaha, which is Arabic for reconciliation.

Musalaha does many things but its original core product is 'Desert Encounter'. This is a cunning plan whereby Israelis and Palestinians are paired up and hike across the desert with a camel, taking turns to ride it or lead it. They spend the day figuring out how to operate the camel, which becomes the common enemy. By the time it comes to discussion round the camp fire, the pairs can share their political grievances constructively, as fellow survivors and friends.

It turned out Sue had met Salim before, at a Christian student conference in Austria. I was keen to understand the situation because of my Middle East background and an interest in the Israeli–Palestine conflict that I inherited from my father. Dad had been in Palestine in the war and always referred to Israel as 'Occupied Palestine'.

The Oslo accords had been signed and I asked Salim what I could do, as a businessman, to support peace in Palestine. He suggested I came to visit.

At first, I saw this as a vaguely philanthropic gesture. Nevertheless, I did some research and contacted the Department for Trade and Industry Palestine desk. I located the Palestinian Chambers of Commerce and contacted them, asking to meet them and individual companies so I could find out how I might be of help. I also discovered the British Palestinian Partnership Scheme (BPPS) managed by the Aid Attaché at the British Consulate in Jerusalem, which could provide grants of up to £40,000. Finally, I contacted the Bishop of Coventry, Simon Barrington-Ward, who suggested I meet a key church leader in Nablus. Armed with this, a room at Bethlehem Bible College, and a British Airways ticket to Tel Aviv, I headed out.

Visiting Palestine was like coming home. Palestine in the 1990s was like Kuwait in the 1960s: the same battered Mercedes, constantly honking horns, smells, and well-meaning but chaotic hospitality. I loved it. There was also a spiritual sense of coming home, that this was my calling. And in the West Bank there was also a feeling of hope, a sense that at last things were looking up.

On the trip I got to know Salim, his wonderful wife Kay (from Bolton), and their growing collection of strapping sons. The highlight of every trip after that was taking Salim and Kay out for dinner. Both have a great sense of humour and were always fun company.

I visited Chambers of Commerce in Hebron, Nablus, Jericho and Gaza, and the 'Bethlehem Group of Industrialists' which was a kind of quasi-chamber of commerce. I had expected one-to-one meetings, but Hebron and Nablus brought in all the local notables: 20 or so older men in traditional Arab dress sitting around the walls, while a man behind a desk offered Arabic coffee or mint tea, introduced the group and politely answered my questions.

It was difficult not to be drawn into the political situation. I was especially moved by my visit to the Gaza Strip. Getting there through the Erez crossing involved parking outside, being processed through the Israeli booth labelled 'VIP' (in practice, all non-Palestinians), walking down what looked like a disused motorway for 300 metres, signing in at the Palestinian booth, then being accosted by enthusiastic taxi drivers hoping you didn't know the correct fare.

Gaza was noticeably poorer than the West Bank. The most visible sign of this were the donkey carts, often driven by children, rarely seen in the West Bank. I was also struck by the market: kids selling live chickens, removing the selected victim and decapitating it on a block with a large knife. There was a vibrancy about the place that you just don't get in UK supermarkets.

I met with Khaled Khatib, who ran the Palestine Chamber of Commerce, Gaza. In 1948 he and his family owned 25 hectares of orange groves and a villa near Jerusalem, but they fled to Gaza as refugees when they heard Israelis were slaughtering Palestinians as they advanced.

He told me that business was difficult for the Chamber's 3,500 members, who were mainly in textiles, plastics, fruit, vegetables and flowers.

'Citrus fruits and vegetables are exported to Europe but this has to be via an Israeli agent who expects a good profit,' he said, 'and often shipments are delayed making it impossible to sell flowers and difficult on other produce, giving Israelis an advantage.'

'The Israelis do not seem to be trying to make peace, but in our hearts we are not against them, despite all they have taken.'

In Hebron, I met with a young man called Nidal, at Al-Juneidi Dairies. He had worked for Express Dairies in Ruislip and spoke perfect English. The factory employed 150 people and worked to European hygiene standards, processing 40,000 litres of milk a day, though capacity was much higher. He was unable to sell to Gaza and had had to go to court to get permission to sell to Jerusalem, and this had only been granted for six months. Recently, he had been to Tel Aviv to meet a supplier, obtaining the correct permits for both himself and his car. Despite this, he was stopped, told he was too young to be in Israel and jailed for 48 hours without being allowed to inform his worried family.

I was impressed by the enthusiasm, industry and hospitality of the companies I visited. I was especially impressed when I locked my keys in the car outside a company in Hebron at 8am. I thought I'd blown my tight schedule for the day. I sheepishly explained my predicament to the CEO, who smiled and summoned one of his men; in two minutes he was back with the keys.

The person I related to most easily was Issa Abueitah, who ran the Bethlehem group. He was married to an Englishwoman, and he took me around. He showed me houses demolished by the Israelis as a punishment, and the route of a new road for Israelis, which was being blasted through the hills to link the growing number of new settlements around Bethlehem.

'In many ways things are worse than in the intifada,' he said. 'Israel has in effect shut their border to Palestinian goods because permits are only being issued to cars, not trucks.' National income had fallen, he said, because now only around 30,000 people worked in Israel, whereas before there had been around 200,000 and thousands more working in the Gulf.

'Our costs are high because the Palestinian National Authority is trying to raise income through tax. Diesel, water and electricity are more expensive than in Israel. It's like swimming against a river. There's a risk that business people will open factories in Jordan or Egypt because of lower costs and larger markets.'

He was passionate about building the Palestinian economy and halting the tide of emigration, which was mainly by Christians, 'who often had one leg abroad'. Unlike the UK, everyone is part of a faith community, irrespective of actual belief in God. It was easier, I was told, for the Christians to move elsewhere and this community, once a majority in the Bethlehem area, had dropped to only about 20 per cent of the population. Issa felt it was important to maintain Palestinian diversity as well as the long-established Christian Palestinian presence.

The overall message from my meetings was clear. There was no shortage of consultants. What they needed was hands-on help. Issa had clear ideas about what was needed. Companies needed to develop exports, and to do that they needed help with product design, graphic design of packaging and marketing material, and assistance with finding clients. He felt – correctly – that most companies had little idea of Western expectations regarding design and quality.

I finished the week by visiting the Consulate Aid Attaché and outlined my plans to get a feel for his response before I prepared a proposal. I said it would cost £35–40,000. I recorded his response in my visit notes.

'I don't want to seem too dramatic,' he said, 'but this is exactly what is needed.' (I know, I thought, I've asked.)

'And it's tailor-made for the BPPS.' (I know, I've researched the scheme.)

As well as the business contacts, I spoke to everyone I met on the trip. Daniel Cohen, a freelance journalist, and Daniella Nathan, an Israeli businesswoman, who both approved of helping Palestinian businesses. An Orthodox Jew I met on the tube to Heathrow said, 'Don't ask me about the peace process.' And a group of settlers to whom I gave a lift, talked about 'this cursed peace' and said, 'Violence is the only language Palestinians understand.' They didn't believe anyone was forced out of their homes in 1947 and 1948. When I quoted a particular example, they said 'maybe in one village' Arabs were forced out. In fact, as Israeli historian Ilan Pappe later described in his book *The Ethnic Cleansing of Palestine*,[14] there was a

---

[14] Oneworld Publications, 2006

systematic village-by-village removal of non-Jews from December 1947: villagers were rounded up at midnight, those connected with the 1936 revolt were shot and the rest of the village were evicted. A Jewish majority was seen as essential for the emerging nation. The direct cause of the conflict is dispossession rather than religion.

When the formal business proposal was accepted, I brought out a small team of consultants and a graphic designer. We gave talks, conducted initial 'business health checks' and worked with 12 companies selected by the Bethlehem group. What became clear early on was that some had no hope of exporting, a couple of businesses could not compete on price and, for many, quality was the key issue. We gave recommendations to all, and where there was potential, we found prospects through telesales and wrote letters for them to send. A young couple, who had met and trained in the UK and were taking over a traditional family-run textile company, wholeheartedly responded to the message on quality and began to export to the USA. For a family cosmetics business, we provided new packaging designs. And George Karra'a, who made antiquated mosaic tables and beautiful tiles, said to me, 'You will always have a friend in Bethlehem.'

The idea was that this was a pilot project and we would repeat the process, with some adjustments, in Hebron, Nablus and elsewhere. However, the Oslo process was falling apart. Extremists on both sides objected. Israeli Prime Minister Rabin, who had signed the Oslo Accords, was assassinated and Hamas started a series of bus bombings. This resulted in regular border closures and a shift of Israeli public opinion away from Peres and negotiated peace. Netanyahu won the 1996 election by a narrow margin. The peace process ground to a halt, the number of Israeli settlements grew, and export became very difficult. Support for export promotion was withdrawn.

I stayed in touch, but eventually Issa and his family gave up and moved to Cyprus. I thought that if he couldn't stay, the situation must be desperate. I wrote to the Israeli Ambassador and everyone else I could think of to say that things were going to explode in Palestine. Several articles I wrote, mainly for the Christian press, were published.

In September 2000 the second intifada broke out. At one point Bethlehem was under 24/7 curfew for six months with just short breaks for the population to dash to the shops. People caught breaking the curfew – sometimes even with Israeli permission – were shot dead. Business, schooling, life, were all on hold.

Meanwhile, I had thrown myself into developing CRT, and the sense of call I had to Palestine faded. Until 2004.

In 2003, we had a wonderful family Christmas in Devon with Mum, Dad, my sisters and their families. However, Mum was in a lot of pain and I sensed this was our last Christmas all together. She had nearly died from kidney failure years before, and then patiently tolerated five years of dialysis before a transplant gave her, for a decade, a new lease of life. Then, after their golden wedding anniversary the previous year, she had started to go downhill. Early in the morning of 13th January 2004, Hannah's 18th birthday, Dad called to say she had died in the night.

Dad was lonely but his death on 3rd July from what medics call 'Triple A' was unexpected. Later, we learnt that after a long marriage it was common for both partners to die close together. He had been sailing with me just two weeks before.

Both had experienced a tough start to life and Dad had also experienced the carnage of Anzio, the stalemate in the fight for Rome. Despite this, they were loving parents, devoted to each other and to us. My sisters Jill and Hilary felt the loss acutely. I always felt close to them and we were good at supporting each other. Our loss, and sorting things out, drew us closer together.

It was a big change and I went to the Christian holiday conference New Wine in July that year seeking a new direction. What came across was not a new purpose but to return to my original calling: Palestine.

One of the exhibitors at New Wine that year was an organisation called Transformational Business Network (TBN).[15] TBN is a network of business and professional people committed to using business to bring community transformation and to bring financially sustainable solutions to the scandal of global poverty. It struck a chord with me. TBN members were doing the kind of thing I had been doing in Palestine. I met the Founder, Stuart McGreevy, and joined.

TBN ran things called Exposure trips or 'expos', to give members an opportunity to visit businesses and projects in a particular area to understand the issues and see how they might be involved. In November 2004 I led an expo trip to Palestine with a small group of business people. It was a fresh start, an exploratory trip, taking new people and visiting mainly new contacts.

In my notes I wrote, 'It's impossible to give a full and adequate account of the differing views and emotional roller coaster of the West Bank trip.' We had 18 meetings in four days. We met with Salim and Kay, of course, and with Rabbi David Rosen, an incisive thinker, whom I knew from the Israeli Government Tourist Office roadshows I had set up.

'What you've got to understand is that round here,' he said emphatically, 'everyone regards themselves as a victim.'

We also met Norman Cohen from the very pro-Israel British-Israel Group. He and his wife lived in Gilo, in effect a settlement in the occupied West Bank, though now incorporated into the city of Jerusalem. Ironically, he proudly showed us a press release they had just sent out saying that settlements were only on land that wasn't wanted.

---

[15] www.tbnetwork.org (accessed 26 June 2013).

Four other meetings especially stand out.

First, a meeting with the Syrian Orthodox community in Bethlehem, set up through Coventry Cathedral. We had expected to meet just the priest. Instead, we were greeted by 15 or 20 people, almost all of them men in their fifties and sixties, and mostly called George. We were presented with gifts and given a tour of their church. They were proud to be an older refugee community than the Palestinians, having fled massacres in Turkey in 1915. We sat in their scout building, which the Israelis had recently mistaken for a Hamas stronghold and therefore smashed all the computers. We enjoyed cakes and cola, while we were told how the business of almost every man had come to a sticky end.

Since the second intifada, the economy had completely fragmented. Palestinians needed permission, rarely granted, to travel just a few miles in any direction. The closures, curfews and restricted movement of people and goods had caused unemployment to rise to 76 per cent, and poverty to rise to the extent that according to a UN report, 50 per cent lived on under $1 a day, and this in a high-cost formerly middle-income country. Palestinian Christians felt especially hard hit.

Second, we also met Nader, a deeply committed Christian who ran a rehabilitation programme, helping children and young people traumatised by violence to work through their anger and find healing. The 'breaking bones' policy of attacking unarmed demonstrators had left 5,000 young people permanently disabled. Almost half of Palestinian children had experienced extreme violence. Many wet their beds. The programme helped them work through their experiences, assessed their skills, and provided appropriate vocational training and opportunities for self-employment. Nader didn't volunteer his own experience until a photograph prompted us to ask. In 1989 he was arrested on suspicion of 'recycling terrorists'. He was taken to Hebron and tortured for 42 days, including 13 days of sleep deprivation during which he suffered days and nights in agonising positions. He said he had forgiven his torturers but added, 'I wish I could tell them what they did to me.'

Third, we met Nihad, pastor of a growing 200-member evangelical church in Bethlehem who also taught at Bethlehem Bible College and ran the Shepherd Society, which alleviates poverty through family sponsorship. During the six-month curfew in Bethlehem, he built a stock of goods in his garage. When he received calls from church members who had run out of say, baby milk, he would ask if there were tanks nearby, phone church members between him and the destination to check if there were tanks near them, then he would pray and go. Sometimes he took his children, too, who were desperate to get out of the house. He smiled and said, 'The adrenaline rush beat any theme park ride.'

Finally, and in the end the most significant of all, there was Ibrahim, a tall man, married with a young family. He described our meeting as a 'divine appointment'. I sensed he was the 'man of peace' we were looking for, someone more interested in asking good questions than persuading us of his credentials. He had a government job and only knew of our visit because his boss asked him to reply to my email and turn down my request for a meeting. He sent a formal email to this effect but also sent a private email asking to meet. He had a MBA through a Fulbright Scholarship to the USA, had worked for a development charity before his current role and was an entrepreneur at heart. He had ambitious plans for business-based development but wanted to work with Western business people.

He fixed another meeting with his friend Johnny. Johnny had built a palatial centre in Beit Jala, which included the first public playground in the area, a café and barbecue area, and a kindergarten with a giant wooden Noah's Ark and other play equipment.[16] He was especially involved in youth work, and a 14-seat minibus brought in kids who lived too far away to walk. Despite being a Christian centre, many visitors were Muslims. In addition, a hi-tech auditorium allowed churches throughout the area to meet together, with a different church leading the worship each Saturday. The centre also incorporated business activities and he expected the project to be self-sufficient in five years.

Ibrahim and Johnny wanted to meet and brainstorm with Westerners, not to talk but to get stuck in with business projects that could function even with the movement restrictions. So in February 2005, I led another expo and facilitated a meeting which aimed to create robust jobs, jobs that would survive in peace or conflict. At first the participants turned to me, expecting me to already have plans, a sign of how aid is often distributed. It took a little while to persuade them that I was just a facilitator with a blank sheet of paper. I wanted to know what they thought was needed.

Several projects and further expos arose out of this. Most projects were not of great significance. We looked at graphic design on the basis that designs could be developed without physical meetings. So we linked this company with publishers in the UK and I started to have our church colour magazine, which I edited, and customer folders designed and printed in Bethlehem. We looked at Christmas cards, and I employed a student to research the UK market and bought 2,000 cards to distribute myself. I also sold around 200 beautiful olive wood nativity sets through friends, family, church and school contacts. One of the problems in the gift sector is that charities and others selling through catalogues charge four or five times the cost price. This put the nativity sets at more than £100 each,

---

[16] http://www.beitliqa.org/eng/eng_home_page.html (accessed 2 July 2013).

limiting the market, whereas I was selling at £40, including £10 for the school doing the distribution.

In this renewed involvement in Palestine, we were especially conscious of Christian division about Israel. Part of the original enthusiasm for Zionism and the return of the Jews to Palestine came from Christians who saw this as fulfilling biblical prophecy. Others put more emphasis on equally biblical themes of justice and compassion. One strand of thinking, especially in the USA, is that countries that blessed Israel would themselves be blessed. My response was to agree, but we don't bless our children by only praising them. I began to research the history, uncovering some unexpected facts – for example, in terms of DNA, Palestinians were indistinguishable from most Jewish groups. Nothing is as black and white as some might wish. We sensed God was saying that Christian division was a blockage to the full blessing of God's spirit on both Israel and Palestine.

I presented a seminar at a New Wine conference on the issue. As a result I was contacted by Geoffrey Smith, deputy director of Christian Friends of Israel (CFI). CFI are seen as pro-Israel while I would have been seen as pro-Palestine, though I see myself simply as pro-human. Geoffrey was a gentle and intelligent man, and we got on well. Together we set about writing a book, covering all the areas on which we agreed, and being specific about where we disagreed. The problem with writing anything alone was that the people we most wanted to reach would be unlikely to read or trust a book from a perspective they did not share. With both of us as authors, we thought we could bring the sides closer together and narrow down the areas of disagreement. In fact, we agreed on almost everything. However, about halfway through the process, Geoffrey came under some pressure to withdraw. He was apologetic and I was disappointed. Later, we contributed to a discussion process, and wrote a chapter of a booklet produced by the peace organisation Concordis,[17] but this part of my involvement in the region remains unfinished.

However, the Big Hairy Audacious Goal from early on was to set up a call centre and, therefore, a whole new sector in Palestine invulnerable to border closure.

In 2005, after the end of the second intifada and election of President Abbas, the international community was keen to promote Palestinian economic recovery. This reflected a long-standing assumption that economic development was crucial to the peace process and to prevent backsliding into conflict. In December 2005, I was invited to an East–West Institute Reception in Mayfair, part of a conference on 'promoting economic growth in the West Bank and Gaza through the private sector' with business people from Palestine, Israel, USA, UK and Sweden. I arrived promptly, to maximise networking time. The large, ornate, high-ceilinged hall was fairly empty, but there was a clump of people around a column and I went to talk with them.

They turned out to be Israelis, including Moshe Allon, Chairman of Calanit Carmon, a call centre company with 600 employees in 17 centres. And Amiram Shore, who had founded a business called Emerging New Technologies (ENT) and who was the Israeli vice-chairman of a Swedish initiative, the Palestine International Business Forum (PIBF). The PIBF, which had a Palestinian chairman, aimed to bring together business people from Palestine and from Israel, Sweden and elsewhere, in order to create jobs and build the economy.

Moshe was a friendly, easy-going character with a round face, receding hairline and ready smile, who admitted he had the perfect job as Chairman: all the fun of networking with top people without any responsibilities. Like many Israelis, he was

---

17 CONCORDIS PAPERS VIII: Christian Churches and the Israeli-Palestinian Conflict, February 2010.

not well informed on the day-to-day situation for Palestinians, and defended Israeli actions by throwing up his hands in a gesture of despair, and saying, 'But what can we do?' He could see opportunities to make money from the lower wage costs in Palestine, and perhaps win kudos from international contacts, but I believe he also genuinely felt it was the Right Thing To Do. It was difficult not to warm to him.

Amiram was a much cooler and more inscrutable character. He was medium height with a wiry frame, a deeply creased forehead and grey sideburns, sharp and intelligent. When I visited his office later, it was full of pictures of him shaking hands with well-known Israeli politicians and with Bill Clinton. After a successful career, he was looking for a legacy.

When I talked about our vision for a call centre in Palestine, Moshe became excited and animated. This was exactly what they wanted to do and they had even prepared a business plan. The PIBF were behind it but they did not have a Palestinian partner.

I contacted Ibrahim who went to Tel Aviv to meet them. They were impressed with him and we began to explore how to take this further. I brought another small group of business people out to Palestine and met up with Moshe, Amiram and others from Calanit Carmon.

The relationship progressed and we gradually persuaded them away from their original plan of having a token Palestinian ownership of perhaps ten per cent and towards a more evenly balanced venture. We eventually agreed to a Memorandum of Understanding giving 40 per cent to Ibrahim and 20 per cent each to Calanit, ENT and my company MSA.

It was a tough time in Palestine. In January 2006, frustrated by the failure of more than a decade of a negotiated approach to peace, and the corruption of Yasser Arafat's Fatah party, the Palestinians stuck two fingers up to the world and voted in Hamas. The champions of democracy had given them the vote and then they had voted for the 'wrong' party. Hamas, an acronym for 'Islamic Resistance Movement', is classified as a terrorist organisation and so aid and tax revenues via Israel stopped flowing, teachers and medics stopped being paid and institutions closed down. Hamas see themselves as something akin to the French Resistance, the British saw former Israeli Prime Minister Begin as a terrorist, and the Israeli Defence Force was once described by *The Economist* as the biggest terrorist organisation in the Middle East, so it's all a matter of perspective. Several rounds of fighting followed in 2006–07; this ended with Fatah taking control of the West Bank and Hamas taking Gaza.

Around that time I met the amazing Brother Andrew, author of bestselling books *God's Smuggler* about smuggling Bibles into the communist bloc and *Light Force* on work in Lebanon and Palestine. He told me he had recently met top Hamas leaders who were open to recognising Israel, but Israel had been barred from speaking to Hamas by the Americans. Already in his eighties, Brother Andrew then headed off for a demo where the Israelis threw tear gas canisters at him.

In the midst of all this was the Lebanon War of July 2006. As I saw for myself a few years later, this was devastating for Beirut and southern Lebanon, but while many in Northern Israel fled, the war had little impact elsewhere in the country. I remember meeting with Ibrahim, Moshe and Amiram at a Tel Aviv café overlooking the beach in the middle of the war, idly discussing whether the Hezbollah would get hold of missiles that might reach Tel Aviv.

To update and extend the Calanit Carmon business plan, I applied for funding for detailed research and to move the project to the next stage. In July 2006, we were offered £45,000 by the British Consulate General.

The plan was to share the work among those best qualified to do it. Clearly Calanit had information on training, for example, that would be easy for them to more or less paste into the business plan. I met with senior people from Calanit and

ENT, a dozen of us squeezing into an office in Tel Aviv with a large boardroom table only marginally smaller than the size of the room. It was easy to sort who would do what. Much was to be handled by an independent consultant called Ron, with whom they worked regularly. However, it proved difficult to get down to the fine detail of cost allocation. Moshe waved his hands amiably and assured me there would be no problem, they would be very reasonable, we could sort the finer details later.

I soon learnt about Israeli negotiation, which seemed to be based on the market stall model: put in an absurd bid and treat every counter-suggestion as a great disappointment requiring a painful act of self-sacrifice on their part to concede. Calanit Carmon wanted pretty much all the money available. Ibrahim recognised that it would struggle to work with them and nearly quit. On the basis that on a market stall you have to walk away to get the best deal, I obtained alternative quotes. They reacted strongly, with a mix of Moshe's disappointment (Jerrrry, Jerrrry...) – I could almost see his hands raised in despair – and Amiram's tough talk on how the knowledge developed in the course of the work should accrue to the joint venture. Their price came down but they still got an uncomfortably good deal.

Ron the consultant's first shot at the market research report was appalling. It looked like he had cut and pasted everything vaguely relevant on the internet into one massive document with no balance or coherent argument to bring things together. Twice I wrote extensive guidance on reworking it, and eventually rewrote most of it myself. It would have taken less time if I had done the lot from the beginning.

One of my roles was to call potential competitors from Egypt, Jordan, UAE and elsewhere. Egypt was especially interesting in that the call centre industry had created 10,000 jobs in five years, initially serving the local market and then increasingly serving Europe. Their costs were not greatly different from those in Palestine. We based our sales projections on $10 per hour all-in charge compared with $10–16 in Egypt, $10–12 in India, and $17–$20 in Israel.

I also called dozens of prospects in Europe and the USA. There was interest from existing call centre companies wanting subcontractors, from Hyatt Global, who were unhappy with the booking service provided from the UAE, and from Logitech, who planned to set up a bespoke technical support centre in the Middle East in the next two years.

Perhaps my main role was to bring together a report which, despite heavy pruning, still totalled more than 100 pages. This included a detailed market research, technology recommendations, a complete operations handbook, a step-by-step plan for business development, proposed structure, financial analysis and a detailed risk analysis. To minimise risk, we proposed locating the server, data and software in the UK, and the centre itself on a site in Israeli-controlled West Bank, where there was access to both the Israeli and the Palestinian telecoms companies.

I presented a draft to David Freud (now Lord Freud), a highly respected banker and former *Financial Times* journalist who was CEO of the Portland Trust, a group set up by Sir Ronald Cohen to monitor and support economic development in Palestine. I was impressed with his straightforward approach. He went through the figures, thinking aloud:

> So EBIT is $2.4 million year four, let's call it $1.5 million... a P/E of six or seven so a year four value of $10 million... discounted at 25 per cent so $3 million value at outset... capital requirement is $1.1 million, let's call it $2 million... that means 50 per cent immediate uplift, so it's viable...

On the funding he said, 'You need $2 million, say $300,000 guaranteed loan, $500 million repayable equity from PIF, $200,000 equity investment perhaps IFC, six $100,000 investors,

$200,000 match funding perhaps from DfID or one of the others, hmm... Should be doable.'

Thus in 30 minutes, he cut our estimated profits by 40 per cent, doubled my estimated investment requirement and decided it was viable. I was encouraged to have backing at such a senior level. Later, I spotted his story in W H Smiths, *Freud in the City*.

The consulate invited me to present the plan to an audience of international donors at the Ambassador Hotel in East Jerusalem on 20th February 2007. What I didn't realise until a few minutes before was that the consulate had also invited the media. They were keen to publicise their role in the development. I knew it would be a problem but it was too late to ask them not to come.

The donors were universally interested and I began a series of one-to-one meetings to win clear support. Unfortunately, when it came to actual funds, this was problematic. The Dutch focussed on agriculture. The EU did not have schemes that fitted. The Swedes were cutting back on the number of programmes. DfID said their whole policy on dealing with the private sector was under review and I should talk to their consultants about it. The Turks loved it but their main man was about to move back to Turkey. The Japanese, Belgians and Germans were supportive but couldn't help financially. The contact at the IFC was about to get married and the project was a bit small for them. The Canadians and Danes explored further but it came to nothing. USAID said we should contact the organisations they supported like PICTI (the Palestine ICT Incubator) and PITA (the Palestinian IT Association) but they were reluctant to give up funds for a third party like us. The Swiss offered 200,000 Swiss Francs for training but then found they didn't have the budget and couldn't give anything.

The most promising source of funding was the Palestine Investment Fund, PIF. They existed to put equity funding into strategically important developments. Although our investment needs were small by their standards, we were strategic, aiming to start a whole new sector for Palestine. Initial contacts were favourable.

Meanwhile, the initiative got into all the local media following my presentation and onto the BBC website. The Ma'an News Agency quoted my talk extensively:

> Mr Jerry Marshall, the project manager, hopes this ground-breaking venture will provide jobs for more than 900 Palestinians across the West Bank and Gaza over the next five years. He expects this new private Palestinian company, named Transcend, to generate annual sales of over US $12 million.
>
> Marshall says the objective is to 'create a substantial and profitable West Bank and Gaza-based Palestinian-led company, offering technical support, customer contact, software development, and business process outsourcing services to local, Gulf and Western clients, in both Arabic and English.'

This put two sets of noses seriously out of joint. Amiram phoned me. He was irritated that the Israeli element was only mentioned in passing without any credit being given to the people and companies involved. He was looking for recognition and thought I was trying to take all the credit. It was true I had underplayed the Israeli link: this was an audience of Palestinians and donors committed to supporting the Palestinian economy.

More seriously, news had got out before we were ready and before we could brief some of the most influential Palestinian businessmen. Palestine is a small country with a small elite holding key positions, often sitting on the same boards, and they like to know what's happening before reading it in the papers. Several of these people were on the board of Paltel, the very profitable, very aggressive, telephone monopoly. Potentially we could be competing with them. As part of the research I had met one of the Paltel directors in order to understand their plans and see if there might be opportunities for partnership, although I had been deliberately vague about our plans. They were planning to set up a call centre for their own customers. Several of the Paltel directors were also on the board of PIF, our best hope for funding.

It was a concern but we carried on seeking backing and customers. I was invited to present to the PIBF conference in Stockholm in May 2007. This was attended by senior Palestinian and Israeli business people and officials, as well as representatives from Volvo, Tetra-Pak, OMX, Ericsson, ABB, Saab, Scania and other leading Swedish companies. Portland Trust, the PIF and the Peres Centre for Peace were there. I even had a film crew in tow, who wanted to film some meetings to sell a documentary on the call centre project.

It was a wonderful experience but completely surreal given that this was about tackling poverty. We had one dinner at the Täcka Udden Mansion, owned by Sweden's wealthiest family, the Wallenbergs. Another dinner was on a motor yacht on a lake. I sat next to Israeli businessmen, PLO members and journalists while being served a beautiful meal by waiters in dinner jackets.

The meat of the event was a series of presentations and discussions. It turned out that the Israeli and Arab electricity industries were working closely together. One person even thanked the Israelis for bombing the power station in Gaza because they got a better one as a result, built with international support. Israel, meanwhile, had been quietly included in a Middle East regional electricity grid. Other presentations covered social housing, insurance, loan guarantees, agriculture and ICT. The call centre presentation was warmly received. I told our story with passion and humour, with facts and photos. Amiram quietly congratulated me; rare and heartwarming praise.

I made good contacts with potential customers, including a Palestinian living in Stockholm interested in investing. I followed up with a further visit, but generating enthusiastic support was easy. Turning it into money, investment or letters of intent on business contracts was a different matter.

I don't know if the premature publicity was a factor in the PIF turning us down. However, I do know that Paltel decided that they would open their new customer support centre to third party customers – in other words, offer what we planned to offer.

We tried elsewhere without success, and in the absence of further soft funding the Israelis pulled out. They had got their money back on their original speculative business plan. Moshe said the Board were not prepared to invest any more in the venture, so what could he do? This was a real blow because we needed their call centre skills and experience, which Ibrahim and I lacked.

We used the remaining money to set up a small test facility at Johnny's place, Beit al Liqa. And I came out to train a group of final year Bethlehem University students and recent graduates in telephone techniques. They were an enthusiastic group, willing to take part in role plays, and several were excellent.

I think we hoped something would just come along. However, it was a long time coming and the business plan began to gather dust. David Freud, who had high level contacts on the ground, told me we should congratulate ourselves for creating a new sector in the Palestinian economy even if it wasn't us blazing the trail.

Meanwhile, another project arose from the workshop back in 2005 and our desire to create robust jobs. TeamStart was the UK programme designed to create high-potential technology-based businesses, which I joined in 1999 and which led to the formation of CRT. It had been successful. For example, in 1999,

Andrew was a student with a business idea to use technology to assist doctors in prescribing drugs. Ten years later the business sold for £35m. There were others with a similar experience.

I was convinced TeamStart was ideally-suited to Palestine. Education standards were high and there was a technology cluster developing in the Ramallah area, a small-scale Silicon Valley, Palestinians would have visitors believe. Right on the doorstep, Israel was becoming one of the most technology-based economies in the world. A paper published by Paltrade and the Peres Centre for Peace in 2006, called *The Untapped Potential*, calculated that Israeli–Palestinian economic cooperation would bring $8 billion additional GDP and more than 500,000 jobs to Palestine and $12 billion and 400,000 jobs to Israel.

I pushed the idea with the Bethlehem University Institute for Community Partnership. This seemed the right body; the director seemed enthusiastic and they were well placed to find the funding to set it up. I wrote a proposal, but nothing was forthcoming from him or the many other people I approached.

Several years later I had a call out of the blue from an NGO called Mercy Corps. They had received an offer of funding for a project of theirs but on the condition that they incorporated 'Jerry's TeamStart Project'. I dusted down the old proposal and fixed a meeting.

As a result, in August 2008 three Palestinians arrived in the UK for TeamStart training. They were from Mercy Corps and from PICTI, who were to run the programme. The first evening I took them for a tour, ending up at Kenilworth Castle. By the time we arrived it was closed, but I explained to the night watchman that my guests had just arrived from the Middle East and he let us in, allowing us to wander the site as it grew dark. It was a small bonus that seemed like a sign of God's blessing, leaving me feeling positive and encouraged.

Over the next few days, I took them for training with Harry Stott, who had managed the programme at the University of Warwick Science Park, and to meetings with former TeamStart 'Venturers' who were now CEOs of successful technology companies.

The next stage was adaption of the programme for delivery in Ramallah. This was tricky because TeamStart is an approach, a methodology, rather than a training syllabus. The detail of the training material was left to the invited speakers, practitioners in sales, marketing, finance and law. The secret to TeamStart was in selective recruitment, helping participants form teams, and in the high pressure mentoring designed to maintain the momentum of business formation. The subtleties were difficult to communicate because training in Palestine tends to take a traditional 'chalk and talk' approach.

One aspect of the programme peculiar to Palestine was building links to Israeli technology companies, giving an opportunity for Palestinians to visit and broaden their experience, and allowing relationships to develop. Israeli companies benefited from local programmers at a cost comparable with India; emerging Palestinian companies benefited from international exposure and potential partners to help them to move up the value chain. This aspect was the most difficult challenge for the programme. There is strong resistance to 'normalisation' by many Palestinians who see the development of this kind of link as giving tacit acceptance to the internationally illegal occupation.

In October 2009, after a couple of programmes had been run by PICTI, I was invited out to review progress. I led one of the sessions and was impressed by the quality of the participants and the creativity of their business ideas, but deeply unimpressed with PICTI. I wrote a scathing report. The immediate issue was that they had reverted to the cultural norm, providing up-front teaching and little interaction and mentoring. The broader issue was that I questioned whether

PICTI senior management were actually interested in helping potential entrepreneurs. After several years and millions of dollars of US aid, they had only actually incubated seven companies. It seemed to me that the top team were more interested in networking with other senior officials at conferences in Dubai.

Nevertheless, TeamStart continues to run in Ramallah and has also run in Gaza. I enjoyed being a catalyst rather than the programme manager, enabling me to achieve something useful without taking up much of my time. After the failure of Transcend, the proposed call centre, I felt I had redeemed myself with TeamStart. However, for Ibrahim and me, the call centre and the idea of 'transcending the walls' was still in the back of our minds, dormant but not dead.

The call centre wake-up came as a result of helping organise the first TBN Gulf conference in Dubai in September 2010, an event set up by Charlie Donald, who had been inspired by the TBN London conference that year. An American called Russ Sandlin responded to the event marketing. He was interested in the conference, though in the end he could not attend. He was a call centre manager working for Gulf Bank in Kuwait, which had just won an award as the best call centre in the Middle East. He seemed to have exactly the skills and experience we needed. I raised the call centre idea with him and Ibrahim, and I invited him to Bethlehem, to get to know him and test his level of interest and commitment.

The three of us met in Bethlehem in December 2010. He even brought his young daughters over, despite the gruelling trek across from Amman (as there are no direct flights from Kuwait to Tel Aviv). We had a meal out and I took them to see the inspiring Banksy drawings: a dove of peace with a flak jacket and a little girl frisking a soldier. Russ was amiable, enthusiastic and had a great CV. He had even set up a website he described as a 'Facebook for the call centre world' and was certain we could find clients.

Between us we decided we could put in a little more than $100,000. I devised a cunning scheme which valued our financial contributions, time we could put in each week without pay and some compensation for earlier work. As I was increasingly busy with the HS2 campaign, and as I would be working remotely, I offered to put in $65,000 – 62 per cent of the capital, return for 28 per cent of the equity, but only three hours a week. This kept my time manageable and financial commitment at a level I could afford to lose. It confused my long-suffering accountant no end but I like to give him an annual challenge. The CRT deal had kept him and the tax advisor well entertained the previous year. Ibrahim committed to a smaller amount and 18 'free' hours a week, both stretching for him, but leaving him with 53 per cent if we went ahead. The balance of 19 per cent was to be held by Russ.

Further support was needed. The most promising source was PSI, part of the Dutch government's overseas aid, who could provide up to 60 per cent of capital costs for private sector initiatives, in selected countries, that would be financially viable in the long term. This was subject to various conditions on wage levels, gender equality, a balance between local and overseas ownership, etc, all of which we were happy to meet.

We didn't exactly fit into the scheme, as it was designed for established companies rather than for individuals to start a company together. To meet the rules I used MSA as the vehicle, even though this had become something of a shell with no assets. However, we were completely aligned with their aims and they were very supportive.

It was a struggle to pull together a new business plan. One challenge was around technology: we came to realise that Russ's knowledge of call centre start-ups was around recruiting and training teams rather than building the centre from scratch. Another was to start large enough to make full use of the grant, yet small enough to survive with our limited capital. We just met the PSI submission deadline at the end of February 2011.

In June 2011 our PSI contact Matthijs van der Hoorn called me at home. They had agreed a grant amounting to €82,439 in three installments. I had mixed feelings. I said, 'That's great news, brilliant, many thanks, we look forward to making a start.' I was actually thinking, 'Oh heck, now we're actually going to have to do this!'

From the start I recognised that it was almost stupidly high risk. Setting up a call centre is itself very high risk. Setting one up in Palestine, with limited investment, added further layers of difficulty. Costs in Palestine are higher than say the Philippines or Bangladesh, the up-and-coming countries for Business Process Outsourcing.

The summer and autumn of 2011 was a curious time of chicken-and-egg delay. We needed premises to show prospects and win their business; but we wanted letters of intent from prospects in order to have the confidence to sign a rental contract for the premises. So Russ was under pressure to deliver the near-impossible from his wide network while Ibrahim set about looking for sites to Russ's size and specification.

Meanwhile, we registered the company. In the UK, this takes five minutes on the internet and around £30. In Palestine, it's ridiculously slow and expensive. At an event promoting private sector development in Palestine I once told Tony Blair and President Abbas that company formation and the high cost of broadband were the biggest brakes on development and asked what they were going to do about it? Like all politicians, they waffled and never properly answered the question.

The biggest problem in forming the company was that my company MSA, rather than me personally, was investing in it. Apparently, the Palestinian Authority (PA) needed to check that the company existed and that there were no connections to

Hamas. At first, we just thought I just had to travel down to the Palestinian General Delegation (ie embassy) in Hammersmith and present various documents to them with proof of identity. But the Deputy Head of Mission explained it was not so easy. In fact, I had to pay a notary £100 to stamp five documents to prove I existed, then I had to pay the Foreign and Commonwealth Office £150 to restamp the documents to prove that the company and the notary existed, and then I had to pay the Palestinian General Delegation £400 to stamp the documents yet again, to prove that the FCO existed. Nice work if you can get it.

Just when we thought we were there, and we had torn most of our hair out, we encountered another problem. Ibrahim emailed me: 'The Ministry now wants your company to register here before it can become a partner. Our lawyer had an argument with the ministry official... This is the most frustrating thing ever but I am dealing with it and I am now obliged to use my connections.' This contradicted what we had been told by the Palestine Investment Agency.

As a last resort, Ibrahim contacted the Minister of National Economy. He emailed:

> Guys, I had a call yesterday from the deputy minister asking me to send my lawyer today with the papers. My lawyer just called me and WE'VE GOT IT!!!! And within only two hours of submitting the papers. This usually takes weeks and the minister had to sign to waive the requirement that Jerry's company has to register first in Palestine. AAAAAAAAAAYYYYYYY.

Eventually, we got sort-of promises of 'pay by results' work and Ibrahim found premises where we were offered a deferred rent. The 400 square metre site, in Beit Jala Industrial Zone Street, had been used as a wedding hall. In Palestine, it's normal for landlords to build the basic structure and leave the purchaser or tenants to put in the windows and complete the building. So we were expecting to put in the actual offices and do the wiring, etc.

Ibrahim got stuck into the nitty gritty of setting up a modern centre: washrooms, canteen, cabling, generator, air conditioning and work stations. It was a mammoth task and took Ibrahim every evening and weekend.

Meanwhile I commissioned and wrote the copy for a website, prepared a sales presentation, talked to potential UK clients and liaised with PSI.

I only really appreciated the scale of things when I came out in early January 2012. My first thought was that it was a much bigger centre than I had in my head. Initially, I had been thinking in terms of a 20-seat pilot centre, but a mixture of the PSI grant and Russ's specification pushed this to a centre equipped for 88 seats including the training room and space for around 120 workstations. Potentially, we could employ 200 or more with multiple shifts. I said nothing to Ibrahim. After all, I had seen the plans, but I had a scary cold feeling in my stomach, not just because of the risk to my own investment, but especially Ibrahim's investment and reputation. Much was riding on the success of the centre.

On the January trip, I worked with Ibrahim late into the night on cash flow projections. We had hoped to open in October, then it was December, then every month it seemed to be about a month away. I asked Ibrahim, whom I saw as an experienced project manager, whether he had done any kind of critical path analysis. He said, 'Everything's critical.' Which I think meant no. I wished I had pressed him. He was, of course, absurdly busy, but knowing the order of installation and lead times for each item would have sped up the process and improved cash flow.

I came out again in February and hired a car, as Ibrahim was not allowed to take his car into Israel. We began to visit potential local customers: the Bank of Palestine, Palestine Yellow Pages and Wataniya. The latter is a Kuwaiti pan-Middle

East mobile phone company that had won the contract to be the first to break the Paltel monopoly. By keeping similar prices but offering much better customer service – which was not difficult – they had quickly won more than 500,000 customers in Palestine. I was impressed by the professionalism of the company and the CEO, who was sharply dressed and spoke perfect English. They planned to outsource all their customer support operations and for obvious reasons did not want to work with REACH, Paltel's new call centre, the one we had helped stimulate. It was a great opportunity to develop a core customer, with potential to meet their customer contact needs elsewhere in the Middle East in the longer term. We agreed in principle to a pilot, providing welcome calls to new clients with upselling, such as adding data to contracts.

We also met with most of the larger Israeli call centre companies, one of which was owned by an Israeli Arab. We established that we were around 25 per cent cheaper, but that the opportunities were limited. We would not be able to find many Hebrew speakers and they did not need Arabic services as almost all their calls in Israel could be handled in Hebrew or English.

The final delay was the fibre optic connection which had to come from Paltel, the former telecoms monopoly. Ibrahim had been playing this very carefully, not revealing exactly what we were doing, which was in competition to REACH. He was getting a better offer at every meeting. Unfortunately, in frustration, Russ jumped in and complained at the delays, letting on that we were both desperate and competitors. Suddenly, negotiation was much more difficult. We solved this by starting with a cheaper microwave solution, which then became the backup.

Russ had been made redundant from Gulf Bank, leaving him with some financial difficulties in part because of child maintenance commitments. He had taken up an offer from a contact in Spain, based on shared profit rather than income. A stormy relationship ensued. At one point, he called me because he had been thrown out of the office and was walking the streets, though he was reconciled to his business partner later in the day. Eventually, he was completely ripped off by this partner and it was agreed he would come to Bethlehem and manage the early stages of Transcend in return for accommodation and a salary that covered his costs and maintenance payments.

Russ's hands-on involvement was a mixed blessing. He had come on board on the basis of a few emails, a meal in a Bethlehem restaurant with me and a meeting the following day with Ibrahim and me. In retrospect, we should have done more checking and team psychometric tests. Russ is extraordinarily hard working and very generous, but also impetuous and emotional, easily hurt, sometimes very self-critical and liable to have an outburst then apologise. He saw himself as a victim and needed affirmation, so Ibrahim's no-nonsense style left him feeling bullied. This seriously damaged open communication at a time when Ibrahim needed to understand the harsh zero-tolerance call centre world, and Russ needed to understand the Palestinian culture and sensitivities of the working with Israelis.

We had signed a contract with Russ's partner in Spain, selling business loans into the USA. When things fell apart between him and Russ we needed to get out of it – but a non-compete clause left us stuck. I prayed about it and an extraordinary thing happened. I felt I should have a fresh look at the contract and for the first time I noticed that the non-compete clause named another company, not us. I presume the contract had been edited for us from an earlier document and this change had been overlooked. I don't know how I had not noticed this before: I had read it several times, but it certainly felt like an answer to prayer. Legally, it meant that there was nothing to stop us doing the same work with another company and, morally, we felt justified in moving.

Following this I formed a small email prayer group. We were clearly going to need it.

Russ took up residence and worked with Ibrahim to recruit the first batch of trainees in April 2012. We decided to train in US hours, 5pm to 2am Palestine time, to prepare the group and weed out those who couldn't manage it. We laid on door-to-door transport home at 2am, but for the women Ibrahim still had to meet concerned fathers and husbands to reassure them. We were very conscious of being pioneers.

I met the first group early on and I was impressed by their enthusiasm and appreciation of what we were doing. Yaman, who became our first home-grown team leader wrote:

> This transcends political barriers and limitations. I really love that. I am the eldest daughter in the family and I am my family's hope. There are many things I wish to achieve through this job. Most importantly, I love it because it makes me feel renewed every day because I learn about other cultures and it helps my English come to life.

We paid fixed salaries but our income was pay for performance, ie commission only. As expected, our results and therefore earnings were low at first. Performance improved rapidly, faster than other new centres, but then plateaued at a rate that was not sustainable. The client sent a trainer over who raised concerns over team management. Part of the problem was that the initial team were not as hungry for work as those in poorer countries like Bangladesh. Several were from reasonably comfortable families, so work was not life-or-death, and they were too relaxed on punctuality and performance. Another part of the problem was that Russ was too busy doing the follow-up calls to be on the floor. This is where we felt he needed to be, listening, encouraging and coaching the agents. Instead of this he periodically vented his frustrations about poor performance at the end of the shift, contributing to demotivation. To free up some of his time, we appointed others to do the follow-up calls and supervise the team.

Despite the challenges, the contract was keeping the team working and learning, and provided a foundation from which we could find other clients. I found some work with CRT, the UK business I set up, but it only required one agent. Our big hope was Wataniya, but progressing this was like walking through treacle; it always seemed to be about two weeks away. The Bank of Palestine and Palestine Yellow Pages were promising leads but they decided to go elsewhere. Our competitors REACH became more aggressive, buying (in our view) a contract with a major car importer at an unsustainable price and putting pressure on some of our prospects. Ibrahim also had a visit from Palestinian Security wanting to check him out. So certainly there were some that didn't like what we were doing.

At one point, a contract in Kuwait looked promising, taking orders over the phone from a major branded takeaway restaurant chain and passing them to the local outlet for delivery. However, just when things were looking good, our contact emailed us from his wife's email address asking for 5,000 Kuwaiti Dinars (£12,000) up front. We offered him an agency and said we would pay commission on any third party contracts he sourced, but there would be no hidden payments for work relating to his own company. We didn't hear from him again.

It seemed clear to me that we were undercapitalised and we needed to invest in marketing. I strongly suggested finding a further equity partner before we started to run out of funds and it became desperate. However, Russ was reluctant to dilute his shareholding and Ibrahim wanted to wait until Wataniya signed up on the basis that this would add value to the company. He was also, I felt, over-optimistic on what the company was worth. However much effort and investment we had put in it, there was no profit stream (the normal measure of value), and our assets would be worth little in a quick-fire sale.

Meanwhile, we approached the Bank of Palestine for a $100,000 loan. At first, it looked like we could get this without personal guarantees. We knew that the loan would qualify for a 70 per cent international guarantee, though they didn't know we knew. Personal guarantees would have wiped out Ibrahim and, from my perspective, it defeated the purpose. I had the money but didn't want to risk everything in this one high-risk venture, especially if the loan was on an 'each and several' basis meaning the bank could go after any one of us for all of any outstanding sums. At the last minute the loan was blocked, and guarantees demanded. Once again the prayer group got to work, and with this and some hard work by Ibrahim, the loan came through secured only against our equipment.

Two other very different issues exercised the prayer group, with encouraging results.

First, a close relative of Ibrahim found she had a tumour on her bladder. A CT scan showed it was the size of a plum. Ibrahim was very upset, her husband was distraught and it was complicated by the need to obtain a permit to go to Jerusalem to have a biopsy done. We prayed, they received the permit and Ibrahim emailed, 'Today God made a miracle... the doctor found nothing...' The tumour had completely disappeared. 'We believe that it was a miracle that she is healed. Thank you so much for your prayerful support.'

Second, Russ went to Tel Aviv and his passport was stolen. He couldn't get another one because it turned out he had fallen behind with his child maintenance when he was working in Spain. Meanwhile, his Israeli visa was about to run out. Israeli visas last for three months and, normally, all that is needed is to go out of the country and come back in again for another three months – if you have a passport. And overstaying the visa would result in him not being allowed back when he next left. It was a complete mess.

The whole issue became a soap opera, except that the plot would have been almost too unbelievable to broadcast. We became embroiled in negotiating with his ex-wife, providing loans and sending Russ off to lawyers to try to extend the visa, which in turn involved having an address in Israel not the West Bank. It also became apparent that there was more than one ex-wife.

Nevertheless, God was gracious, loans were made, payments were transferred, ex-wives were mollified, the visa was extended and Russ was despatched to a hotel in Jordan for a night. It was booked for a different night to the one Russ arrived for, but he managed to get out and back into Israel. Another miracle was logged.

It was a far more difficult journey than any of us could have imagined. We continued to burn through money, with insufficient sales to pay overhead costs. By January 2012, the bank account was almost empty. Despite the many answers to prayer, I could not, humanly speaking, see how we could avoid bankruptcy.

However, a pilot contract with Wataniya was finally signed and later, a major extension was agreed. A sales trip to Dubai in January 2013 produced promising leads from the Dubai Outsourcing Zone. In June 2013, the Palestinian Investment Fund purchased a significant minority share in the businesses. Now, we are confident we will reach 200 employees and go on to develop further sites. In any event, we have undoubtedly been a catalyst for a new sector in the Palestinian economy.

On a visit to Gaza in December 1996, I stayed in a Guest House and saw a poem written in cross-stitch in a frame on the mantelpiece. It deeply moved me. It seemed to sum up so much in so few words. I scribbled it down and pinned it to my noticeboard to remind me why I was doing what I was doing.

I walk between darkness and light
The long night of exile
and shining memories of home
The land I knew is given up to strangers
There, in the sunshine, do they know any shadow?

Reflections

- Be patient and persist: if the first attempt doesn't work, keep the plan at hand and look for other ways forward.

- Think about who could support you, and who might have the power to stop you.

- Understand the team using psychometric tests and obtain references on potential partners.

- Aim to have access to twice as much capital as you think you need (because it will take longer and cost more than you think).

- Be a catalyst: use your time in the most efficient way.

Chapter 8: Business solutions to poverty

I slipped in and sat at the back of the class, an open area with a white board and drawings on the wall. About ten young teenage girls, mainly wearing t-shirts and skirts, were spread out in relaxed postures on the cool marble floor. They were responding to a smiling and encouraging teacher, an earnest young woman speaking with warmth and passion. An older woman sat on my right, looking after a baby who belonged to one of the girls. Unexpectedly, I felt a surge of emotion, fighting back tears, both for the contentment I could see in front of me and the pain that must have been.

We were in Phnom Penh, Cambodia. All the girls had come out of trafficking. All had been sold or kidnapped or tricked into the sex trade. The older woman was the 'mother' of one of the makeshift 'families', made up of small groups of girls. The organisation behind this is called Hagar, after the abandoned servant who bore Abraham's son Ishmael. The abused girls Hagar takes in can be as young as four.

It was late 2007 and I had just been appointed Network Development Director for Transformational Business Network (TBN), the organisation I had joined as a member back in 2004. I had been somewhat pushed out of CRT and the development work for the proposed call centre with Calanit Carmon had ground to a halt. In a conversation with Marisa Dallamora, the efficient yet warm-hearted TBN Operations Manager, I discovered she was leaving and TBN were planning to appoint a CEO. This was something I, and others, had been pushing for. The Trustees were very busy with their own work and it felt like TBN was drifting. I jumped at the opportunity and Marisa encouraged me to apply.

I went to see TBN Founder and Chairman Stuart McGreevy in his company office in Wimbledon, which was shared by TBN. We agreed a fair salary but TBN was on the edge financially and could only afford me two days a week. I took it knowing I would work on it more or less full-time; this was close to being my dream job. In time, membership and income grew, and my pay was increased to three days a week. The CEO title, however, was downgraded in our discussions, first to MD then to Development Director, for reasons that did not seem entirely satisfactory.

The administration seemed exceptionally complex, split between the Wimbledon office and accounts in India. It was also split between two companies (the charity TBN Foundation and the trading company TBN) and it was difficult to piece the two sets of accounts together to understand what was really happening. I sidestepped this and left it with an assistant, Jennifer, to avoid being sucked under by day-to-day operations with no time to develop TBN strategy.

Almost immediately, I had an opportunity to get to know the trustees and experience someone else's 'expo' trip (covering most of the costs myself). I joined a TBN conference in Kuala Lumpur and then continued to Phnom Penh on an expo led by TBN Trustee Mike Perreau and his wife Deborah. They had been especially involved in supporting Hagar.

I went earlier than the others to spend a day with Mike Hill and family, a missionary linked with Westwood Church. It was an eye-opening first day in one of the poorest countries in the world. We were driven back from the airport in a tuk-tuk, a motorbike with a trailer, two bench seats facing each other, open sides and a canvas roof. This seemed to be the main form of urban transport, along with motorbikes that carried up to five people plus luggage.

I loved travelling in the open air and seeing the extraordinary city sights. There seemed to be few rules of the road. At T-junctions, a fist of traffic from the side road would gradually squeeze its way out onto the main road, narrowing the available passageway for the main traffic until the flow stopped, leaving triumphant side traffic to burst out in all directions. At once, the main traffic responded by pressing forward until the side traffic flow was, in turn, choked to a halt. Then the cycle repeated. On one occasion there was complete gridlock as the ebb and flow unexpectedly fused together. The situation looked completely hopeless but a few people went on to the street, took charge and shouted instructions. The opposing strands of traffic untangled and we headed on our way.

The TBN connection was through the range of social enterprises being run by Hagar. These provided vocational training and initially sheltered employment so that women rescued from trafficking could find a long-term sustainable future, rather than just being sent back to the streets. We saw women making beautiful handbags out of silk and colourful shopping bags out of old rice sacks. We visited the soya milk factory, which made a range of health drinks, and saw adapted bicycles developed for micro-franchise street distribution. And we ate at the excellent training restaurant, part of Hagar Catering, which provided catering services to many of the top offices in Phnom Penh.

Visiting the 'Catch up School' and seeing the young abused girls broke my heart. I could not trust myself to speak in the car as we drove back to the hotel. As I became increasingly involved in mundane areas of finance and business plans, the picture of those kids in class served as a reminder of what the mission was all about.

While we were there we also met Trevor Sworn, founder of a social business called Yejj. The business started by providing IT support services and computer training, where commercial prices paid by corporates paid for training for the poorest groups. Trevor then added Café Yejj, a beautifully designed bistro-style restaurant that provided training and employment especially to women from 'at risk' and vulnerable backgrounds. Later, he added renewable energy, web and software development and outsourcing.

Back at base, I took my usual consultancy approach to refining TBN strategy. I phoned current and lost members, and anyone else I could find, to ask what they thought and what they wanted out of TBN. Several messages came through. The most important was that the conferences were inspiring but people often didn't know what to do next. There were 'expo' trips – which were crucial to igniting a passion to help meet the needs of the areas visited – but most members were just not as entrepreneurial as the founders and needed more help to know how to get involved. There were also concerns about the cost of membership, which had been set at £30 per month to ensure we attracted reasonably serious players. And there were concerns about transparency: no one knew how TBN was doing financially.

Essentially, I refined what we did under three headings:

1. **Inspire** more people to want to use their skills and resources to use business to alleviate poverty and transform communities, through TBN conferences and speaking at relevant events.

2. **Engage** those who had come in contact with us, helping them set up a project or get involved in others' work, through expo trips and communicating opportunities via eNews, on the web and at member events.

3. **Support** members and their projects through personal encouragement, mentoring and funding.

In particular, I took a similar approach to the one that had worked for Administry: I introduced a new member category at £7.50 per month and recategorised existing members paying £30 per month as partners. Essentially the difference was that partners received free personal support, conference discounts and extras such as free business cards. I also introduced a corporate membership category.

Initially, this worked well, with all membership groups growing and few existing members downgrading from partner. Later, when the recession hit, the number of partners did begin to fall.

I had an old version of the Goldmine customer contact system on my computer and I transferred all our contacts to this. The main benefit was that I could send personalised (mailmerged) emails to everyone or to specific groups. I deliberately moved away from the previous very corporate style and took a personal, friendly and sometimes humorous approach. I was somewhat embarrassed to realise that quite a few people thought these emails were personal one-off messages. However, it generated real interaction. Goldmine also meant that when someone called, within seconds I could remind myself who they were and what they were doing.

On the transparency issue, I introduced KPIs and included these and a summary of the financial situation at every Members Day Conference. At the first event I set up, there was a warm impromptu vote of thanks at the end.

There were some inspiring projects. One of the largest and most impressive projects was Kuzuko, led by TBN Trustee Dr Kim Tan. The vision was to create a 'Big Five' safari game park combining conservation, job creation and social transformation in one of the poorest parts of South Africa, an area of over 70 per cent unemployment and endemic poverty.

Twenty-two farms were purchased totalling around 40,000 acres. The first stage was clearance, including of 230 kilometres of farm fencing, dozens of old buildings and 20 tonnes of metal. Meanwhile, a team of 70 men erected 70 kilometres of fencing, and were then helped to set up their own fencing business.

In partnership with the South Africa National Parks, game was introduced. Antelopes, zebras and buffaloes were released when the vegetation had begun to recover. Predators were introduced when there was sufficient game to sustain their numbers. And, after an absence of 150 years, elephants and black rhinos were added.

In partnership with Legacy Hotels, a luxury lodge was built on a hill with stunning views. As well as construction jobs, 80 permanent jobs were created. All the work was done by local contractors or from nearby towns using local material where possible. Kuzuko set high standards in staff housing, wages, working conditions, insurance and share ownership through a Workers Trust. A pioneering programme was set up to enable young adults from broken backgrounds to take an 18-month course in ecotourism work.

The Kuzuko Foundation was formed as a charity to continue with the work of conservation, education and healthcare. It funds projects such as a leopard sanctuary, school visits, healthcare and educational activities of local communities.

The project was formally opened by in November 2008 by Archbishop Desmond Tutu. Since then it has gone from strength to strength, with glowing customer reviews on booking sites.

Most projects were more modest in their aims but we looked for every opportunity to achieve replication and scale to achieve a significant impact. I could not help enthusing, encouraging and supporting members who got in touch. The creativity and variety of projects was astounding.

The first project that challenged me was Touch Nature in Nepal, perhaps because unlike Kuzuko I could relate to it, as it was on a scale I could have managed myself. Touch Nature was a project to provide work for single mothers, and had a crèche and childcare facility to help them keep their children. Main products were natural handmade aromatherapy soaps and candles. When a TBN member visited, the project was struggling. A sales outlet was needed and a $10,000 loan meant that the project could rent a retail unit in Kathmandu, enabling more than 50 women to be employed and their children educated. A TBN corporate member, who was in the business of wet room and shower installation, linked with Touch Nature and imported the products, giving them away as a 'thank you' to customers. The project has now moved to India and works with Nepalese women rescued from trafficking, women who had been sold into the sex trade by parents or husbands for a few hundred dollars.[18]

Other projects that impressed me included a low-cost primary healthcare venture in India, where tiny regular contributions paid for regular visits from a local health worker. Six weeks of training enabled the health workers to deal with most common issues and refer others to a doctor. Another project was a not-for-profit company manufacturing flat-pack bamboo coffins in an area of chronic poverty in Bangladesh. An abundance of bamboo grown on otherwise wasted scrubland allowed the business to tap into the growing Western market for 'green' funerals by providing handmade coffins from natural, renewable materials.[19]

Then there was a young graduate from the Orkneys, Julie Hagan. Her pending career in architecture was interrupted by a gap year experience in Zimbabwe.

> I was living in Zimbabwe working alongside a local Church, and I kept meeting with ladies who were making beautiful products but with no way of marketing them or knowing what would sell well outside of Zimbabwe. I had some basic experience of working for friends of mine as they built up their craft business on the island of Westray in Orkney, Scotland, and I've always loved design and making things with my hands. So the

---

[18] http://touchnaturejo.wix.com/touchnature#!home/mainPage (accessed 26 June 2013).

[19] http://www.oasiscoffins.com/ (accessed 26 June 2013).

idea started to form that maybe there was an opportunity to work with some of these ladies. Gogo Olive started as a simple vision of a group of women singing and laughing together while creating things with their hands, a vision that is fulfilled every time we meet together!

After starting with six women, the project grew and at the time of writing there are now around 60 women employed, making absolutely beautiful and highly original knitted animals. I bought the giraffe and took him around to show him off when I gave talks on TBN.[20]

The other item I took around with me was the Toughstuff solar power kit, which comprises a small solar panel, an LED light, leads for mobile phone charging, a small storage battery and a cunning device that substitutes for any number of D cell batteries. It was designed for areas of Africa without mains electricity, which is most of the continent outside cities. It was a substitute for kerosene lamps, which are dangerous, polluting and expensive to run; a replacement for disposable radio batteries; and a means of charging mobiles. Unlike mains electricity, everyone seems to have a mobile phone and they typically cost 500 Ugandan shillings (12p) to charge.

Although I acquired a Toughstuff set for talks, it was also a valuable camping accessory and (I felt) something of a status symbol. Who could not be impressed by our green credentials? It was useful for my nautical ventures as well: I tacked the LED light onto the cabin ceiling of my boat, the solar panel thrust through the forehatch, to save the boat battery.

The kit is now distributed by thousands of village entrepreneurs, through a micro-franchise package, often in partnership with a micro-finance institution. The kit retails at around $35, while consumers typically spend $100 a year on kerosene, batteries and phone-charging. So a real win–win.

---

[20] http://www.gogo-olive.com/ (accessed 26 June 2013).

Toughstuff aims to be financially sustainable but work on low margins and bring social and environmental benefit.

The company was already established when I met with Andrew Tanswell, the entrepreneur who started the business with an investor. TBN helped by advising on the micro-franchise model and finding contacts, local investment and markets.

My favourite event was the annual Members Day, which generally took place on a Saturday in November. Given that membership was concentrated in London and the South East, I looked for a location near the M40 and M25. The Chartered Institute of Marketing HQ in the pretty village of Cookham became our regular venue. The event had a relaxed atmosphere with time for networking and renewing contacts. I introduced a resources marketplace where anyone could have one minute on the microphone to offer or request a skill or resource, and several other regular features.

The most memorable section was usually the members' case studies. Naturally, these were mostly success stories but there was a level of honesty that meant difficulties could also be shared. At one event, a member shared his experience in Africa in his dry Scottish wit that had us creasing up with laughter. He had actually been successful but you might not have believed it from the many valuable lessons he brought back. Afterwards I summarised them and sent them round the network:

The developing world entrepreneur believes that...
- the social entrepreneur is some idiot with pots of cash to fund their latest project

- it is not necessary to write or even verbally explain a business plan

- all they have to do is make something and people will buy it

- the only reason their last business failed was because they were unlucky

- the solution to every failed business is more money

- the alternative solution to every failed business is to come up with a new wonderful idea which only lacks money

- the social entrepreneur is the barrier to progress if he or she doesn't accept the idea presented

- the quality required for Western markets is the same as local quality requirements

- production does not need to be the same as the sample

- a deadline is when they happen to finish the work

- an order size is whatever they happen to have produced

- the final price does not have to be the same as the one they negotiated

- loans do not have to be repaid

- the task of an NGO is to provide them with money to start a business

- when they run out of money, they just need more money

- the concept of return on investment or cost of capital is irrelevant to them and hence it is not necessary to save for capital replacement

- they should not trust another developing world entrepreneur

- poverty is their most marketable product and hence will 'sell' it with great expertise

- Social entrepreneurship is another word for charity.

Conclusions:

1. Forget the term social entrepreneur; just be a businessman. The 'triple bottom line'[21] is *your* agenda not theirs; there is no need to share it with developing world entrepreneurs. Focus on the business.

2. Do not throw your business discipline away due to your compassion for the poor. It's more important to be rigorous and disciplined than compassionate. Compassion does not make things successful.

3. Avoid grand plans. They normally lead to grand failure. Think small until people have developed a track record with you, and bear in mind women are infinitely more reliable than men.

Of course, one cannot tar every developing world business person with the same brush and I met some remarkable entrepreneurs who had overcome massive obstacles to build a successful business. Nevertheless, there was more than a ring of truth for many working in this area.

Africa Invest was one project that was successful at first, but was later a victim not of problems in Africa but the vagaries of Western capitalism. Jon was an investment banker who decided to use his skills to fight poverty. Someone told him Malawi was poor, so he headed out and bought a farm. He found investors and, in a short period of time, Africa Invest owned seven farms, employed 1,000 directly and a further 5,000 outgrowers, organised in small groups. Outgrowers were earning up to $1,000 a year more than before, making a huge difference. The farms acted as testing and training bases. Unlike most large African farms selling cash crops like tobacco, these farms

---

[21] The idea that businesses should seek a social and environmental as well as a financial 'bottom line'.

produced staples, and also paprika and chillies. Hundreds of local children were also provided with a meal and education at the farms. Jon then decided to take this model to several other African countries, develop the product marketing and set about raising funds from investors. The story looked good: African farmland was cheap, food was going up in price, it seemed to be a good investment and thousands of families were benefiting as well.

Meanwhile, however, his UK funds got into difficulty. The problem came from offering a liquid investment (ie investors could cash in any time), and investing the proceeds in illiquid assets, assets that could not be sold quickly if there was a sudden demand for cash. In normal times this would not normally be a problem, but the 2007 credit crunch was another matter. Demands from investors wanting to cash in led to the suspension of the entire UK investment range.

Investing in farms carried the same risk, so to prevent this, a locked-in long-term institutional investor was recruited to provide a solid foundation to the new Africa Invest fund. However, they pulled out the day before the fund launch and the Trustees pulled the plug. In the end, the Malawi assets were sold off at a massive loss, investors lost out, and Jon's name was dragged through the mud.

The main annual event was the London conference. It was our shop window. After the first year, I settled on the TUC Congress Centre in central London. This was central, smart, good value for London, without lots of expensive extras for basic PA. Steps led down from the modern entrance to a reception area and organisers office. Delegates could then move through to a large coffee area, where smoothies and fruit, as well as coffee and pastries, were provided on arrival. This led out to a wide conference hall with wings that were ideal for exhibitors.

We managed to attract some top speakers. Trustees knew some leading business people including Sir Peter Vardy, the philanthropist who had built up and eventually sold the Reg Vardy car dealership for more than £500 million; and Lord Brian Griffiths, vice chairman of Goldman Sachs and a former adviser to Margaret Thatcher, especially on privatisation. I suggested Midlands businessman Bob Edmiston, now Lord Edmiston, and as he was in the same business as Peter Vardy we managed to contact him through this connection. Later, I got to know him through HS2 and other links.

Several of my past contacts had gone up in the world and I persuaded them to speak at a TBN conference. Michael Hastings, my Evangelical Enterprise mentor for CITEE, was now Lord Hastings. He was head of KPMG's Corporate Social Responsibility department and seemed to be on every important committee known to man. I took the opportunity to sell him TBN corporate membership for KPMG. He asked how much and without a second thought I said £10,000. KPMG was well off the scale for our corporate membership fees. We settled on £5,000. Another ennobled past contact who spoke was David Freud from Portland Trust, now Baron Freud and a shadow minister in the House of Lords.

I was especially pleased that Professor Paul Collier responded to a cold contact and spoke at a conference. I loved his book *The Bottom Billion* on the factors behind extreme poverty, the linkages between natural resources, corruption and conflict, and the failure of governments and NGOs to deal logically and patiently with the real needs.

In 2008, a TBN member in Northern Ireland, David McMillan, asked to put together a conference in Belfast, and I worked with him. About 40 people gathered for an excellent event with a warm feel about it, including David's brother Phillip, who had set up an essential oils business in Nepal, selling for example elderflower oil to the Bottle Green brand. A good-sized and active Northern Ireland TBN group emerged from this.

On the back of the Belfast success, I targeted Edinburgh for a similar event in 2009. In early summer of that year I was interviewed for a *Songs of Praise* programme on entrepreneurship. When it came out, I found that one of the other entrepreneurs interviewed was Sir Tom Farmer, the Edinburgh-based businessman who founded Kwik-Fit. The next day I called his PA, explained we had been on a programme together the night before, and invited him to speak. Yet even with a big name speaker it was hard work to get delegates. I had some good contacts, but unlike Belfast the conference was not initiated by a local person, and that seemed to make all the difference. Nonetheless, we had quality if not quantity, and a local Edinburgh TBN group was established afterwards.

Local transformational business groups (TBGs) were a mixed bunch. On the basis that entrepreneurs never follow instructions, we didn't provide any. So different groups took different approaches. One group, misleadingly called South Kensington (they met in central London), worked together on a project in Albania. This was on the basis that Albania was just about the nearest place with extreme poverty and, therefore, presumably the most affordable place to get to. Another group, Southampton TBG, pooled funds and invested in projects. East Anglia TBG put together an impressive business start-up course, originally for Uganda. Coventry TBG existed to provide moral and sometimes practical support for the projects of several individuals, some members heading to Palestine, Turkey and Ghana. Every other meeting was simply a meal out together and we had a summer barbecue at my house.

I attempted to spot clusters of members where there were no TBGs, then would call everyone in the area together for a one-off event with food, and then try to persuade a couple of people to take it on as a new group. My attempts to be a catalyst had mixed results: a couple never got off the ground but several were quite successful. Against this, TBN Trustees, the mainstay of running expos and TBGs, gradually pulled back. I had warned them that this was a danger when I joined. It felt like swimming against the current.

The highlights of my involvement were trips overseas. Mostly, they were not essential to the job so I generally covered the costs or the parts of the costs I couldn't justify. I wanted to have a feel for the regions of the world where we operated. Before TBN I had not been anywhere in East or Central Asia or to any of sub-Saharan Africa.

The first African adventure took me to Kenya and southern Africa in late summer 2008. I flew to Nairobi and met Luke and Mary Kinoti. Luke introduced me to the two projects he ran. Risiki is a microloan project serving Kibera, the slum of a million inhabitants without mains water, sewerage or power. Sixty per cent are children and there are 100,000 orphans. The other programme, Fusion Capital, is a fund for small and medium enterprises.

Viewed from above, Kibera is a brown sea of rusting corrugated iron roofs. We crossed a small river where a family and a couple of goats were living in what looked like a giant tin can; a laden washing line was strung to a post. We climbed a hill, following a small grey stream-cum-drain filled with neat little plastic bags, tied off and filled with excrement. Around us were huts with mud walls crumbling off light wooden frames. We cut across a narrow gap between huts. A toddler sat in the mud in a dirty sweatshirt and skirt. We reached a bustling main street: general shops with strings of single sachet packets of shampoo, 'hotels' that were actually cafés selling chapattis and where you could buy a cup of tea for five pence, mobile phone charging stalls, lots of shops selling charcoal, dentists, clinics, and booths with blackboards advertising the opportunity to watch English Premier League football matches on TV.

We met several of the Risiki clients including Husna, one of the first Riziki borrowers. She was wealthy by Kibera standards. She still lived in a mud hut, but Luke and I were shown through a small courtyard to a sitting room with a three-piece suite. She gets up at 3am to make chapattis for workers, then sells charcoal, then runs a dressmaking business, using cloth she imports from Tanzania. And she wanted to start more businesses! After repaying earlier loans, she is now able to borrow 25,000 Kenya Shillings – about £200. I felt completely humbled by her hard work and enterprise.

Later, we visited Fusion Capital, which operated from an office tower block in central Nairobi. At the time there were 262 clients who were unable to obtain bank loans, but had borrowed a few thousand pounds from Fusion. Clients pay 15 per cent interest – less than any other source – so it was commercial and profitable, therefore sustainable, providing a reasonable interest to investors in the UK.

One client we met was Margaret. She had been in business for five years, manufacturing wigs and selling beauty products, and now had ten employees. We also met Joseph and Janniffer, who ran a shop providing printing and photographic equipment and services. They had been in business three years and had five employees. When we walked to their shop in a dodgy part of Nairobi, the pavement was covered with street vendors selling shoes and other wares displayed on cardboard mats on the pavement. While we were talking with Joseph and Janniffer, we heard shouting and whistles. A police van stopped outside and there was a whiff of tear gas. By the time we left, the street vendors had gone. Joseph and Janniffer were unsympathetic. Street vendors were unfair competition to formal sector businesses like theirs, businesses paying rent and tax.

The highlight of the trip to Nairobi was very personal. I managed to track down my mother's cousin David Thomson and his wife Eleanor. David was suffering from cancer. There was an instantaneous warmth and a sense of recognition at our meeting, and a shared, slightly provocative sense of humour with David. It was as if I had known them for years. I prayed for them before I left, and came away touched and feeling a kind of inner warmth at meeting this relative for the first time. David died a few months later.

From Nairobi, I flew to Johannesburg and stayed in a smart hotel with a pool near the airport. The next day I returned to the airport to meet my daughter Jo. After spending most of her gap year on a Christian leadership and discipleship course and working part-time at Hobbycraft, she had travelled with a small group to spend a few weeks at a project near Durban. As I waited at arrivals I saw someone who looked similar to her, and had an irrational fear I wouldn't recognise her, or somehow we wouldn't find each other. Then I caught a fleeting glimpse of a bit of her on the other side of the doors, immediately knew it was her and rushed forward to meet her and give her a hug. I was so happy to see her.

The next day we flew to Maputo, capital of Mozambique, for part of the trip not directly related to TBN. Ever since reading There is Always Enough,[22] we had both wanted to see Heidi and Roland Baker's amazing work with orphans – Iris Ministrie This couple are people of extraordinary faith who ga everything and, at times, were completely destitute. Perhaps a result, they have seen stunning miracles. It reminded me of biblical text:

[22] Chosen Books, 2003

The blind receive sight, the lame walk, those who have
leprosy are cleansed, the deaf hear, the dead are raised,
and the good news is proclaimed to the poor.[23]

Iris Ministries have seen all of these things.

I was flicking through their book on the Westwood Church
book stall when Peter, the vicar, said he would buy it for me if I
promised to read it. It was the most challenging and inspiring
story I have ever read. The title comes from an incident when
they had been evicted from the orphanage they were running
and were in their small house in Maputo with dozens of
children. A woman from the US embassy came with a meal for
four, not realising there were far more than her immediate
family sharing the home. Yet, like the loaves and fishes, they all
ate all they wanted. In God's economy, they concluded, there is
always enough.

Their base consisted of long single-storey buildings which
were dormitories and classrooms, and a central building where
food was served – usually rice and some kind of sauce. A
separate guest area on one side of the site consisted of a small
courtyard with male and female dormitories furnished with
metal bunk beds and a kitchen area where guests could sign up
for different activities. Jo and I packed in everything we could,
travelling by minibus in small groups to different ministry
activities, buying food on the way.

First, we joined a trip to the local prison. Jo went to the
women's building, and I joined three or four people in a small
courtyard outside the men's building. The prisoners emerged. I
was asked to preach. The deal was they listened then we
handed out food. The prison did not provide food so they
depended on visitors to survive. I spoke for a few minutes on a
guy in the Bible I had just read about, someone who had
completely messed up his life but reached out to God and

---

23 Matthew 11:5.

found forgiveness and new life. I can't remember who it was, just that I was grateful that I was well gemmed up on him. Someone translated into Portuguese. There were similar trips to homeless people living in squalor on the streets, to a youth group, and to a hospital. At the hospital, we bought bananas and visited the kids' ward. Many kids were badly burned from stoves and lamps. We asked permission to pray for them, then handed out bananas.

The most moving visit was to the rubbish dump ministry. We walked down a track to a simple wooden church, then climbed a steep bank up to the dump itself, which was about the size of four football pitches. The stench was gut churning and it seemed to cling to everything. A couple of trucks were dumping fresh rubbish, while maybe a dozen people gathered around the back of the truck, keen to get the best spoils. There was a woman collecting string from the rubbish and unravelling it for resale. I walked in the direction of a child, perhaps a year old, sitting on a mat of cardboard. He was completely covered with a cloud of flies. Next to him was a small pile of stuff, a corn on the cob and banana skins, presumably collected for food. Softly I said, 'Hello.' He immediately started to wail and began to crawl off the mat. The ground was covered with broken glass. In a panic I shuffled around making friendly noises, trying to work out whether to walk away to stop him crying or pick him up to stop him crawling on the glass. Then I saw a woman, presumably his mother, turn and come towards us. I backed off and felt a complete idiot. I wanted to give her all the money I had on me, but Iris had strict rules: no photos and no personal hand-outs.

Later, we headed to the church, a hut with a straw roof and benches, for a short service. A child in a dirty dress with strange black oily stuff on her leg befriended me and climbed onto my lap. She didn't seem to have any adults looking after her. After the service I took her to the medical assistant so her leg could be examined. Then we distributed bread. When we got back we had to wash every item of clothing we wore. They say poverty is something you smell, rather than see. It was one of the most moving experiences of my life: when I feel grumpy about some problem I try to remember how these people live.

Back at base I met August, a boy found on the rubbish dump eight years earlier. He wanted to be a pastor. I also met Gabriel and his brothers, who had also tried to survive by living on the dump. He wanted to be a doctor and had had visions of being called by name and a promise he would be a blessing to Mozambique.[24]

Jo and I also signed up for a mission in the Bush. When the day came we collected a tent and waited for hours while the details, venue and people kept changing. Then we were off, about eight of us in the back of a small truck. I loved travelling in the open and for much of the trip I sat on the side corner, legs wedged in and holding on tight while the truck bounced along a sandy untarmacked road for mile after mile. At first the road was wide, with groups of people walking along it and occasional cars or trucks piled high with passengers. Then we turned onto a smaller road. Then we got stuck in the sand. By this time it was dark.

We carried our tents and luggage and walked down a track in a long line. Eventually we arrived at our designated

---

[24] Now, five years later, I'm Facebook friends with him; he's not a doctor, but he is involved in hospital ministry. This week, he prayed for two blind ladies who received their sight and posted their pictures.

Just now that we are in the hospital... God delivered the healing into these women eyes... They could not see but they seeing now.
Jerry Marshall Tell us more? What happened exactly?
Gab-g F. Paco It was so amazing that the lord has used us to heal them. Oh, just keep us in your prayers because we want to have an really kind work on the streets too, with the boys around there. This is what Heidi Baker left in our hearts... Pray and God will heal. That was Iris Ministry of Zimpeto long ago when Mama Heidi was very close to teach. Thank you God for her life in Mozambique.

homestead, a collection of African huts with different purposes: sleeping, cooking, washing, and a pit latrine. Chickens clucked freely around the site. Children watched us with curiosity. First we were invited to visit the local chief, visiting his hut a few hundred metres away. Our group leader explained what we were planning and received his permission. Then we returned to our homestead to put up the tent. It was pitch dark and there was a strong wind. That's when we discovered there were no tent pegs in our tent bag.

We borrowed three pegs and attached one corner to the bottom of a hut and slept until a cockerel about a metre outside the tent decided it was dawn.

Our host family were exceptionally hospitable. We used the pit latrine, lifting the wooden lid and squatting on the sand. Then we waited round a fire to take turns in the washing hut, drinking black tea and eating breakfast. In the hut there was a plastic washing-up bowl on a stand, with warm water heated on the fire.

In the morning we split into twos and threes and walked around the village homesteads, essentially subsistence farms scattered around every few hundred metres. I was introduced and asked to speak while one of the Iris team translated into the local tribal language. Remarkably, there was always something that made speaking easy: to a woman called Mary I talked about the very special qualities of Mary, the mother of Jesus; to two women round a well, I talked about how Jesus met a woman by a well.

In the afternoon I was asked to preach at a birthday party. Apparently this is normal. There were lots of parents and children sitting on the ground in a broad semicircle next to the huts, while the leaders completed the circle on chairs in the shade. Chickens clucked and there were a couple of black baby goats. I lay back with my straw hat over my eyes, just drifting off in the sunshine when proceedings got under way and it was time to speak. I talked about dismantling an expensive watch as a kid but my father forgiving me and still loving me, and how the heavenly Father loves us. There was a very happy, informal and welcoming atmosphere. Life may have been hard but there was simplicity, a beauty in families doing things together and a community feel that we lack in the UK.

After Maputo we caught a bus to a project linked with TBN in Swaziland. Bulembu is both beautiful and amazing. The stunning views are reminiscent of the Lake District – but without the rain. The 4,000-foot elevation gives the area a pleasant climate. The guest house, where we stayed, is the sort of place you could go to on honeymoon, eat delicious fresh food in the garden, and hike in the hills and waterfalls. It was a welcome change and refreshing rest after Maputo. But it is a town with a story.

Bulembu was a mining town. Rows of small, colourful, wooden workers' houses still line the hillside. However, the company that built it mined asbestos, and when the market collapsed, the town was abandoned. Now it's being brought back to life by Bulembu Ministries, with a particular focus on orphan care and education. Swaziland has a 43 per cent incidence of HIV, the highest in the world, and life expectancy has fallen to just 31.

The town is full of abandoned buildings that are gradually being renovated, with help from Murray Bell, a TBN member who is an architect based in Northern Ireland. The guest house was where visiting company executives stayed and was one of the first buildings to be renovated. Another TBN member, a chef, had helped improve food quality. Jo and I walked around an abandoned cinema, pushing open the door and exploring in semi-darkness, climbing the stairs to find a massive old projector. Next to this there was what must have been a club building with a wide balcony, and beyond that, a swimming pool yet to be brought back into use.

As well as the guest house, several businesses had been set up to provide employment and help pay for the social aspects of the project. A sawmill was the largest employer, harvesting timber in the area in a sustainable way. A honey business was growing towards 2,000 hives and had a processing facility. A horticulture business grew a remarkable range of fruit and vegetables, thanks to the temperate climate. And a new business was beginning to bottle spring water for the local tourist market.

Before returning to Johannesburg and home, Jo and I toured the different activities and visited the orphanages and the school. The head girl and head boy took us round and we met the very impressive head teacher, Jon Skinner. Because of the vast differences in levels of education of newly arrived pupils, study was mainly individual using an established home schooling plan with one-to-one support and a high teacher ratio. This meant pupils could stay in classes with their own age group. Jon's aim was that the school would create the next generation of leaders for Swaziland.

Back home, I was keen to encourage expo trips to areas new to TBN. So when I was contacted by Jonathan Holmberg, who was running a small business micro credit organisation in Tyre, Lebanon, I asked if he was interested in hosting a group. Sue had a long-standing interest in Lebanon and for me it was another part of the Palestinian story. So I led a trip there, and she joined me, undaunted by our inability to obtain travel insurance for Lebanon south of the Litani river, and my need for a second passport without any Israeli stamps.

Tyre is an ancient Phoenician city, a UNESCO World Heritage site and a Mediterranean seaport visited by Jesus and St Paul. There are pockets of both wealth and poverty, with two Palestinian refugee camps and problems of street kids and child labour. Roman ruins are scattered around the wide sandy beach, the port and the city, and attract little attention. But one site does attract visitors. There is a Roman road in good enough condition to walk down, through a necropolis with hundreds of ornate stone and marble sarcophagi, through a massive monumental arch and into one of the largest Roman hippodromes ever found. Alongside this is a 480-metre long stand that seated 20,000 spectators who gathered to watch the death-defying sport of chariot racing. We sat in the seats overlooking the race track and imagined being part of the crowd.

As well as seeing the sights, we visited some of the businesses benefitting from loans: we sat in a car mechanic's workshop just off the street, drinking Arabic coffee and learning about the issues and challenges of business in Lebanon. We visited a banana farmer, devastated by the 2006 war with Israel, saw his fields and met his family. We visited one of the refugee camps, where life seemed even more dire than in camps in Palestine.

Jonathan hired an old bus and we went on a tour. We visited the Home of Hope Orphanage in Beirut, which mainly takes in children who have been picked up off the streets by the police, often arriving in handcuffs. Some have been abandoned or their parents are in prison. Some of the older children need help coming off drugs.

We then headed across the mountains and dropped down into the Bekaa Valley, the rift valley that extends through Galilee, the Dead Sea, the Red Sea and through East Africa. We were just in time for the last hour of opening at Baalbek, where we wandered unhindered round and on and in the stunning array of temples: the massive 22-metre high columns of the Great Temple of Jupiter, the almost completely preserved Temple of Bacchus, the gem-like Temple of Venus.

The following day we headed down the valley, past the vineyards, to an A Rocha project. The Bekaa valley is an important area for migrating birds but wetlands have been much reduced over the years so the area is being protected and improved. Water buffalo have been reintroduced. We walked round with Chris Naylor and reflected on plans for a visitor centre and an eco-lodge. Then we continued back to Tyre, through the Cedar of Lebanon State Park.

That autumn, 2008, TBN administration began to unravel. My assistant Jennifer had moved back to America and handled the Gift Aid and membership admin from there. She liaised with the office in Wimbledon who scanned documents and sent them to the bookkeepers in India. For a while this seemed to be fine, with communication by email and Skype, but then she went AWOL. For weeks I couldn't get hold of her, then she popped up and disappeared again. Eventually, all I wanted was a copy of the last Gift Aid claim so we could pick up where she left off, but even this was not forthcoming. Meanwhile, some change in personnel in India had meant that membership renewal reminders had stopped being sent out.

Including IT support in Serbia, we were operating from five different locations and stuff was falling unnoticed down the gaps. We needed to bring everything together. It happened that the Trustees were working on a cunning plan to develop a fund to support TBN Partners' projects. To enable this to happen legally but without FSA regulation, a new company was formed called TBN Business Growth Services, of which I was a director. In the event, the fund recipient requirements and loan size was so tightly specified that only one loan was ever made. However, the company had one redeeming feature: it was a start-up, which meant it qualified for a small subsidised office three miles from my house with my favourite landlord, the University of Warwick Science Park. That in turn meant I could cycle to work, a cobweb-clearing 12-minute downhill run there and an 18-minute aerobic exercise back.

Since Sue was familiar with QuickBooks, which seemed the cheapest and simplest way to manage the accounts, I brought her in part-time to sort out finance and administration. Originally this was on a temporary basis, at minimum wage to deflect charges of nepotism, but the Trustees didn't think this was a problem and, in the absence of anyone else, she carried on. So I was working with Sue, based in a building with old Science Park contacts and friends, and gaining the support of a small group of wonderful receptionists who were always volunteering to help. The powerful photocopier printed and stapled delegate lists at breakneck speed, a boon in the lead-up to conferences. And two Rachels took over and massively improved the café, serving with a friendly smile. The café was extended to a conservatory area, which became a convenient meeting venue for TBN Members if I wasn't meeting them on a trip to London. The deal was that if they came to me I bought them lunch, saving me time and saving TBN mileage.

With an office base, there was now an opportunity to try to ramp TBN up to the next stage of development, to increase membership to the point where we benefited from economies of scale and could do more for members. The best option seemed to be the John Templeton Foundation, not least because one of the Trustees was heavily involved with them. In early 2009 I worked flat out on a wide range of documents, setting a schedule and avoiding looking at emails until the day's target was reached, in order to meet the submission deadline of 13th March 2009. In the event, though, the application arrived at the lowest point of the stock market and they pulled back significantly from new grants. It was a blow. There did not seem to be any other source of funds that could provide substantial support to the organisation and our work as a whole.

However, membership was increasing, expenditure had been kept low, conferences were generating a profit, and we were out of the hand-to-mouth financial existence we had been in when I joined. In fact, we had a reasonably healthy balance. I presented a plan to the Trustees for organic growth, taking on two further staff to develop the website and social media and to push corporate and other membership. However, there were cautions around this and the Chairman was keen to begin paying off the substantial debt to him, built up at the beginning. I felt the goalposts had moved. Nevertheless, we did eventually take on a new person part-time. Harrison Brown was fresh out of university but he had already set up a small IT business. A friend had already introduced us to Dropbox to share files, and to Campaign Monitor for our emailings, but Harrison took it from there. He did wonders replacing the old TBN website, over which I had little control, and a portal site that never quite developed the usage needed for it to work, with a single site with a mass of information and resources. As well as conference presentations and videos, we began to collect case studies in a standard format including questions on impact, lessons learnt and scope for expansion and replication.

Autumn 2009 was a busy period, with the Scotland conference, launching TBGs in the Thames Valley and Scotland, recruiting MBA students to develop a corporate campaign and a Palestine visit on TeamStart development. I also managed a trip to Kazakhstan to help train 150 entrepreneurs based at a dynamic 5,000-member church in Almaty.

I was pleased to have this opportunity to visit central Asia, to see a former Soviet country. Almaty is a modern concrete city, with beautiful parks, a stunning mountain backdrop, and a mixture of people of Russian and Korean origin. I knew little of the forced people movements under Stalin that was so evident, and I was intrigued that the heating system was city-wide and switched on at a particular date in October regardless of the actual temperature. I was also surprised at the level of control the government had over churches. We gave talks to the whole group of business people and aspiring entrepreneurs in the morning and evening, and one-to-one consultations in the afternoon. Especially poignant were questions about doing business honourably in the face of corruption.

With the sale of my shares in CRT, I felt God's gentle challenge that my response to new-found wealth should not just be about the P&L (profit and loss statement) but also about the balance sheet – in other words not just giving, but also lending. Giving – at least ten per cent – remained important. However, although it was right to keep capital for family and pension needs, I knew I should make some available as loans.

One of the first opportunities came through a TBN member working with Becky Johns, founder of 'Who made your pants?' – a project employing marginalised women in the UK. The need was too urgent to pass to others and I had the funds at hand. So over the phone, with a complete stranger, without paperwork, I agreed an interest-free £6,000 bridging loan. I'm not sure whether this was a worthy step of faith in response to a poke from the Almighty or just plain reckless. Nonetheless, Becky repaid. And borrowed again and repaid again. I still haven't met her or visited the project but it looks fun and definitely A Good Thing.

I made other loans, UK and overseas, some with interest and some without, mostly on the strength of an email. Typically they were around $10,000 – too little to justify the legal expense of doing it properly. I found it surprisingly liberating. Stuff the rules and common sense; go with your heart and character judgement, though only with sums I could afford to lose.

A loan to a Ugandan called Livingstone, matched by another TBN member I talked into it, had a powerful impact. Livingstone's story also demonstrates the potential of business to fight poverty.

Livingstone was one of 20 children born into a polygamous family in extreme poverty in rural Uganda. Half his siblings died as children. At 14, he moved to a slum dwelling in Kampala to live with his uncle. He studied hard and worked in a laundry, eventually becoming a laundry manager. Then he started his own laundry business, initially taking laundry from hotels and subcontracting it to appropriate cleaners. Good customer service helped build the business.

One year in, he faced a crisis that by rights should have destroyed the business. His van was hit by a tanker run by a large company. He was badly injured and taken to a government hospital where his broken leg was set so badly he had to pay for a private hospital to have another attempt. He was off work for a year, faced huge medical bills and still walks with a limp. The large company only agreed to pay for the damaged vehicle, and taking them to court was beyond his reach. Nevertheless, Livingstone's business grew, he took out a loan from Barclays at 34 per cent interest a year, and bought his own washing machines.

His contact with TBN was through TBN member Mike Clargo and the East Anglia TBG who had created a superb course, initially for Uganda, called 'Setting up a Biblically Based Business'. This could be delivered over four mornings with exercises such as market research in the afternoon, or delivered over an intensive weekend. The course helps potential entrepreneurs think through their resources and opportunities, and, therefore, what business they could establish. It then enables them to do their sums to see if the proposed business is viable and how much money they would need to borrow. Six out of every ten people on the course are running a successful business – defined as able to support a family – one year afterwards. Livingstone ran this course as a volunteer pretty much every month in different parts of Uganda.

The loan we provided enabled him to buy dry cleaning equipment, and over the following year his business grew from 15 to 35 employees. In 2011 he spoke at the TBN London conference and by a curious coincidence his brother-in-law Doug found himself on a plane sitting next to Bex Holt, the daughter of our very good friends and neighbours Mike and Dorinda, and they married in 2012.

My first trip to Kampala was actually through another Ugandan called Hamlet. Or rather the Hon Rev Canon Dr Hamlet Kabushenga Mbabazi, Chaplain to the Ugandan Parliament, former MP, and entrepreneur. He was launching a microfinance bank at a big event with bishops, business people and the Ugandan Prime Minister. I was invited to speak. This was the event where I promised to bring my family.

So I fixed an expo in December 2009 and brought Jonathan Bamber, from Toughstuff, who gave a superb talk and presented the PM with a set of the Toughstuff kit; and also Andrew Richardson, CEO of Metalrax plc. Initially, Andrew was uncertain over whether the time would be well used and whether he could justify it as an expenses-paid business trip. His top criterion was that his company wanted to meet with the Joint Clinical Research Centre, the main medical and research group. As it happened, I knew the Deputy Director, who had been a Warwick University PhD student and a friend of ours at Westwood Church years before. The particular value of this to us was that Andrew paid for a light plane to fly us to south-west Uganda, to Hamlet's beautiful lodge at the edge of the Bwindi Impenetrable Forest, saving 12 hours on very rough roads. We dined on a veranda, with the sounds and darkness of the forest, wrapped in traditional African cloaks as it got colder, eating beautifully cooked and beautifully served dishes. We had to cover our own costs, of course, but I felt privileged to have this experience. We still had to drive back, an especially long journey because a key bridge was clogged by fallen-over lorries. Andrew was particularly moved by the trip: he realised he could have so much more impact in Uganda than in the UK. Later, Andrew's company developed a stove for Toughstuff.

Two people spurred me into co-leading an expo to West Africa in February 2010. The first was an enthusiastic and passionate Ghanaian prophetess, Betty, of an international ministry based in London. She wanted me to speak at a conference in Ghana. It was apparently going to be massive but the precise details were worryingly vague. The second was a rather more humble, more impoverished but equally passionate Ghanaian church minister in London who wanted to help get TBN members to Ghana. So we brought together a group of people and I attempted to cover both needs with one visit.

The first part of the trip centred on running the business start-up course at a church in Kumasi, the second largest city in Ghana. This went remarkably well, aided by an experienced trainer, Kate, and a cash flow enthusiast, Susie, who handled the financial sessions. Anyone who can be enthusiastic about cash flows has my full support. In the mornings, the trainees sat in red plastic chairs around wooded tables, listening and doing exercises, a mix of experienced and aspiring entrepreneurs on each table. In the afternoons we visited existing businesses: a pig farm, a tourist shop, a seller of natural health products. Then we headed for the twin cities of Takoradi and Sekondi on the coast, where the main group went to help a lady called Gifty, founder of an over-stretched and underfunded micro credit fund, while I joined Betty.

It was not a comfortable experience on several levels. First, the speakers were expected to sit in smart high-backed chairs at the front, which I felt went against Jesus' teaching on servanthood and against pride and status. Second, despite the heat and humidity, speakers were expected to wear a full suit (preferably three piece) and tie, which left me sweating so profusely that one woman at the front got up to give me tissues to wipe my brow mid-sermon and looked seriously worried. Third, the preaching style is to shout a lot and generally harangue the congregation, which is in stark contrast to my rather English, borderline Boris Johnson approach. Fourth, the times and content in the itinerary I had written out, and confirmed with Betty, did not match what was expected on the day, and somehow I felt that this mismatch was assumed to be my fault.

More seriously, I deeply disagreed with the lead speaker. She was preaching a Gospel of Abundance which I felt amounted to prosperity theology, whipping up emotions, getting the congregation to repeat phrases after her. It was all very money orientated, about developing multiple income streams and promising material wealth for those with the right attitude and enough faith. It was a promise I felt sure would disappoint in the cold light of reality, not because of any lack of generosity or abundance on the part of God, but because facilitating extravagant lifestyles is not on His list of priorities. I countered it where I had the opportunity, while avoiding directly contradicting her. At one point Betty swept up to the front and announced we were going to wash the speaker's feet. At the Last Supper, Jesus, creator of the universe, washed the feet of the disciples to make a powerful point: Christian leaders are called to serve, not be served. Washing the feet of the star preacher seemed to completely miss the point.

Nevertheless, there were some good moments. I enjoyed speaking to a hall of medical students at the local university and was warmly received. It was moving to see something of the Gold Coast and slave forts on the way back to Accra. And the guilty highlight, going against everything I believed about status, was being motorcaded across Accra in the rush hour. Our three white luxury 4 x 4 vehicles were met at the outskirts of Accra by one of the President's motorcyclists. We followed behind his flashing blue lights as he took us the wrong way down dual carriageways, skipping queues and traffic lights. I loved it. The next day we joined the President for a service in his chapel and met him privately afterwards. The conference speaker prayed for him at length then monopolised the time afterwards, pushing her company, which invests in real estate, mining and commodities. Thankfully, the rest of the TBN team had a more productive, if exhausting, time.

A few days after we returned, my world changed with the announcement of the HS2 High Speed Rail route, and later that year with the rebirth of the Transcend project. Though I didn't know it at the time, it was the beginning of the end of my role at TBN. This was not just because new activities caught my time and attention, but also because there were frustrations with TBN. It seemed to me there was a mismatch between the Trustees' aims and activities and the needs of members, and there had been a pullback in Trustees' interaction with members through TBGs and expos. Stuart's contact with me was sporadic and I proposed a structure in which he became Founder-President and chaired an advisory group and annual dinner with the great and the good, while a management committee of members worked with me on TBN development. However, this proposal spent more than a year going nowhere. In addition, the Trustees wanted to focus more on impact investment, out of the reach of many members and not my area of expertise. Several incidents left me frustrated or demotivated. Meanwhile, membership started to fall, partly as a result of the recession and redundancy, but I was depressed that some of the members who left had received much from TBN. The final straw was finding (through Campaign Monitor's excellent campaign statistics) that none of the Trustees had opened eNews, our primary communication, for months.

Harrison's involvement meant that as my HS2 campaign involvement deepened, I was able to cut back to a day a week on TBN. When I was in a position to refocus on TBN, I wasn't sure I had it in me. I couldn't face organising another London conference. Logic suggested I carry on part-time while I finished the Transcend set-up and looked for my next role; but this would not have been fair to TBN. In many ways it was a dream job, and I loved encouraging and supporting members, but it was time to push myself off the hilltop and see where the track would take me next.

Reflections

- Enterprise is the sustainable solution to poverty.

- Look for ways to bring organisations together for win–win solutions.

- Go somewhere in the developing world to see issues first-hand, meet real people and explore what you might do together.

- Passion changes the world!

Chapter 9: Travels with an inflatable elephant

11th March 2010 started like any other day, listening to the *Today* programme. I had no idea it was the beginning of a journey that would lead me to being interviewed on the self-same programme.

The newsreader said the government would announce at lunchtime the route for HS2, a proposed high-speed train between London and Birmingham. I said nothing but made a mental note to check the route announcement.

HS2 had not previously registered on my consciousness. Nevertheless, a lot had been going on behind the scenes. Despite the 2006 Eddington Transport Study advising against a new high-speed line and recommending the upgrade of existing lines, the Labour government announced the formation of HS2 Ltd in January 2009 to look at a possible new railway line between London and the West Midlands. Councils and other stakeholders were contacted and sworn to secrecy before the emerging route was discussed with them, concluding with a briefing by the Secretary of State for Transport, Lord Adonis, at Birmingham Airport on 15th January 2010.

At lunchtime on 11th March I checked the news and found the route map. I could see the line went between Coventry and Kenilworth which meant it had to be extremely close to my village, Burton Green. It was an hour or so before I found the detailed map which showed it went through our small back garden. Meanwhile, *BBC Midlands Today* had already sent a crew to Burton Green, delivering the news and filming the reaction of neighbours who, up to that point, had no idea that their homes were under threat or that village life was about to be turned upside down.

Burton Green is a village a few miles south-west of Coventry, with a village hall, pub and school serving a population of around 800. There is an active village life, for example, the legendary curry night with Bhangra dancing, and a wine club where we all have a good time even if we fail to gain much expertise on wine.

Through the middle of Burton Green is a former railway line, a victim of the 1960s Beeching cuts. Now it's a Greenway, much used by walkers, cyclists, riders and wildlife. The track extends from Kenilworth to Balsall Common, entering Burton Green in a deep cutting under Cromwell Lane and backing onto all the gardens on the south side of Hodgetts Lane. The proposed HS2 route cuts through ancient woodland before converging on the Greenway and following its route through Burton Green.

As a Christian, I faced a moral question and concluded that if HS2 was in the national interest I should not campaign against it. Therefore, as a businessman, I began to work through the 'Command Paper' which presented the case for HS2.

Two days later, I wrote and distributed a one-page response entitled, 'The devastating flaws in the case for HS2'. The case was based on what seemed to me to be a completely unrealistic growth in demand, from 45,000 travellers per day to 145,000 per day on HS2 alone; the cost was, I wrote, 'eye-wateringly high'. The benefits assumed that time on a train was completely unproductive even though those who wish can work on trains, so saved time is less valuable than assumed; the 'wider economic benefits', the report itself admitted, were 'uncertain'; and on carbon emissions the report concluded the impact was 'highly uncertain' and 'likely to be marginal'.

All these arguments were studied, developed and quantified over the following two years. In due course, the forecast growth in demand was cut back and the estimated benefits reduced, but what was remarkable is that it took so long for so many people in government to come to the conclusions that were glaringly obvious from just a few hours looking at the Command Paper.

It took a month for the Burton Green campaign machine to roll into action, mainly because the Residents' Association Chairman, Chris, was swanning around Australia and New Zealand, where every winter he is paid to take people on holiday. When he returned he dropped by for a coffee, suggested that an HS2 group become a spin-off from the Residents' Association, and that I should chair it.

Burton Green had successfully defended itself before, notably against a proposed massive opencast coal mine, including using the Greenway for coal trains, a campaign that was won before we moved there in 1992. More recently we fought off a radio mast, though this was possibly an own goal, as the telecoms company then went off in a huff and we've had terrible mobile reception ever since. The government clearly had not studied our form. I especially liked the BBC TV news report that concluded, 'What is certain is that the decision on HS2 will be made in Westminster, not in Burton Green.' HS2 certainly put Burton Green on the map. But all that was still to come.

On the evening of 13th April 2010, more than 200 people crowded into the village hall, itself facing demolition as a result of HS2. Chris introduced the meeting, I talked about the business case and our objectives and the three Parliamentary candidates spoke. The Conservative candidate, Jeremy Wright, who was subsequently re-elected, explained that his party was in favour of HS2, but he felt this was the wrong route and HS2 should follow an existing transport corridor. Speakers also included Graham Long, from another affected village; and John Whitehouse, a Liberal Democrat Warwickshire County Councillor. Both were to become significant figures in the campaign.

Around 50 people volunteered to be on the committee, which was organised along the same lines as other emerging action groups, ie:

- Fundraising

- Media, marketing and IT

- Community liaison

- Policy

- Economic and financial

- Wildlife and environment

- Mitigation

- Technical

The idea was to enable groups to work together nationally, but some of these sections didn't really work. For example, the economic case was best developed by a small number of specialists nationally rather than a sub-group locally. The mitigation group started work straight away with the Exceptional Hardship Scheme consultation: a scheme supposed to allow those affected by blight, and with exceptional reasons to move, to sell their house. The fundraising group, led by Deirdre Vernon, was also outstanding, with five fundraising events in the first two months alone.

A logo was produced with the name 'Keep Burton Green'. It was jokingly suggested that our neighbouring town Balsall Common should take the same approach. A glossy newsletter was sent to every house. Bookmarks, banners and greetings cards were produced, the latter with pictures of the Greenway, bluebell woods and other places that would be destroyed by HS2.

Tim Sanders produced a superb cartoon for the *Independent* – a white elephant pulling a train, with the words, 'OK, it's a white elephant but it's a fast white elephant'. So we contacted him, bought the original and the rights for £100, auctioned the original, had mugs and bags made using the cartoon and produced a white elephant enamel badge.

A highlight of the first few months was the Burton Green Rally, efficiently organised by Archie and Rona Taylor and team. My daughter Hannah, living in Liverpool, posted a picture on her blog with the following comment:

> This week my family were involved in the poshest protest I've ever seen. If your village was about to be destroyed to make way for a high speed railway would you get a marching band? Or would you think 'I shall juggle my clubs in anger' like my sister? I saw the whole news item on *Midlands Today* and in front of the marching band were three or four tractors. I think the people of Northern Ireland and Gaza could learn a lot from the people of Burton Green. Their posh protesting might not get them anything but at least it is fun for all the family.

The *Coventry Telegraph*, and other local papers, gave significant coverage from the beginning, broadly supportive of our position. Outside broadcast units became regular features of the Burton Green landscape, parked outside the village hall or on my drive.

One thing we learnt was the significant delay resulting from transmission by satellite. On one occasion Sky News filmed a live piece in the garden when Hannah was at home. She threatened to ride her unicycle across the patio at the back of the shot, but in the end contented herself with playing her ukulele sitting in the dining room window. After a few chords she shot into the sitting room in time to see herself in the background 'live' on TV.

The regional BBC news programme *Midlands Today* and local edition of *Politics Today* covered the issue but tended to present it as Birmingham business leaders against NIMBYs ('not in my back yard'). I recorded an interview on the impact of HS2 on jobs, pointing out that most of the anticipated new jobs would be in retail and office developments by the new stations and therefore mainly transfers of jobs from existing high streets and malls rather than genuinely new jobs. During the filming, I naively complied with their request to walk down my garden and peer down at the Greenway. This served as an introduction with a voiceover saying, 'This man stands to lose his house and garden', which implied that my main point, though drawn from the Command Paper, was suspect. After that I started to refuse to use my garden as a venue.

Elsewhere, many were making a significant contribution. Joe Rukin, who had a background in National Union of Students campaigning, organised a public meeting in Kenilworth. Lizzy Williams walked the entire route and with Joe's help attracted considerable publicity. Graham Long helped other action groups (AGs) form in Warwickshire and went on to organise meetings between Jeremy Wright MP and AG Chairs, fix regular meetings with Warwickshire Country Council and email Warwickshire Councillors with frequent updates.

An area where we could have done better was collecting email addresses. The Burton Green team did not want to exclude those without email addresses, so they preferred to use printed newsletters. However, this meant we could not send urgent messages beyond the committee, for example, links for comments on online coverage or polls. It was a couple of years before email distribution was organised. Nationally, a petition was organised by Joe – and eventually taken to 10 Downing Street – but email addresses for those collected on paper were difficult to read and we never had a national shared database we could use effectively for communication, mass action and fundraising. Communications went via a Yahoo group to the AG Chairs and through them to local committees and lists. Next time, one of the first volunteers I would look for would be a national database and petition manager.

The backbone to the campaign, in my view, was the rigorous analysis of the business case by Hilary Wharf and Bruce Weston of Wharf Weston, a rail consultancy based in Great Missenden, one of the small Buckinghamshire towns blighted by HS2. They established HS2 Action Alliance (HS2AA) very early in the campaign, set up monthly meetings with the Chairs of emerging AGs, produced valuable advice for the Exceptional Hardship Scheme consultation and dug deeply into the flaws in the case presented for HS2. In due course, their detailed report was peer reviewed by a team from an independent consultancy company led by Vicky Pryce, a former head of the Government Economic Service. (She later achieved unwanted fame and a prison sentence after a perjury case about taking speeding points for her ex-husband Chris Huhne.)

As well as quantifying the more obvious areas I and many others had spotted at the outset, notably that time was not unproductive on trains, HS2AA identified other issues few would have spotted. In particular – with apologies for all the abbreviations – it seemed that the Department for Transport (DfT) were using an old version of the Passenger Demand Forecasting Handbook (PDFH) and the latest version would cut the Benefit Cost Ratio (BCR); the average business passenger earning figure used (£70,000 per year) was an overestimate; and the projected 18 trains per hour did not provide a safe space between trains and was significantly more than achieved elsewhere in Europe. Their work generated BCRs of less than one – ie, costs exceeded benefits.

Where HS2AA was weaker, however, was at presenting their complex information in a reasonably simple or memorable way. To be fair, they never claimed this was their skill and when Hilary appeared on *The Politics Show*, and couldn't give a clear, concise summary of why HS2 did not stack up, I switched off the TV: I couldn't bear to watch. However, it encouraged me to find a role in interpreting the business-case arguments for a range of media opportunities.

On 22nd September 2010, the then Secretary of State for Transport, Philip Hammond, toured the route, meeting with different groups with the intention of learning about local concerns and providing reassurance. I worked with Graham Long and Jeremy Wright on the first of these meetings, booking the venue and leading our presentation. He was surprised that all the groups attacked the business case rather than raising local concerns. By the end of the day he refused to listen to any further opinions on this and began to put out the view this was just a mask for what was a NIMBY campaign.

On 3rd November, I presented the business case to the influential Warwickshire County Council (WCC) Overview and Scrutiny Committee, as part of a small team. The WCC position was that they were only interested in local concerns, and they would not express a view until after the HS2 consultation the next year. So I emphasised whether or not HS2 was in the national interest was crucial to how they responded. Eventually, the hard work from Graham Long and Cllr John Whitehouse paid off and Warwickshire came out against HS2 before the consultation started.

On 5th November, I presented at a Coventry and Warwickshire Chamber of Commerce event on HS2. Mindful that most businesspeople know how to massage a business case to make them look better to investors and shareholders, I focussed on how HS2 were pulling large amounts of wool over our eyes.

Manipulating a business case: A how-to guide

Rule #1 – Up the forecast demand: HS2 were forecasting a 267 per cent increase compared with the Independent Transport Commission's 35 per cent and Network Rail's 70 per cent (later, HS2 cut their forecast, but extended the forecast period, in order to obtain the doubling of demand essential to give a benefit–cost ratio that would work).

Rule #2 – Add unrealistic benefits: include benefits up to 2085, assume time travelling on trains is wasted, inflate benefits at two per cent per year and assume impossible levels of crowding without HS2 in order to add impossible 'uncrowding' benefits.

Rule #3 – Stretch the rules on costs: use a lower optimism bias correction than normal, ignore finance costs and ignore the need for operator profits.

Rule #4 – Assume no competition: assume there is no competitive response from other rail operators and airlines and, therefore, assume a high demand and price.

Rule #5 – Ignore disbenefits: eg, slower, less frequent, Virgin service that would add 25 minutes for Coventry travellers.

Rule #6 – Don't learn from mistakes: eg, HS1 running at a third of forecast demand and sold at a third of the cost '…at a cost of billions of pounds… passengers in Kent have seen their service transformed into the worst they have ever known' (Andrew Gilligan, *Daily Telegraph*).

I finished off by pointing to growing problems and bankruptcies with high-speed trains elsewhere and my own growing use of video calls and webinars. Given that the commercial use of the internet had only started 15 years earlier, how could we have any confidence about rail demand in 2085?

The other two speakers were pro-HS2; I was fortunate that they were seriously boring and lacking in passion. I felt that the audience were on my side, though the Chamber CEO was disgruntled and issued a press release to say that HS2 would have to do better at presenting the case in favour. I went on to speak to several other Chambers of Commerce.

The only Chamber of Commerce that refused to allow a balanced debate was Birmingham. At their televised event with Philip Hammond I was refused the opportunity to speak, but as a compromise was allowed to ask a question. I brought flyers but was told they could not go on the seats with other material. They were taken by security, who promised they would be put at the back, but instead they were binned. One of my biggest regrets of the campaign was not to have had the courage to take to the podium when I was invited to ask my question. I could have made some strong points on better alternatives before security dragged me off and, as it was being televised, it might have received good coverage. Nevertheless, my views became known in Birmingham and at one event I was advised 'not to walk around the city alone after dark'. They were only half-joking.

The very weak business case was the HS2 Achilles' heel. It was also the area on which I could speak with the most confidence. It did, though, cause some tension within the Burton Green group. Several people saw me and HS2AA as the 'intellectual' approach and they felt that the decision would be made on political or economic considerations. While this was true, the detailed cost–benefit analysis was a foundation for everything else: it fed into the political campaign. Others believed it was the environmental aspects that would fire up the public. A number of unhelpful emails went around the Burton Green group. I tried hard to avoid being drawn into personal criticism and thankfully, in time, the group drew closer together.

Nationally, tensions also developed. This was almost inevitable. Most successful campaigns involve 'insiders' trying to change the views of decision-makers within the system; and 'outsiders' shouting and waving banners. Typically, the two groups mistrust each other and don't value the other's contribution, but you do need both. Hilary and Bruce at HS2AA were respected within the rail industry and knew the people and the methodology used to assess transport projects. They set out a professional image, challenging the HS2 case and resisting being overtly against it until their initial work was done so as not to have seemed to have pre-judged the issue. Others wanted to get on with waving the banners, with an unambiguous logo and concise summary:

STOP HS2
No business case
No environmental case
No money to pay for it

In addition to the difference of approach, there were many other layers of difference that came close to splitting the core campaign: differences of geography, class and politics. I once spoke at an anti-HS2 media event where the other panellists included the Green Party, the RAC Foundation and the TaxPayers' Alliance – an extraordinary set of bedfellows.

Perhaps more than anything, a campaign collects strong characters who are all convinced that their approach is the right one. In the early part of the campaign, spring and summer 2010, HS2AA took a lead role in the monthly gatherings of AG Chairs. HS2AA were organised and knowledgeable while most were still trying to get their heads round what a campaign would look like. However, their instinct was to follow their own agenda, maintain control and keep their activities fairly private, unless there was a reason to go public. There is good reason for discretion, especially over strategy and developing media stories. However, there is also a need to keep the broadening group involved, informed and feeling valued and listened to.

Over the summer, those who wanted to get stuck into campaigning action became increasingly frustrated. Several models for campaign structure and strategy documents were produced. Different people chaired each meeting so there was little follow-through and we seemed to be going over the same ground every meeting. In July, it was agreed we create a 'national Stop HS2 Campaign' to 'complement, exploit but not replicate existing organisations', releasing Penny Gaines, Joe Rukin and Lizzy Williams to organise the campaigning they urgently wanted to do and at which they were very competent.

However, that didn't solve the frustrations. They worked hard but tended not to tell others what they were doing or present proposals for funding by AGs. Some began to worry that there was no accountability to the broader group. To formalise accountability, and provide financial protection for those campaigning, a separate company formed, Stop HS2 Ltd.

Although we continued to meet together, and many people were effectively involved in different aspects of the campaign, it was clear that our structure was not fit for purpose. Things came to a head at the November 2010 AG Chairs' meeting. We recognised something had to change. Before the meeting, one of the AG leaders approached me and suggested I volunteer to be permanent Chair. I was in fact down to chair and host the next meeting anyway. When the topic came up, I suggested an election at the next meeting and said I would be prepared to be considered. To my surprise, I was elected there and then. I'm glad I said I would only do it for six months.

It was a baptism of fire but I had had some preparation. I was grateful now for my media training; the vociferous opposition to some of my work in Palestine; and that I had read Julia Middleton's book, *Beyond Authority: Leadership in a changing world*.[25]

The latter is a guide to leading when you have no line authority. This was my position at TBN and we were fortunate that Julia agreed to speak at a TBN conference, where her non-corporate style gave her the unique position of getting both the

---

[25] Palgrave Macmillan, 2007.

highest and the lowest delegate ratings. Here's my take on the key points from her book.

Leading 'beyond authority'

- Overall, lead with humility and self-belief.

- Learn to understand and cross cultures (private/public/voluntary sector) and be 'multilingual' in your communication to different groups.

- Be courageous, but make a stand on the right things.

- Jettison: giving instructions, intellectual rigour, strict hierarchies and the instinct to tidy.

- Know why people follow you: position/intellect/personality/ideas/communication/or your ability to invest or connect.

- Know your role: are you a rebel or a transformer? Are you going to lead from the front, back, middle or side?

- Expect and cope with the vitriol – there will be strong voices ranged against you.

- Accept and give feedback even when it's uncomfortable.

- Establish and protect your personal brand.

- Don't be in it for yourself – enjoy the achievements of others.

- Build a support group: people who encourage you and tell you the truth; include outsiders with a different perspective.

- Build coalitions: this takes patience and compromise but does not require consensus.

- Delegate someone to sort emotive but less important issues.

- Be patient, and ready for the right time.

- Creativity and fun: people stay with leaders who are brave – and fun; count the laughs at meetings.

Almost immediately there was a massive falling-out over giving evidence to the Transport Select Committee (TSC), which was running an enquiry on Transport and the Economy, including current methods for assessing and prioritising proposed transport schemes. This was relevant to the assessment of HS2 and Bruce and Hilary of HS2AA had done a lot of technical work on problems with the HS2 assessment. They had submitted written evidence, but the committee invited Joe Rukin of Stop HS2 to give oral evidence. This caused fury from Bruce, who felt that his hard work over the previous eight months was about to be thrown away. Joe responded robustly, arguing that it was all about politics and that the Select Committee were MPs who would never get their heads around the finer points of the HS2AA arguments. My attempt to douse the flames had the opposite effect; I was roundly criticised by both sides, including a passionate dressing-down from Bruce.

I kept calm and carried on, wading through up to 200 emails a day. 'Expect the vitriol,' Julia Middleton had written, and I took the view that if both sides shouted at me I had judged it about right. Our public affairs consultancy, Quiller, briefed and prepared Joe, who gave evidence on 30th November and (I was told) ignored most of the preparation. I listened to the first few minutes online then switched off; I couldn't bear it. Reaction was mixed: Joe's supporters praised the excellent job he had done, and others complained he had significantly set back the cause.

Passions were at their height at the first AG Chairs' meeting that I chaired, in Burton Green Village Hall, on 5th December. The Burton Green group were supportive and prepared food to break up the meeting – food always helps when there is tension – and I arranged the seating around small tables in order to run a 'Wisdom Café' in the second half of the meeting, to collect views from everybody. Several people were praying for the meeting and, throughout, I was asking for God's help. I felt comforted that, whatever happened, I was still loved by Him.

In my introduction to the meeting I listed a number of changes, mainly to make more efficient use of time – for example, circulating updates in advance rather than lengthy presentations. The minutes also record the following:

> [JM said] ...contributions should be kept short and constructive. If a contribution was not going to change anything then the meeting would not discuss it. To that end JM was not going to allow a discussion on the events at the TSC earlier in the week. It would not be constructive. It had been discussed with the parties concerned, lessons learnt and built into the Code of Conduct. There followed a brief exchange between BW and JM at the end of which the meeting voted not to discuss what happened at the TSC.

The final sentence is diplomatically phrased. The atmosphere was explosive, but in a rare flash of inspiration, I called for a vote which was overwhelmingly in favour of moving on. It was a make-or-break moment.

We covered a lot of ground at that meeting. We agreed papers previously circulated on the purpose and structure of the emerging federation of AGs; agreed that Stop HS2 was to be the campaigning arm; HS2AA was to be the research and analysis arm; and the purpose of the Federation was to coordinate opposition organisations and identify gaps in the campaign. We agreed a code of conduct, mainly to prevent negative and provocative emails being circulated to all.

We also needed to agree a name. I had proposed that we used the white elephant cartoon and the name, 'White Elephant

Federation: Organisations opposing HS2'. My logic was that the name itself would communicate a memorable message and the strapline would enable us to broaden the membership beyond local action groups. Initial sounding suggested that this would attract strong support, but concerns were raised and instead, the name AGAHST (Action Groups Against High Speed Two) was suggested and agreed.

As I walked home later, I regretted not pushing the White Elephant name more. I had hoped to create a kind of 'Make Poverty History' broad alliance. Much later, the misspelling element of AGAHST (rather than 'Aghast') was humorously picked up by the *The Now Show* on Radio 4, but their coverage was well balanced, and I felt getting on *The Now Show* meant we had really arrived on the mainstream.

Quiller had been hired at a very substantial monthly fee by another anti-HS2 group, Transport Sense, who were well connected with well-off individuals. This itself was a source of tension: those with access to funds could take the campaign their way. However, as I worked with the team of three at Quiller I was impressed by their knowledge, enthusiasm and integrity. Their focus group research was especially useful: it told us the message that most resonated with voters was HS2 was the 'wrong priority'.

Meanwhile, there were several encouragements for us. The first was that the NIMBY label Philip Hammond and the pro-HS2 lobby loved to pin on HS2 opposition was wearing thin. We had argued that it was in fact Hammond who was a NIMBY, given that his election leaflet had declared his opposition to the Heathrow third runway and support of HS2 as a more acceptable alternative to his voters in Runnymede and Weybridge. However, a more powerful argument emerged: groups that could not be labelled as NIMBYs were adding their voices to the opposition: the influential TaxPayers' Alliance; the Adam Smith Institute; Institute for Economic Affairs; the Sustainable Development Commission; the Green Party; the

New Economics Foundation; the Wildlife Trusts; the Countryside Alliance; the RAC Foundation; the Conservative Transport Group. Some of these we had briefed. There were also some leading journalists opposing HS2: Andrew Gilligan, George Monbiot, Simon Heffer, Simon Jenkins and the rail author and journalist Christian Wolmar.

A second encouragement was that it became increasingly apparent that High Speed Rail was struggling in Europe, China and the USA. Those in favour of HS2 loved to say how we had fallen behind our competitors, conveniently ignoring that the West Coast and East Coast Mainlines and Great Western were all designated 'high speed' by EU standards and in fact the new ICE line between Frankfurt and Cologne was similar in journey times to the Virgin Pendolino. One of the team began to list overseas problems and keep this up to date. The Netherlands and Taiwan both had to rescue ailing high-speed lines because passenger numbers were way below forecast. In Spain, the €3.5 billion high-speed line between Toledo, Cuenca and Albacete was axed after attracting an average of only nine passengers a day. In France, the minister of transport announced that all TGV projects not under contract must be re-evaluated. Belgium, Portugal and Poland all cancelled high-speed rail plans.

From early on, Stop HS2 Director Penny Gaines had been actively using social media, attracting up to 3,500 visitors a day to the website and using Twitter and Facebook. Penny wanted more support and, in January, several people managed to find funding, generate interest, hire a consultant and pull together a social media strategy.

Joe Rukin, who was giving the campaign masses of time without charge, objected on the basis that consultants were expensive, probably knew no more than he did, and he could have done the training. This was true but it hadn't happened. Joe was brilliant at implementing things on his own, but not at putting proposals to the committee, so he often felt unsupported. And while most of what he did was valuable, at times he went off the rails, ranting at anyone who might be listening. Once, he sent me an email listing his grievances that ran to 20 A4 pages. So many kept him at a distance.

Using social media with an agenda was new to me. I was allocated the task of writing a blog suitable for journalists, questioning HS2 and taking a professional and relatively balanced approach.[26] We also set up a related Twitter account – HS2_Questions. I quickly became a regular blogger and tweeter, though I found it difficult to be as balanced as the consultant wanted. We immediately attracted a response from pro-HS2 activists. Some were people I knew, notably John Morris from Birmingham Airport, who was just doing his job, supporting something that would benefit Birmingham Airport, while expressing sympathy with local residents. We understood each other and there was a mutual respect. Others on Twitter were abusive and sometimes ill informed, calling us liars and NIMBYs. It was difficult to have a rational argument and it often wound me up. I tried to avoid pointless discussions and returning personal criticism. Joe occasionally reminded us: 'Don't feed the trolls.'

I bought a video camera in order to put some of my talks on YouTube, and a couple of times I was inspired to prepare a humorous video, not least to encourage the team.[27] On one occasion, I happened to have a bamboo coffin in the office for a couple of hours, an eco-friendly product made on a TBN-linked project in Bangladesh. So Sue and I recorded a hasty deadpan 'HS2 Confidential Briefing', which turned out to be uncannily accurate in its prediction, ending by panning to the coffin, labelled 'HS2'. I stood in front of a white board, drawing a graph of money against time, with a downward line for benefit

---

[26] http://hs2questions.wordpress.com (accessed 26 June 2013).

[27] This and some other talks are on YouTube, search for 'Jerry Marshall HS2' or look for my channel audaciousstuff.

and an intersecting upward line for cost. The core script was as follows:

> In March 2011 the total benefits were said to be £67 billion. A year later this has fallen to £44 billion. We expect this benefit denigration to continue at a similar rate as all the drivers around DfT enlightenment are still in play. In particular, the assumption that time on trains is unproductive still has a long way to go, and when the DfT discover that the laptop and wireless devices have been invented this will massively cut the apparent benefit from time savings.
>
> On the cost side, we have adjusted for inflation.
>
> So as you can see these two lines intersect at the Financial Crunch Killer Date.

I wrote FCKD on the board at the intersection.

> Of course this is only a forecast. There are a number of hard to predict variables which could change things. It is possible that the DfT decide to apply the correct PDFH or up to date income figures which would hasten benefit degradation. It is also possible that the full NIMROD[28] cost overrun corrector is brought into play, though this is considered unlikely.

Drawing a line down to the date axis, I continued:

> So on balance we forecast FCKD as September 2011. This is the point at which Hammond moves to another department and some other poor sod has to sort out the mess.

---

[28] A patrol aircraft project that had been cancelled not long before at a cost of £3.2bn.

In fact, Hammond moved to Defence in October 2011.

The Coventry MP and former Defence Secretary, Bob Ainsworth, came out in favour of HS2, so I wrote to the *Coventry Telegraph* and challenged him to a debate. He agreed on the basis it was on neutral territory, I paid costs and it was not packed with the 'anti' brigade. It took place on 11 February 2011. I didn't know quite what to expect; he was, after all, a seasoned politician and former cabinet minister. I need not have worried. His presentation was vague and devoid of facts. He had clearly done little research and simply had a vague idea that the proposed station near Birmingham Airport (between Coventry and Birmingham) would have some knock-on benefit for our region. It was a confidence boost, but on the other hand, I lost any remaining deference I had for cabinet ministers. The thought that Bob Ainsworth was once in charge of Defence was scary.

I was struck by the variety of abilities within the House of Commons. I was impressed with Jeremy Wright, who consistently held the position that the specification speed (250 mph) should be lower, so the route could follow existing transport corridors. He was always friendly, wise and helpful, despite being a government whip and therefore required to take the government position. One meeting reminded me of the *House of Cards* TV programme, as he advised us on what he would do if he was in our position: 'You may say that but I couldn't possibly comment.' I was also impressed by Dan Byles (North Warwickshire and Bedworth), and by Graham Brady, Chair of the powerful backbench 1922 Committee, who was completely professional but seemed sympathetic to our views. On the other hand, I was deeply unimpressed with Jim Cunningham (Coventry South); he eventually came out against HS2, but I suspect this was more a reflection on the way the wind seemed to be blowing.

A convention held at Stoneleigh Park on 19th February 2011 was a highlight, though not without problems. It was a Stop HS2 initiative amid many HS2AA reservations: they wanted to focus on an expected new business case and were nervous the convention would go off half-cocked and damage our cause. I therefore agreed that the event would be developed jointly with AGAHST, and met with Lizzy Williams to produce a proposal to reassure AGs and clarify aims. Unfortunately, when the meeting took place, Joe Rukin was not there, and it turned out he had very different ideas for the event. As a result he (temporarily) pulled out of Stop HS2, the first of several resignations.

The convention was a triumph, with speeches, stands and workshops, 700 delegates and good media coverage. With some pushing from me, HS2AA took part and they gave a clear and devastating summary of the business case. Christian Wolmar was the leading speaker, and it was good to get to know him a little and buy his history of the railways in Britain, *Fire and Steam*. I found this fascinating and it provided useful background, especially against Pete Waterman's defence of HS2 on the basis that the railways never made any money (they started out as highly profitable private enterprises).

The convention was the first outing for a life-size white elephant that my daughter Hannah had made. It was willow framed and clad in cotton sheets stiffened with PVA glue and paint, with flappy ears and tail, and each eye was made out of a golf ball inside a green balloon skin and stuck inside a shuttlecock, then inserted in the cotton 'skin'. Four helpers wore a kind of willow-framed skirt then stood inside the body, taking the weight of the frame on shoulder straps. 'Ele', as we christened her, was rather sweet but the rigid body and trunk made her difficult to transport, she could not easily stand on her own and she required five people to operate her. But she did attract the attention of TV cameras and photographers. However, she was not waterproof and that summer she was accidently left outside all night in heavy rain, leaving her in a sorry state. She was replaced with a much more practical eight-foot tall £2,000 inflatable elephant, and then ceremonially cremated in a bonfire in Burton Green on 5th November.

It was eventually announced that the HS2 consultation would start on 28th February and a new business case would be released that day. The night before, I was asked to speak on Radio 4 *Today* programme in the morning. I worked hard deciding on the key messages and trying to anticipate the pro-HS2 points. Richard Houghton, a PR professional, gave me advice including bringing water, and card rather than paper to write on (paper can make a crinkly noise).

The BBC sent a car to take me to Birmingham. I climbed the steps to the BBC reception desk and was led through to a tiny studio. I sat alone, wearing headphones and facing a desk microphone. I listened in to the programme until someone cut in to check I was there. I found I was debating against Julie Mills from pro-HS2 group Greengauge 21.

I knew there would be millions of influential people listening; but what made me most nervous was a fear of letting down my fellow campaigners. I prayed, went through my possible answers, and felt at peace.

In the event, Justin Webb gave me good openings to make the case and I don't think Julie Mills was expecting robust opposition.[29] I summarised the problems with the business case and countered the points she made. The final question from Justin Webb was one I had anticipated.

'Jerry Marshall, in a word, can you get a U-turn on this from the government?'

---

[29] Many of the interviews, including this one, were placed on YouTube by 'Gordyfin'. Search YouTube for 'Jerry Marshall HS2' and add the programme to find a specific interview.

'We will do; our fear is that it will be into the next government and this will be a Nimrod project and we'll have squandered millions of pounds before finally the government comes to its senses.'

I felt elated when the interview came to a close. It was an overwhelming win on a day expected to go the way of the government. Immediately, I began to receive congratulatory text messages, starting with my sister Jill, and it raised my profile well beyond the action groups. I started to field many of the mainstream news programme debates, something I thoroughly enjoyed. However, I suspect it was the spark to start a much more aggressive pro-HS2 campaign.

A new group emerged – The Campaign for High Speed Rail with the slogan 'Yes to High Speed Rail', directed by David Beggs. David was the CEO of *Transport Times* and on numerous transport groups. The government undoubtedly had a role in this development as we know a DfT official was phoning business people to enquire about sources of funding for pro-HS2 lobbying support. It was said that companies were asked to contribute £10,000 to the fund. Many supporting companies had vested interests in the development or had rail franchise renewals coming up.

I was surprised by the extent to which the DfT seemed to be fiddling the figures, or giving misleading or contradictory information:

- Using the wrong PDFH (which anyway was designed for short-term not 35-year forecasts)

- Using an income figure for business travellers that was too high

- Continuing to assume time was unproductive on trains and that all saved time would be productive

- Breaking their own rules by not comparing HS2 with the best alternative

- Extending the forecast by ten years to boost the flagging business case

- Claiming they could run 18 services per hour each way, which the European authorities said was impossible

- Revising upwards the costs of the 'RP2' alternative that we had been pushing, by assuming that developing existing services was as risky as the completely new HS2 development

Politics was a darker and murkier world than I had thought.

The new business case, published on 28th February 2011, presented us with excellent PR opportunities. HS2AA were keen not to blow them all at once, so I sent out an email asking for others in the campaign to hold fire, in order to make the most of each of the issues being uncovered. This was taken badly by Lizzy Williams at Stop HS2, who thought I was now being 'dictatorial'. My relationship with her deteriorated even further at the start of the HS2 roadshows, which were billed as part of the consultation but were actually a propaganda exercise. The first one was at Euston. I was busy helping prepare literature for our 'shadow roadshow' response and, knowing there would be a good team on site from London groups and Stop HS2, I decided there would be no added value from me being there. At the time, I saw myself as leading from the middle, facilitating the campaign and bringing groups together. Lizzy, however, was shocked by my absence: she led from the front and thought I should be doing the same. It was the final straw for her and she resigned from Stop HS2 and the Federation.

On the fun side, someone suggested a spoof rail ticket and I enjoyed putting together the initial copy. The different fields on a regular ticket fitted our message well.

In terms of strategy, I compiled a list of next steps and asked AG Chairs to rank them, giving a 15-point wish list. I also tried to pull together champions for different activities, though this turned out to be difficult: despite our best efforts, some roles remained unfilled and others continued to be filled by more than one person, often with little coordination.

One key area was spreading the message beyond the route, where many had not heard of HS2. We needed to get the message across on cost, which we calculated at more than £1,000 per household in the UK (later the TPA put the total cost to taxpayers at £45 billion so we increased this to £1,700).

Another vital need was to have an alternative to HS2 to meet growing rail demand. Former Strategic Rail Authority director Chris Stokes began to pull together a plan for the newly formed 51m group of local authorities opposing HS2 (so-called because of the £51 million cost per constituency). HS2AA were closely involved with this. It became clear that all the forecast capacity needs could be met through train lengthening and dealing with a small number of pinch points. In fact, it was possible to treble the number of standard class seats and also double capacity to Milton Keynes, a congested route that would need to be dealt with before HS2 arrived in 2026.

A major boost came when the Transport Select Committee decided to specifically investigate HS2. At least this time we could be more coordinated.

On the media side, the highlight at the time was a live half-hour ITV debate with Philip Hammond and myself on the panel and a studio audience. We were led into a dramatically lit old industrial building with bare bricks and pipes. The Secretary of State argued that there was no alternative; the West Coast Mainline would be full by 2022. I was so irritated by this nonsense that I was fired up with passion:

> That there is no alternative is absolutely absurd, we can treble capacity on the West Coast, East Coast and Midland mainlines... what is really important is that this is the biggest white elephant since Nellie the elephant packed her trunk... this is going to cost more than £1,000

for every household viewing this programme... and the jobs are completely illusory, these are shopping centres around stations that are sucking jobs from high streets.

When I started as Chair I cut TBN time down from three days to 2½ days a week, but the HS2 role was becoming full-time. I was glad I had thought to limit my stint to six months, especially with the TBN conference at the end of May. However, my impending retirement focused minds and I agreed to continue if I could drop my TBN days to a day a week and AGAHST made up my pay.

June 2011 was my full first month as a paid Chairman. Chris Stokes and I met with Maria Eagle, the Shadow Transport Secretary, and we seemed to get on well. I thought she was very open to our view. I met with business leaders in the North West (though failed to convince them), with the Coventry City Council and with the CEO of the British Equestrian Federation at Stoneleigh Park. With help from the public affairs consultancy Quiller, I wrote to MPs on 'the Y', the expected route to Manchester and Leeds, and to MPs in Cornwall to point out that HS2 would not benefit them and electrification to Penzance would be better use of funding. Later we took a similar approach to other regions. I was interviewed on *Politics Today*, *Midlands Today*, *The Jeremy Vine Show* on Radio 2, spoke on a debate for BBC CWR which was also televised in part, and was on a *Railway Gazette* panel on HS2, broadcast over the internet from the Stock Exchange.

Early July brought four highlights.

First, Boris Johnson replied to my letter on HS2 and, after checking with his office, we placed this with Patrick Hennessy of the *Sunday Telegraph*. I was learning that offering a story as an exclusive to a selected journalist could be more effective than the old press release approach. It was front page news on 3rd July:

Boris: why I no longer support high speed rail
The future of the planned High Speed 2 rail link has been thrown into doubt after Boris Johnson described the project as 'perverse' and 'inadequate' and said he 'cannot support it.'
... Mr Johnson listed his objections to the project in a letter to Jerry Marshall ...

This led to further publicity in the *Evening Standard* (where Ken Livingstone said he had been against HS2 long before Boris Johnson) and the influential Conservative Home website.

The second highlight, also on 3rd July, was speaking at a fundraising event at Waddesdon Manor (the Renaissance-style château that has been the Rothschild home since 1874). Though many AGs raised thousands of pounds through village events, funds from wealthy individuals had enabled us to employ Quiller and pay for other expensive items. Most of these people wanted to stay out of the limelight – one told me he didn't want to jeopardise an impending peerage – but many were willing to contribute to costs. My invitation letter made it clear we wanted to raise £100,000 that evening, and with around 100 there it was easy to do the maths. We also paid for the inflatable elephant at this event: she was auctioned to the highest bidder and we made a profit.

Thirdly, on 11th July, we publicised the expected eight years of chaos at Euston as a result of a complete HS2 rebuild with an advan poster, 'Euston we have a problem'. Camden MP Frank Dobson spoke, we brought the white elephant and volunteers handed out a flyer-sized version of the advan poster. Rallies in London need to be huge to attract media attention; this more focused approach worked better.

Finally, the following day I gave evidence to the Transport Select Committee and was interviewed outside Portcullis

House for *Newsnight*.[30] Quiller had prepared me for the TSC session, stressing the need to stay cool and professional. It was televised, and it felt strange being on the same bench that was familiar on the news with the phone hacking enquiry. The TSC sat in a u-shaped configuration, facing a long desk with four seats for those giving evidence, with the public seated at the back.

It felt like I'd been called to the headmaster's office for being naughty. 'HS2 campaigner given rough ride by MPs Transport Committee,' reported the *Coventry Telegraph*. The vibes were not good and the committee had just come back from a tour of European high-speed rail and, predictably, none of the European officials that showed them around said they had made a huge mistake.

I felt that they were constantly trying to twist my words or catch me out, but I was well-briefed.

> **Iain Stewart:** Some experts in the rail industry have calculated that at peak times, which are obviously when the main capacity demands are, RP2 will only increase capacity by 25 per cent and will not even come close to meeting the forecast increase.

> **Jerry Marshall:** It is just a matter of arithmetic. It is not really complicated. The peak-time standard class number of seats between 4.30 and 6.30 in the evening out of Euston on the InterCity services is under 6,000 at the base level 2008 timetable. By making the various changes we are suggesting, we get the seat numbers up to just over

---

30 http://www.parliamentlive.tv/Main/Player.aspx?meetingId=8867 (accessed 27 June 2013).

13,000. That is an increase of more than 130 per cent where you need it: standard class peak-time capacity.[31]

Kwasi Kwarteng picked up the TSC European trip.

Kwasi Kwarteng: As you know, the Committee went to France and Germany and looked at how high speed rail had developed there. Not once did anyone say, 'Don't do it. This is going to be a disaster.' On the contrary, people suggested that they were trying to extend their networks... What do you say to that?

Jerry Marshall: There are two main differences. One is that 92 per cent of passengers in the UK are very satisfied with journey times. That is higher than France, Germany and all our main competitors. It is the second highest in the EU. We already have a very good system that people are very happy with.

Kwasi Kwarteng: Rail is so good here that we don't need it.

Jerry Marshall: That is only one factor. Secondly, our cost per mile on the route to Birmingham is £160 million. In France, it is between £11 million and £16 million per mile. The cost structure in the UK is very different. That is partly to do with density of population and partly to do with distances.

The prize for twisting words went to Paul Maynard.

Paul Maynard: It is fascinating to listen to you all so far. I have to congratulate Mr Marshall on his incredible ability to be more productive on the train than he is in the office.

---

[31] The transcript of this meeting is available at http://www.publications.parliament.uk/pa/cm201012/cmselect/cmtran/uc1185 -iii/uc118501.htm (accessed 27 June 2013).

Jerry Marshall: I am not saying that; I am as productive.

Paul Maynard: I am sorry. I have not actually finished. Can you possibly be quiet and listen for a moment rather than talking to me?

And the prize for least attentive MP went to Julie Hilling. Towards the end, after we had all spent a great deal of time on how our alternative would provide the capacity we needed, she suddenly asked how we were going to deal with the capacity problem. I noticed even the Chair looked exasperated.

The focus for much of July was on completing consultation responses. HS2AA, Stop HS2 and others produced suggested responses to guide others. There were seven questions, starting with:

> Q1. Do you agree that there is a strong case for enhancing the capacity and performance of Britain's inter-city rail network to support economic growth over the coming decades?

> Q2. Do you agree that a national high-speed rail network from London to Birmingham, Leeds and Manchester (the Y network) would provide the best value for money solution (best balance of costs and benefits) for enhancing rail capacity and performance?

They were leading questions that would certainly not pass Market Research Society guidelines. The biggest problem was the final question, on compensation:

> Q7. Do you agree with the options set out to assist those whose properties lose a significant amount of value as a result of any new high-speed line?

Three options were set out but only the Property Bond approach came close to meeting the government promise that those blighted by HS2 would not lose out. HS2AA advised respondents to choose this, but STOP HS2 suggested answering 'no' to every question. As a result, although 98 per cent of those expressing a preference said Property Bond, the government had enough wriggle room to opt for a cheaper scheme that left most people unable to move before 2027, except by selling their house at a much reduced price.

[A Judicial Review in March 2013 concluded that the HS2 compensation consultation was 'so unfair' as to be unlawful.]

That month we also published a document called *A Better Railway for Britain*. This was mainly designed to move from a negative campaign (Stop HS2) to a positive campaign (Better than HS2). Positive campaigns, we were told, are more successful then negative campaigns. It was sent to the TSC and the concurrent Labour Transport review. Chris Stokes wrote it, drawing on the 51m 'Optimised Alternative'. HS2AA edited it; I refereed and wrote a foreword to cover other broader issues. The need for a referee arose from the deep desire to show that our alternative was also 'High Speed', to make it politically more acceptable to the government. The West Coast and East Coast Mainlines were already designated High Speed by European definition but were limited to 125 mph because of external signalling. With in-cab electronic signalling this could be lifted, enabling 140 mph on parts of the WCML and 150–160 mph on parts of the ECML. Nevertheless, Chris was keen not to overstate the case. The document was jointly branded, printed and launched on a new website, www.betterthanhs2.org.

Once the consultation was out of the way, the key issue was party conferences. Quiller felt that party conferences were poor use of limited funding. There was so much for the media to cover that it was difficult to be heard, and the key MPs we wanted to influence were generally too busy to attend much of their conference. Quiller thought a great deal could be achieved at low cost through 'guerrilla' tactics: having an advan in place, especially on the first day as people register; leafleting queues outside and putting leaflets through hotel room doors.

However, many thought we should attend and, rather late in the day, we raised funds and booked a stand at the Tory conference. Stop HS2, with a contribution from AGAHST, booked a stand at the Labour conference. There was some tension around the arrangements and poor coordination of leaflet production, although there did need to be differences. For the Conservatives, I favoured an A5 flyer we could thrust into everybody's hands with just four key points backed up by quotes.

High Speed 2: 'Fundamentally Flawed'
'The coalition has accepted a fundamentally flawed scheme.'
– Conservative Transport Group

HS2 is not a sound investment
'There is a significant risk that High Speed 2 will become the latest in a long series of government big-project disasters.'
– Institute for Economic Affairs

HS2 will not bridge the north/south divide
'Official documents suggest that … capital is likely to flow from Manchester and Leeds to London rather than the other way round.'
– Camilla Cavendish, *The Times*

There are better, more affordable alternatives
'The burning need in public transport is not for sexy, pointy-nosed high speed trains whose economics simply don't stack up. It's for boring unglamorous improvements to the services we actually use.'
– Andrew Gilligan, *The Daily Telegraph*

The flyers were supported by much more detailed documents from HS2AA on particular issues, plus our *Better Railways* report and a reprint from *The Economist*, entitled 'The Great Train Robbery' that said Britain should ditch HS2. We designed a simple stand, booked an advan – with a poster making the link between HS2 ('His 7.45') and police cuts ('Their P45') – and arranged a fringe meeting.

The Labour event led by Joe had long, densely written handouts and a large but rather amateur-looking stand with a motley collection of posters. However, it worked well in that we looked like a poorly funded protest group rather than the image the 'pros' were putting about that we were rich southerners concerned about our lawns.

We left the Lib Dem conference to a group of Councillors who organised a fringe event and distributed leaflets. We supported them on the first day by bringing the elephant.

For the minor and regional party conferences, Joe picked up some money from me and did a single-handed tour of the country, with the elephant. This was typical Joe: last minute, little planning, working alone rather than organising support: but it was enormously valuable to get a presence in all these places, and I doubt anyone else could have done it.

This is what worked well:

- Having the inflatable elephant on the first day as people queued to get in and handing out leaflets. This worked better than the advan because the police allowed us to get it nearer the entrance. The highlight was the Manchester police providing an escort as we carried Ele into position.

- Leafleting the long queues that started to form a couple of hours before the leader's speech. This worked especially well at the Tory conference. I worked my way along the queue saying, 'Would you like a free reprint from *The Economist* to read while you wait?'

- Attending every fringe meeting that touched on anything related to HS2 and in the question session making a short point against HS2 disguised as a question ('Given [fact about HS2], does the speaker agree that the best way to achieve [Speaker's purpose] would be to ditch HS2 and focus limited taxpayers funds on [HS2 alternative that contributes to speaker's purpose]?')

- Networking at events and talking to everyone going past the stand, to inform, persuade and learn their views. It was interesting to find that many MPs agreed with us but it was not an important enough issue for them to vote against it. We also learnt that although Lord Digby Jones supported HS2 he didn't think it would do anything for Birmingham other than enable it to be a dormitory town for London.

- Tackling party leaders with a key point when they did their formal tour of the exhibition.

It was good to have an anti-HS2 fringe event on the agenda at the Tory Conference and it was packed out, although unfortunately many were 'pros' who quietly distributed specially printed flyers outside until I asked them to go away. They had every right, I suppose, but I had not expected it, and felt angry that they were taking advantage of something for which we were paying. I was chairing the event and the questions were ill-tempered.

There was one other conference activity that was useful but we didn't do ourselves. Certain people with friends in high places bought a drink or three for the aforementioned friends and pumped them for information. From this we learnt, for example, that Ed Balls, the Shadow Chancellor, was very concerned about the cost of HS2.

One disappointment at the Labour conference was Shadow Transport Secretary Maria Eagle's speech, which confirmed their support for HS2 – though taking a different route through

Heathrow – on capacity grounds. I had thought she had 'got it' and wondered what was going on.

The best way to find good volunteers is to harness the ones complaining that we should be doing more in an area they thought was vital. The best example of this was John Lee, a maverick landowner and campaigner who wrote short but colourful emails in some quantity, sometimes sending me more than 20 a day. His passion was that PR was key and we were not doing enough, especially at the 'red-top' tabloid end of the market.

Many people were unhappy about our PR efforts, in part because they didn't understand how it worked. Some thought you just had to send out press releases and it would all appear in the news. Others complained that some of the coverage was not helpful, not recognising that we did not have editorial control. One group demanded to know in advance exactly what we were going to get for our PR agency fees, which is impossible to tell. The red-tops posed particular problems: they were just not interested in something as technical as the case against HS2.

A friend involved in the media once gave me a useful *aide memoire* for getting coverage, 'TRUTH':

TOPICAL –   ie news
RELEVANT – eg a local paper, a strong local connection
UNUSUAL – not what you would expect that group of people to be doing
TENSION – an element of jeopardy, eg a risk, it might fail
HUMAN –   about people, not ideas

This last point was the reason it was so difficult to get away from a NIMBY story of troubled residents and onto the business case.

Despite the frustration, there was a lot going on in the background. Quiller helped fix meetings with editors and place stories for HS2AA. Stop HS2 sent releases out, though some journalists complained about what they saw as rants that were too long and too frequent. I built up a list of media contacts and had lunch with the transport correspondent at *The Times*.

Apart from reacting to HS2 developments and uncovering uncomfortable truths in the business case, we created useful coverage in a number of ways: events (like the convention); lighting a series of beacons (as a 'national warning') on the day the consultation was announced and having a helicopter film it; a demo in Old Palace Yard or College Green outside Parliament with the elephant; sending a release to local media on the cost of HS2 apportioned to their local authority and compared this with local cuts; and paying for an omnibus telephone survey question and releasing the results both regionally and nationally.

On the telephone surveys, YouGov did these for us for around £1,000 per question and the results were taken seriously because they would not permit an obviously biased question. By the autumn, around 50 per cent of the whole country was against HS2 – a major shift in opinion.

To improve general PR, we agreed to hire Aspect Consulting. London MD Richard Houghton had been helping the campaign on a voluntary basis before he joined Aspect so this put the relationship on a professional basis. His team were invaluable, especially at peak times. However, their strength was at the broadsheet and broadcast end. To get into red-tops, we believed the best route would be to find supportive celebrities. The actor Geoffrey Palmer had helped but was not exactly the youthful image we were seeking. Sophie Dahl had the right image and was from Great Missenden, one of the towns affected, but unwilling to get involved. We had made a few attempts to spread the net but it was an uphill task. Agents are not interested in encouraging unpaid roles, for obvious reasons, and were keen that any links to voluntary activities would support the celeb's brand in some way. In terms of campaigns, that meant being linked to a campaign of interest to their target audience and one that was likely to win.

John Lee worked hard to obtain the backing of a small number of wealthy Warwickshire individuals to develop red-top coverage and find celebrities. We hired PHA Media, run by Phil Hall, a former *News of the World* editor, allegedly sacked by Rupert Murdoch in 2000 for running a story about Jeffrey Archer that Murdoch had not wanted to appear. Between us, we assembled a target list of 100 possible celebrities and the PHA team worked though the list. We ended up with Bill Oddie, with whom I spoke but, in the end, he did not get actively involved; and the Phelps brothers, who we already knew were anti HS2. James and Oliver Phelps had played the Weasley twins in the Harry Potter films and were very popular, especially among my daughter Sarah's age group.

PHA found it hard to place interviews with the Phelps brothers but we did gain some additional coverage and, as they each have more than 300,000 Twitter followers, feeding information through them was a bonus. They also took part in a film I was invited to make with the BBC *Inside Out* team. This was a completely different media experience – two days' filming and more time doing voiceovers and taking part in the final edit, all for ten minutes' output.[32] James and Oliver joined me by Skype from a hotel in Australia, to make the point that it was no longer necessary to travel to meetings. Unfortunately, their internet connection was poor, so it was not the advert we had hoped it would be.

Wendover was an active action group from the beginning, uneasy with our approach to PR and both keen and able to fund their own initiatives. They decided to get involved in the faltering 'off-route' campaign by working with a sister

---

[32] http://www.youtube.com/watch?v=swKabV-ZW-o (accessed 27 June 2013).

company to Quiller to develop an online tool. This enabled anyone to identify their MP and generate an email to send to them, which they could personalise if they wished.[33] The emails were not all the same, as the tool pulled together a selection of paragraphs from different categories (business case, environment, etc). I was writing personalised emails to MPs via Goldmine CRM software on my computer, enabling me to write to all MPs very quickly with different messages for different parties, but emails from constituents to their MPs were far more valuable. We used this tool to encourage campaigners to call friends and family off route and ask them to do this on the spot. It was a clever system but it was expensive to set up and difficult to inspire people to get their friends to use it in the quantities we wanted.

The resignation of Liam Fox as Defence Minister on 14th October and replacement by Philip Hammond was a moment of excitement. I was driving back from a *Politics Today* interview in Leeds at the time and I whooped at the news. Hammond had nailed his colours to the mast and we couldn't see how the government could do a U-turn on HS2 with him in place. He was replaced by Justine Greening, who carefully kept her options open, so a barrier was removed and there was some cause for hope. Her Treasury background was a plus, though her active opposition to the Heathrow third runway was a problem given that Hammond had suggested HS2 could be an alternative to the runway.

Greening had been outspoken in her criticism of the previous government not listening to a consultation:

> We have had a consultation, to which residents have responded overwhelmingly by saying that they do not want the plan to go ahead. Despite all those points,

---

[33] www.highspeedrail.org.uk (accessed 27 June 2013).

ministers still seek to override people's will. That is deeply worrying.[34]

Ministers must ask themselves what is more important — saving face and sticking with a bad decision, or having the courage to admit that this is wrong, and change course. It is time to listen to the people, including my constituents, who responded with their grave concerns to the consultations.[35]

Sadly, her response to the HS2 consultation as minister was different from her approach in opposition, and the glimmer of hope with her appointment turned out to be misplaced.

In early November we were told by the TSC secretary that their report would be published on Tuesday 8th November, and we would receive an embargoed copy at 8am the day before. So on Monday 7th November I was at work for 8am to read the report. My heart sank when I saw the headline: 'Good case for High Speed Rail.' However, this was in sharp contrast to the body of the report, which was highly critical of HS2. We prepared a press release.

All morning the phone was buzzing. Every time I was on a call, my mobile and the extension also rang. Sue and Harrison were fielding the calls and stacking them up for me. It reminded me of the air control game on my phone: after a while, it's a struggle to land all the incoming planes without them crashing.

The theme of my notes for broadcast interviews was that TSC had endorsed much of what we had been saying, and had

---

[34] www.theyworkforyou.com/debates/?id=2009-01-28b.299.1&s=heathrow+speakerper cent3A11771#g341.3 (accessed 27 June 2013).

[35] www.theyworkforyou.com/debates/?id=2008-11-11c.641.0&s=heathrow+speakerper cent3A11771#g724.1 (accessed 27 June 2013).

produced a series of damning criticisms which destroyed the case for HS2, in effect, sending the DfT back to the drawing board. They called for a 'lower value attached to time savings', they raised concerns over attempting to run 18 trains an hour, and they said that viable alternatives to HS2 had not been investigated thoroughly. Finally, they said HS2 must be part of an overall transport strategy.

The team at Aspect did a brilliant job in pulling together a schedule for the Tuesday. Timing was tight. After a Paul and Gaby interview on BBC London at 6.20am, the only way we could fit in the next two and a Radio 4 *Today* programme interview at a farm belonging to Paul Hunt was to take them from Paul's sitting room. Radio 4 were getting panicky and sent a runner to fetch me just as I was finishing with Radio Manchester. I jogged across just in time and the cows mooed obediently throughout the interview.

Sue was standing by to chauffeur me to Coventry station. I had to catch the train and didn't think I would have time to park. Oliver Cann from our Aspect Communications met me at Euston, where Richard Lister from BBC News was set up and waiting to film an item with the Euston sign in the background. Later, Joe Rukin sent me an email to say this piece was a 'perfect report'.

Oliver took my phone to field interview requests. A taxi bike was standing by to get to Millbank for an ITN slot at 10.15. Then I was in the hands of BBC Millbank, who had arranged an interview every eight minutes for two hours. The day ended back in Burton Green, with a live BBC *Midlands Today* interview at the village hall. It was a wonderful, adrenaline-filled day.

Later, we acquired a paper from the 'Yes' campaign, complaining that they had received a good report from the TSC but the news story had been 'hijacked by the antis' and 'we must never let this happen again'. The paper then laid out a £25,000 PR campaign to support the expected announcement in favour of HS2 along with the consultation results. This was clearly prepared in close conversation with ministers. It had been sent to me by one of our campaigners. I didn't ask where he had got it from.

Working with Andrea Leadsom, we organised a 'lobby day' in the Grand Committee Room at Westminster on 28th November 2011. The idea of a lobby day is that voters write to their MP, asking them to join them at the event. I drafted a letter for people to encourage their 'off route' friends and family to send to their MPs and this was included in the Wendover online tool. I included quotes from *The Economist*; from Coventry Labour MP Geoffrey Robinson, a successful businessman and former Paymaster General; and from Archie Norman, who was ITV Chair, founder of the Policy Exchange, a former senior politician and a star recruit to the cause.

> HS2 is the most extraordinarily expensive 'grand project' and could cost every taxpaying household £1,000 each ... The likelihood of cost-overruns is high and the damage to countryside and communities certain and permanent. Scrap HS2 now and announce instead £17 billion of spending – half the amount – to bring about the biggest improvement in history of Britain's existing railway. (Archie Norman)

Andrea and Geoffrey spoke at the event. The two of them made a great cross-party double act and were always very helpful. I summarised the business case against. Unfortunately, numbers were small, but it was good to have Dominic Grieve (Attorney General) there and to see Steve Baker again. Steve was the strongest voice against HS2 on the TSC and had spoken at our Tory conference fringe event.

Furthermore, in the late autumn I had an invitation to a private meeting with Cheryl Gillan, who was Welsh Secretary and MP for Chesham and Amersham. She was taking a lot of stick from constituents who felt she was not supporting them enough in fighting HS2 and wanted to know when she was going to resign from the government. I was ushered in from the Portcullis House entrance, down the steps, under the road and along a cloister that passes under Big Ben, a point marked by a lantern, then up to her wood-lined study. On the way out, the passage has an exit straight into the back of Westminster underground station; it reminded me of Narnia or Hogwarts. I'm not really sure why she wanted to meet, possibly she just wanted to understand feelings within the campaign and stress the value she provided on the inside, saying there were several cabinet ministers that were secretly anti-HS2. She was ousted from the Cabinet in the reshuffle of September 2012, and was immediately outspoken in her criticism of HS2.

We had been expecting an announcement on HS2 from Justine Greening in December but it was postponed. Eventually, it happened in January, a few hours after I returned from Palestine. By that stage we knew it would be in favour of HS2 and the original route, rather than through Heathrow.

I drove straight from Luton Airport to my sister's house in Chiswick in the early hours on 10th January 2012 and got some sleep before a BBC car collected me. Oliver Cann met me at Television Centre and took charge of my mobile, as before, to field interview requests.

I was filmed live on BBC network news before the announcement at 8am and again as the expected announcement was made. After that it was the BBC Breakfast TV couch, with music mogul and rail enthusiast Pete Waterman.[36] Pete responded to my opening summary of the case against by saying we were all 'bloody bonkers' and that you couldn't make investment decisions on rail by looking at the finances (see introduction). He started shouting, which was great. I just had to keep calm and carry on making more substantive points.

---

[36] http://www.youtube.com/watch?v=0Rtgk-pIU1w (accessed 27 June 2013).

Then it was straight on to BBC Millbank, who had again arranged an interview every eight minutes for two hours, as they had done before. This time even a Chinese TV channel wanted to interview me, for a business programme. I told them not to bother bidding for contracts. Whatever the government said, HS2 was never going to happen.

A stack of reports were released at the same time as the announcement: the consultation analysis, a new business case, and a response to the TSC. By the time we had worked through them and found the weaknesses, the media had moved on. Nevertheless, we had a lot of helpful publicity. Now that the government had formally decided to go for HS2, more groups seemed to wake up and come out against it.

At that point, the campaign moved to a new stage: judicial reviews and patiently informing MPs. This was not particularly my area of interest or skill. I had agreed to work as executive Chairman on a paid basis for six months and had formally resigned at an AG Chair meeting in December (effective from the expected announcement). After the meeting, Sue and Sarah suddenly appeared and I was presented with a magnificent HS2 cake train (pulled by a white elephant), a box of very nice wine, other cakes, flowers for Sue and a beautiful card.

Meanwhile, I had worked on a revised structure including incorporating AGAHST, appointing a campaign director (earlier, I had approached Deanne Dukhan, one of the most respected campaigners), and setting up a Board which allowed for a growing number of groups across the country when the 'Y route' was announced. I agreed to chair the Board during the transition to Deanne.

Judicial reviews (reviews by a judge on whether the government has broken the law) were a key next step. HS2AA headed up a group launching two reviews, on the environment and on compensation; a six-figure sum was raised to pay for this in the first few months of 2012. Meanwhile, 51m, the

Heathrow Hub group and a golf club each initiated reviews on other grounds.

Meanwhile, three pieces of information emerged that seemed to me to change everything.

First, the business case was re-issued for a fourth time in April, with a BCR on the London–Birmingham phase of 1.2 (£1.20 of benefit for every £1 invested), reduced from 2.4 in March 2010, well below acceptable limits for government funding. Even this was overstating that case: using the latest forecast handbook, the correct figure for business passengers' earnings, and making realistic assumptions on the value of time savings, would cut the BCR to under 0.5; meaning that the cost would exceed the benefits. The alternative proposed by 51m had a BCR of over five.

The second key piece of information was thanks to Margaret Hodge, Chair of the Public Accounts Committee, who grilled DfT officials using words like 'shocking', 'biased' and 'bonkers'. Clips were set to *I'm Nobody's Fool* and posted on YouTube.[37] What emerged was that the Major Projects Authority has given the HS2 project an amber/red rating, meaning, 'The successful delivery of the project is in doubt, with major risks or issues apparent in a number of key areas.' Margaret Hodge also asked for the BCR to be recalculated with the latest (lower) GDP figures, which would cause it to fall for a fifth time.

Thirdly, a DfT report was unearthed which backed up earlier research we had done. It showed that long-distance rail services to Euston were at just 60 per cent of capacity for the three hours of peak morning demand, and just 64 per cent in the busiest hour. This made Euston the least busy long-distance service; Paddington and Waterloo were both at over 100 per cent in the peak hour. Furthermore, promised new carriages would mean Euston utilisation would fall further. And as the 51m alternative delivered more capacity than the DfT forecast, there

---

37 http://www.youtube.com/watch?v=gmc_2BEGKlU (accessed 27 June 2013).

was no capacity crunch on the West Coast Mainline for many decades, if at all.

I tweeted that the HS2 White Elephant was now a dead duck, and at the end of the Jubilee weekend I sent a personalised email to every MP about these three 'official killer facts'. I concluded by saying:

> HS2 is not needed and makes no economic sense. HS2 Ltd is recruiting £100,000 per year publicly funded jobs like there is no tomorrow. There is no tomorrow for HS2. The government should abandon the project now before more money is wasted. David Cameron should have the common sense to take a fresh look at the more affordable alternatives, which will increase capacity and cut journey times for more people, and more quickly than HS2, as well as creating the jobs and growth we urgently need.

I resigned as Chair of the AGAHST board in October 2012 to take on a new full-time job.

In September 2012, Patrick McLoughlin was appointed as Secretary of State for Transport. And despite the West Coast Mainline franchise fiasco, revealing DfT incompetence on figures, he is apparently keen to 'crack on with HS2'.

Since then, HS2AA won the judicial review on compensation and lost on the environmental case (the court decided the Strategic Environmental Assessment Regulations did not apply to HS2), though leave to appeal was given.

In May 2013, the National Audit Office (NAO) confirmed what we had been saying about the business case for years: the report disputing every argument in favour being made by the government, and pointing out that the DfT had not applied their latest information on demand, and working on trains, to HS2. 'On the scale of damning, the NAO report into #HS2 is around nine out of ten,' tweeted Christian Wolmar.

Stephanie Flanders, the BBC's economics editor, said she could not find an economist who thought HS2 would 'rebalance the economy' (ie bring jobs to the north and the Midlands). *Newsnight* covered the flaws in the business case in detail, with a film of David Cameron and Patrick McLoughlin, 'doing something impossible ... working on a train ... and the document they're discussing is the plans for HS2 which, remember, assumes you can't work on a train, oh the irony...'[38]

Also in late May 2013, just before a bank holiday, the Major Project Authority confirmed that yet again, HS2 had received an 'amber/red' rating.

In June 2013, the government increased their estimate of cost to more than £50 billion (including trains), leaving their calculated benefits at barely more than cost, even with the assumption that no one works on a train and every minute saved will be productive. Meanwhile, the New Economics Foundation produced their criticism and comprehensive alternative.[39]

It's madness, but at the time of writing, HS2 is still going ahead. Nevertheless, whatever the outcome, we have run an effective campaign. Opinion in the country has changed from being mainly in favour to mainly against. The media began to describe it as 'the controversial HS2 project' and then the 'highly controversial HS2 project'. Key media have written against it in the strongest possible terms. And I've had a fascinating insight into broadcasting, leading 'beyond authority' and the sometimes murky world of politics.

---

[38] See Youtube or link from www.hs2aa.org (accessed 27 June 2013).
[39]   http://www.neweconomics.org/blog/entry/is-hs2-really-the-best-way-to-spend-33bn (accessed 2 July 2013).

Reflections

- Understand the different leadership qualities needed when you don't have 'line authority': lead with humility and self-belief.

- Encourage others and make sure there is an element of fun.

- Find a database manager and obtain the supporters' email list right at the outset.

- Understand what the media are looking for in their coverage and be ready to make your key point in less than half a minute.

- Seek influential allies and build alliances.

- Find your inflatable white elephant to rally round.

Chapter 10: Missing the Manacles

Over the centuries, more than a hundred ships have been wrecked on the notorious Manacle reef, east of the Lizard peninsular in Cornwall. More than a thousand people have drowned on this unforgiving shore. During one terrible night in 1809, 110 bodies were washed ashore, and many more were unaccounted for, when the transport ship *Dispatch* was dashed to pieces there. The ship had been carrying part of the 7th Dragoons, fleeing from Napoleon's forces advancing on Corunna, overcome by fatigue and semi-starvation after a long and arduous march. In 1855, the emigrant barque *John* sank, drowning more than 120, and in 1898 the liner *Mohegan* sailed at full speed on to the reef, with the loss of 106 people.

On a sailing passage there are two parts to passage making. First, there is the passage planning: deciding in advance the destination, looking up the tides, checking the forecast wind direction, setting the course and the waypoints. Then there are the adjustments along the way. The weather may not be as forecast, or might change. The speed of travel might be faster or slower than expected, so the tidal streams are different and the course must be adjusted. A good rule of thumb is to adjust the course every time you halve the distance to the destination. Sometimes, I even change the destination, to benefit from a safer or more pleasant journey.

Life is a journey with similar characteristics. Passage planning and some flexibility are necessary to avoid getting lost, going round in circles or hitting the rocks.

At the beginning of the 1990s, before Sarah was born and while we still lived in Cannon Park, I was at an event where we were challenged to write our epitaph. I wrote:

Here lies Jerry from Cannon Park
He treated life as a bit of a lark
He was married to Sue
Had daughters two
And on the world he left his mark.

Hardly great poetry but it made me realise that family, fun and some element of significance or fulfilment was important. So I wrote ten life goals.

I cheated. I included things that I had already achieved, but they were things that had been significant goals and it was encouraging to tick a few things off right at the beginning. Some were a bit vain or corny, and I kept them private, even from Sue.

This was my list, exactly as written:

1. Study at Cambridge

2. Stay married to and faithful to the same woman (as long as we both live)

3. Have kids who love God, love me, and will make a difference in the world

4. Start a successful business

5. Have a book published

6. Be interviewed on TV

7. Achieve a £500,000 pension pot and no debt

8. Initiate some things that make a difference in the lives of others

9. Have fun along the way and forgive myself when I mess up

10. Be God's friend forever

I could tick off numbers one, four and five straight away, and I was in the process of setting up CITEE so that counted as number eight. On number six, the first interview was with Pam Rhodes on a *Songs of Praise* programme on entrepreneurship.

On number two, at the outset I wasn't sure I could manage it, given my track record. Now, however, we have been married for more than 30 years and I can say I have not acted inappropriately to any other woman. So that qualifies for a tick.

Number three is ongoing, but they all chose adult baptism and are fully involved in their local churches. Hannah met her husband Dan at Frontline Church in Liverpool where they now run what their Pastor said was his 'favourite small group', based around creative arts. Jo has already used her medical training on a First Response team as well as with Street Pastors. Sarah shows strong leadership skills, is a worship leader in two churches and is taking a gap year with a Christian organisation in the Isle of Man, working with schools and churches.

The last goal to be achieved was number seven, which I reached in 2010 with the sale of my CRT shares. So I've reached the target. Now I feel like I'm in 'bonus play', extra time to play the game of life and follow new goals.

It's tempting to look back and try to fit my experience and random discoveries into some kind of deep and philosophical framework.

Uncle Gerald saw himself as successful, and few would argue with this. He built up a successful business, sold it and retired to Malta as a tax exile. He was my role model when I was young. Nevertheless, although he was generous, he was obsessed with minimising tax, he married and divorced twice, and in his later years I suspect he was often lonely and unhappy.

It seems to me that the conventional view of success is one dimensional. I was struck by a paragraph from well-known American church leader and author Bill Johnson:

It is hard to gain favour in [the business world] without prosperity. Prosperity is a primary measure for success in that arena. With that in mind, the world is also full of stories of great financial success that were disasters in every other way. People instinctively want both – outward and inward success. Most of those in business want much more than money for their labors. Simple things like joy, a happy home life, recognition, and meaningful friendships are an important part of the life of true prosperity.[40]

Generally, investment success is seen purely in a financial rate of return. But in recent years, 'triple bottom line' or 'impact' investing has become popular, where success is measured by not only the financial 'bottom line' but also by social or environmental returns.

As a teenager I wanted to make pots of money. My measure of success in life was purely financial. Since then it has widened to something that might be said to be three dimensional.

Earlier, I wrote that money, sex and power are key areas that are not wrong in themselves but they have a dark side, and can become destructive addictions. To protect against these temptations, the old monastic orders had three matching vows: poverty, chastity and obedience. These may be fine for a medieval monastery, but not for modern life within our community. Who do we obey? What if we are married? How can we be part of our community without, say, a car or a mobile phone?

However, there is a modern, virtual, ecumenical order that has updated these vows to simplicity, purity and accountability: living simply and decluttering our lives; building faithful relationships that last through thick and thin; holding to our deepest beliefs and purposes through a relationship-based accountability.

[40] Bill Johnson, *Dreaming with God*, Destiny Image Publishers, 2006, chapter 5.

It seems to me that these are the key to three-dimensional or 'triple bottom line' success:

- recognition and career success
- family and relationships, loving and being loved
- joy from spiritual fulfilment, a 'prosperity of the soul' (ref 3 John 1:2, KJV)

These add new dimensions to our measure of success: outward recognition, inward contentment and upward fulfilment. In summary:

Life in three dimensions			
Dimension	Out	In	Up
The dark side – potential addiction	Money	Sex	Power
Counterbalance	Simplicity	Purity	Accountability
Success factor	Recognition and career success	Family and relationships, loving and being loved	Spiritual fulfilment – 'prosperity of the soul'

So that's the philosophical bit.

Of all my reflections, I think two stand out.

The first is to set one audacious new goal every year. To do something courageous. To go beyond my comfort zone.

An Australian nurse called Bronnie Ware spent several years working in palliative care, caring for patients in the last weeks of their lives. She asked about their reflections as they looked back on their lives and it seems that 'common themes surfaced again and again'. The biggest regret was, 'I wish I'd had the courage to live a life true to myself, not the life others expected of me.'[41] It's easy to get comfortable or to feel imprisoned by others' expectations, and not work to realise our dreams until it's too late.

Currently, I have two audacious goals: to save the taxpayer a net £50 billion or so on an unnecessary and pointless high speed rail scheme. And to establish a successful contact centre in Palestine. Meanwhile, another goal is emerging, related to a new role.

The second reflection is this: what or who is going to stop me achieving my goals? The answer is no one except me. It's easy to think that other people might be able to do this or that, but I could not possibly do it; but why not?

What is needed to change the world? When we think of the people who really made a difference – Mahatma Gandhi, Martin Luther King, Nelson Mandela – what did they have that enabled them to have such an impact? The key thing was passion: passion about the injustices of their day.

I love the World War II poster of the woman baring her arm with the strapline, 'We can do it!' And why not? Sometimes I have imagined unwritten rules that I could not break, or boundaries that I could not go past. Yet I have found that if I push the boundaries, if I just get on with things, few object or try to stop me. It is said that it's easier to obtain forgiveness afterwards than permission before.

Set an audacious goal. You can do it.

It's been quite a ride, and it's not over yet. After spending most of 2012 fully employed but with no income, I've now moved into a new area of work as CEO of the Arthur Rank Centre,[42] which supports rural communities and churches. It came about in a remarkable way, at just the right time for both me and the centre, typical of God's timing and provision. For rural

---

[41] Reported by Susie Steiner, *The Guardian*, 1 February 2012.
[42] www.arthurrankcentre.org.uk (accessed 27 June 2013).

churches, this is an exciting period that requires a re-imagining of rural mission and ministry; and there are some remarkable people and places where different approaches are working well. For rural communities, the struggle is to remain a balanced community rather than a ghetto for commuters and the retired, with issues of affordable housing, isolation, hidden poverty, poor transport. It will require all my experience of entrepreneurship and working with disparate groups. It's a daunting task but there is an excellent team in place.

Meanwhile, I continue to support Transcend, taking time off to make a series of sales appointments in Dubai in January 2013. I found that most of my prospects were in the Dubai Outsource Zone, and if I bluffed my way past security, I could roam a building looking for potential clients. In one building I targeted AXA Insurance. In the lift up to their floor I asked someone in the lift, heading for the same floor, if he could tell me the name of the boss. Armed with this, I went to reception, explained I was over from the UK for a few days, and said I would like to speak to Dr Sherif. I enjoy a challenge, and some good leads came out of these endeavours.

We remain members of Westwood Church, which continues to be a growing, vibrant and youthful community, experiencing extraordinary healings and other remarkable answers to prayer. We partner with other churches of different denominations across Coventry in *Kidz Klub*, 'healing on the streets' and a city prayer house. Because of HS2 work, I pulled out of leading our local village congregation but now co-lead a business-focussed group, one of dozens of small groups and communities. We meet together to deepen our understanding of the Bible and pray for each other. Once a month, we meet in a pub for 'Beer Mat Mentoring': an open opportunity for old hands to encourage a new generation of aspiring entrepreneurs, whether or not they have church connections.

The children are now all adults: Sarah turned 18 in November 2012. The event was duly recorded in typical Marshall banter on Facebook.

> **Hannah Jones** In the middle of the night 18 years ago I was woken up by the sound of a baby crying, after ten minutes of wondering why, I got out of bed to discover that Sue Marshall had given birth to Sarah Joy Marshall with the help of Jerry Marshall because the midwife was lost on the motorway. Happy 18th birthday for 12.30am tomorrow Sarah!

> **Sue Marshall** All my children are now adults!!! That's not to say that they're all grown up, I can't see that happening any time soon

> **Hannah Jones** I think Joanne Marshall is the most grown up. I made a deer out of papier mâché today while she did medical exams.

> **Sarah Joy Marshall** I had to have a nap today, I don't know if that makes me not grown up at all, or really really grown up (ie old)

> **Hannah Jones** I had a bath at 6pm that's not very rock and roll

> **Joanne Marshall** Yeh but my exam today involved me trying to get a kid to stop eating my stethoscope long enough for me to listen to her chest and explaining to an actor that his fictional daughter was probably having migraines not a brain tumour. It was a weird kind of exam.

On the night of Friday, 31st May 1985, Sue and I were sailing a chartered 27-foot yacht from the Isles of Scilly to Falmouth. The wind was against us, blowing force six, and we had two seasick crew. In strong winds, steering is hard work. Sue was expecting

Hannah so she stayed down below and I helmed from 11pm, when the seasick crew handed over and went to their bunks.

It was before the days of GPS, and the conditions – strong tide, headwind, indeterminate leeway the boat was making, and lack of help – made it impossible to plot our position on the chart and work out an accurate course to steer.

I knew we were going to have to tack through the wind and sail northwards to Falmouth at some stage, but I could not be sure that we had cleared the notorious Manacle reef. The only answer was to carry on until I was sure we were safe. That meant hours of extra sailing, missing the tide at Falmouth, and being late handing over our yacht.

I had resigned myself to this, but at 1.30am I had an overwhelming feeling that we should tack round and steer a course of zero degrees magnetic, due north. I have never navigated on impulse, but was absolutely certain that this was God's guidance. I tacked onto the new course.

At 5am, Sue emerged from the cabin with hot chocolate and ginger biscuits, and noticed the yellow outer Manacles market buoy behind us. We had sailed just a few hundred metres outside it. Then we spotted the Falmouth lighthouse dead ahead. For the first time ever, I did not need to adjust course as we approached land. We were still steering zero degrees at 6.45am when we sailed through the middle of the Falmouth harbour entrance.

We moored at about 7.15am. A man caught our mooring line and said, 'You're cutting it a bit fine!' If we had been just a few minutes later we would have run aground, and we would have had to wait several hours for the tide to come in again.

That seems to me to be a picture of my experience of life. Take a risk, listen for God's still small voice and He will steer us in the right direction. He knows us, He knows our hopes and dreams, and He will keep us clear of the rocks.

Ian Knox, an evangelist, lawyer and former Westwood Church member, once said that becoming a Christian is like giving God the steering wheel and moving to the passenger seat. After all, He's a much better driver. I don't think that's quite it. I see myself as on the helm. I'm steering, but God is there to my side and slightly behind, just out of sight, careful not to restrict my field of view. He's the Skipper and knows these waters well. Every so often He puts a hand lightly on my shoulder and says quietly, 'Bear away a touch,' or, 'Now would be a good time to tack.'

I feel blessed, not as a result of my efforts, but by the grace of God. As far as I know, Christianity is the only religion where heaven, or paradise, or nirvana, comes as a free gift in response to simply saying yes to God's gentle knock on our door. Any good works are a thankful response rather than a pre-requisite for salvation. I was fortunate to be a British citizen and have loving parents. I'm especially blessed by the love and support of Sue, and my three lovely daughters, and by my two wonderful sisters. I stumbled across some truths and took an unexpected direction. As a result, I can say that if I die tomorrow, I'm satisfied.

> Cowes Yacht Haven, this is Yacht *Lucy*. We're looking for an overnight berth. 24 foot, lift keel, over.

> *Lucy*, this is Cowes Yacht Haven. No problem, come in through northern entrance, berth N7, November 7, port side to.

Sue and I were spending the bank holiday together in the yacht I now share with a couple of friends. It was mid-morning, after a gentle sail up the Solent from Yarmouth.

Once we were tied up, I cooked a brunch of bacon and eggs, with fresh coffee; we ate in the cockpit in the sunshine, and planned our day.

We walked lazily up Cowes High Street, festooned with bunting for the Round the Island Race. The Tea 'n' Biscuit Boys were singing enthusiastically, playing a tea chest and guitar.

Sue took a photo. We continued round the headland and along the beach to Gurnard, stopping to eat ice cream. An International Moth sailing dinghy was launched in front of us, then rose up on its hydrofoils, flying past conventional boats, a couple of feet above the water's surface.

On the way back, we spotted and waved at *Ocean Venture* coming in, the boat I'd sailed to Brittany, and later to the Isles of Scilly with Sue.

We ate out, sitting next to a window. We talked, watched the boats and enjoyed the sunset.

It was a simple but perfect day. As we fell asleep to the sound of the water gently lapping against the hull, I reflected that I have run the race and, so far, managed to clear the hurdles without falling over. Whatever challenges lie ahead, I can enjoy the rest of the ride, knowing that in the end, my true home and treasure are secure.

instant ap◌stle

Join the Instant Apostle community!

Visit www.instantapostle.com and sign up for our newsletter
Follow us on Twitter @instantapostle
Find us on Facebook: Instant Apostle

Check out some of our other great titles!

Building the Kingdom Through Business, by Bridget Adams and Manoj Raithatha

If it's business that shapes the world, then how can we use it to shape the world for good and for God? Against the background of an international debate on business ethics and more just societies, this book looks at godly business in biblical, historical and practical ways.

ISBN 978 0 9559135 1 8

Potholes and Belly-flops, Susie Flashman Jarvis

Susie was a rising star of the modelling world. But she was a private failure, addicted to Class A drugs and promiscuously jumping from one broken relationship to another. Then God...

ISBN 978-0-9559135-8-7

I'm a Christian – so what do I believe? Ken Gardiner

Ken Gardiner has a passion for Jesus Christ and a passion for truth. Drawing on his rich life experiences of God and his deep biblical knowledge, he invites us to re-examine the essence of the Christian faith.

ISBN 978-0-9559135-9-4

A Book of Sparks, **Shaun Lambert**

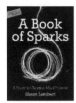

Shaun Lambert weaves the ancient disciplines of contemplation with his modern understanding of psychology to unlock a biblical wisdom. Transformation comes through what he calls 'mind*Full*ness', the practice of being filled with the awareness of the presence of God.

ISBN 978-0-9559135-3-2

Less than ordinary? **Nicki Copeland**

Our life experiences, personality and self-opinions shape who we become. Having struggled for much of her life with low self-esteem and lack of confidence, Nicki Copeland shares her personal journey into self-acceptance and growing belief in herself.

ISBN 978-1-909728-00-4

A Thorn in My Mind, **Cathy Wield**

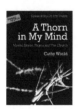

Cathy Wield is uniquely qualified to write on the subject of mental illness as a doctor and a patient. This is her testimony to ongoing healing and maturity while learning to live with serious illness. A must read for those who are affected by mental illness and those who run churches or communities.

ISBN 978-0-9559135-2-5

Sometimes I write words, **John Hermon**

This anthology comprises carefully crafted poems that chronicle the writer's experience of bereavement. It is inspired by a mindfulness of God and a sense of wonder at His creation that will speak to every season of your life, whether read in the quietness of your home or as part of the church's liturgy.

ISBN 978 1 909728 02 8

The Never Ending Journey, Antoinette Anthony-Pillai

Antoinette Anthony-Pillai's future was mapped out. But a routine operation went horribly wrong, and her brain was starved of oxygen A moving account of Antoinette's fight to regain control of her life.

ISBN 978-0-9559135-6-3

Turning the tables on mission, Rev Israel Olofinjana (ed)

This book documents the experiences of contemporary missionaries coming to the UK. Their candid, personal accounts challenge many stereotypes and form a rich resource for collective learning.

ISBN 978-1-909728-03-5

Ten things you must know about Jesus Christ, Michael A. Dada

Using Scripture passages from the traditional King James Version, this book sets out to explain exactly who Jesus is and what he can do for us.

ISBN 978 0 9559135 4 9

Ernie Gonzales: The Determined Dreamer, Beth Shepherd, illustrated by Lisa Buckridge

Ernie Gonzales is a small, ordinary snail with a big, extraordinary dream! Ernie sets out on a daring journey to find a legendary snail paradise and is soon swept up in a more exciting adventure than he ever dreamed of.

ISBN 978-0-9559135-7-0

The Tails of Ginger and Tom, Lynne Bradley, illustrated by Susan Briffett

A heart-warming story of two energetic kittens, their friend Amber, and her Special Friend who looks after them all. Be transported to a world where cats get their paws into everything!

ISBN 978-0-9559135-5-6